JUSTICE APPROXIMATED

Dispatches from the Bottom Rung of the Judicial Ladder

JUSTICE
APPROXIMATED

Dispatches from the
Bottom Rung of the Judicial Ladder

L. Phillips Runyon III

Grove Street Books

Peterborough, New Hampshire

2017

Library of Congress Control Number: 2017936303

L. Phillips Runyon III
45 Main Street, Suite 204
Peterborough, NH 03458
www.runyonlawoffice.com
prunyon@runyonlawoffice.com
603-924-3050

Book Design by Cassie Baron
Cover Design by Cassie Baron
Printed by Kase Printing

Grove Street Books
P.O. Box 117
Peterborough, New Hampshire 03458

www.grovestreetbooks.com

Grove Street Books is an imprint of Bauhan Publishing, L.L.C

Manufactered in the United States of America

For Cathie, LP and Grier,

so they'll know what I was up to all those years.

CONTENTS

OPENING STATEMENT

I was pretty sure the person standing three feet in front of me was a woman, but it was hard to tell for sure because the whole head was covered by a sweat-stained military gas mask. You know, one of those old canvas contraptions with a metal canister dangling from a rubber hose, like World War I doughboys used to wear. And the gender ID was further complicated by camo pants and calf-high combat boots, topped with a white sheet over the head and torso—a la Casper the Friendly Ghost.

Actually, the determination was more than idle curiosity, because I'm a judge—that's what this is about after all—and nailing down whether the person I'm looking at is the same one mentioned in the criminal complaint I'm reading from is a big part of the job description. Plus, making the identification might help me come up with a link between this carefully-accessorized outfit and the strange assortment of stuff the woman (I could see evidence of mascara now) had snatched— that is, allegedly snatched—from our local discount store.

When no one offered a lifeline, and the woman just kept staring blankly at me through the cloudy eyepieces, I figured I was on my own. I asked anyone within earshot whether there was a profound statement being made here, like maybe "war is a terrible waste of human life" or "cops are stinking pigs." Still total silence, or at least nothing more than the woman wheezing through her jiggly snout like a terminal asthmatic.

In the moment, what came to mind was trying to make sense of *Ulysses* in the 10th grade. In fact, this really seemed harder because there were no Cliffs Notes. No matter what I blathered, I couldn't get a nod or a grunt or a twitch of any kind out of the woman, not even a "not guilty by reason of poison gas." She just stood there.

Finally, I noticed someone who looked like he might be the woman's husband. He was standing way off to the side and concentrating on his shoes, hoping, I'm sure, that I'd leave him entirely out of this. He was no help either, though, offering with an eye roll and a shrug that "she isn't speaking to me today either." The best I could figure, he was there just to straighten her sheet.

After some time-killing paper shuffling and lip pursing on my part, I decided to see how the cops were doing. After all, they'd brought the charge, so they had some responsibility for creating this moment of avant–garde theatre. Their eyes were like hubcaps, but at least they confirmed that the woman's weird contraband was back on the shelves for other strange shoppers to select—and maybe pay for next time.

Somehow, that showed me the way. I quickly tabled the case for six months, telling the woman that I'd deep six it for good if she kept her hands to herself in the meantime. All I could think of, though, was that if she fell off the wagon, there was no telling what kind of get-up she'd appear in next time. The cops exhaled audibly at that plan, no doubt wondering where they were going with this not-quite-capital offense anyhow.

Still, the woman wasn't tipping her hand a bit, even in the face of this pretty favorable result. Then, as she departed silently, with her snout bobbing and her hubby sputtering that "she's on her own if she has to come back here again," the woman shot me a quick glance, and I swear I saw a blurry smirk inside the mask. Or maybe it was just gas. I vowed then and there to take another crack at *Ulysses*.

OK, to reiterate (because that's what lawyers do), I'm a judge—of sorts. The sort who would contend with the Gas Mask Ladies of New Hampshire on a pretty regular basis.

I thought I'd start with that visual, because when a lawyer makes an opening statement, she's hoping to make it interesting enough so the jury isn't dozing before she gets rolling. Thus, *State v. Gas Mask Lady*.

I mean, if you've only got one chance to make a good first impression, you've got to go for broke right after "May it please the Court" or the folks in the jury box will start making out their grocery lists. Even then, if you're up against *Court TV, Law & Order* and a baker's dozen of other "high content" courtroom dramas, your chances of getting the channel surfers to pause, even momentarily, are slim at best. People's eyes glaze over in a nano-second these days and once they've moved on, it doesn't matter how impressive the testimony sounds; they won't be there to hear it. Also, to stick with the TV metaphor, it's just human nature to pay more attention to the major networks than to some community access cable channel. If that's where you're focused, though, you're going to miss the busy ant hill of activity down here near the bottom rung of the judicial ladder, where you probably can't even see the TV.

It's likely occurred to you at some point that there are thousands of judges in this country. Indeed there are. And many of them are very thoughtful and deliberate and paid attention in law school, so they really know their stuff. Many of them also deal with the great questions of the day, making decisions that re-direct the course of American life. Just think of the Supreme Court justices who decided *Roe v. Wade, Brown v. Board of Education* and *Bush v. Gore,* for starters.

Then again, I'm guessing that few of those legal leviathans have ever faced a challenge like *State v. Gas Mask Lady,* much less several times a day. Plus, while I may not do anything as earth-moving or robe-popping as those top-rung deciders, at least I'm not responsible for undermining the country's respect for an independent judiciary—like the majority in that last case I cited. When top-runger Justice Antonin Scalia was asked about that one, he just said "get over it", as if it was no big deal that his guy sent a ballpark full of soldiers to their deaths in Iraq because he had a hunch there might be some "nuclear" weapons there. Might as well just get that out on the table right here, 'cause let's face it, if you're using your lofty perch to advance a personal agenda in the guise of legitimate judicial decision-making, you have to expect those of us way down the ladder to look straight up your robe and see what you've got there.

Maybe if I was a federal judge of any rank or stripe, I'd be nervous about dissing the bosses—but I'm not, a federal judge, that is. I'm not on my state's supreme court either, so no bonehead decision from me is going to ruin the lives of lots of Granite Staters. In fact, I'm not even a full-time judge. I'm the part-time judge of the 8th Circuit Court-District Division-Jaffrey (until recently just called the plain old Jaffrey-Peterborough District Court), in what's still a pretty rural chunk of southwestern New Hampshire. I think they gave us the fancy new name to make up for paying us less, but I'll get to that.

Most people think of this lowly rung as "traffic court", or maybe "muni court" in some places. If we convened after dark, you might be reminded of TV's old *Night Court*, but without the laugh track. Whatever you call it, it amounts to the bottom rung of pretty much any judicial ladder, certainly the ladder stuck in the mud here in New Hampshire. Hence the subtitle I came up with for this "res"—which, in order to get you in the right frame of mind, is legal jargon (Latin, of course) for "thing".

Wow, my ears are burning already, as I sense you asking yourself, "Why did I spend good money on a book by a faux-judge like this, and if I plead insanity, will they let me return it?" More to the point, "Why in the world would I—should I—might I, conceivably—give a . . . . whit, a bit, a s***t about what happens in this jamoke's class D minor league outpost of justice, or about what he might have to say on the state of American legal stuff?"

Good questions all. In fact, just the kind of perceptive inquiries we lawyers work so hard to develop in law school. Hold onto those thoughts, and keep reassessing the wisdom of your decision as (that is, if) you read on. If you opt to bail now, thanks at least for considering spending some time with me here, and best of luck with any future run-ins you have with law enforcement—thanks to modern DNA testing and GPS technology, I now know who you are and where you live.

Alright, then, if there's anyone still with me, let's go back to that second question up there: Why would anyone give me the time of day about a job I don't even do full-time? To begin with, I've been perched on this lowly rung for almost 27 years now, since the reign of Bush the

Elder, which is more than Chief Justice Roberts can say. Also, unlike the cases he hears where everyone is expensively coiffed, fashionably clad and scrupulously prepared, I've had a lot more chances than he's had to see those same people just after they've rolled out of bed, before they've taken their first look in the mirror, splashed on some water, and plastered down the sputniks on the back of their heads. In other words, I get to see those silver-tongued Supreme Court mouthpieces after they've been stopped for speeding on their way to the dump—er, recycling center—when every word they say isn't quite as carefully rehearsed and eloquently uttered. And I also see their poorly-behaved spouses and kids at what would not be considered their finest moments either.

One more caveat (as in the Latin caveat emptor). This account of things legal and courtly won't nourish, expand or tax your cerebral neurons; that is, you could read it at the beach without feeling like you were still at work. On the flip side of legal prose, I was browsing our fine local bookstore last week and noticed a really dense and brainy treatise called *How Judges Think*, by a distinguished federal judge. I leafed through a few pages, reading a paragraph or two here and there (like you may have done with this res), and my quick take was that he and I are operating in distinctly different judicial universes. He's up there on one of the top rungs, looking at the judicial landscape from a lofty and rarefied perspective, while my moth-eaten robe is dragging on the ground and I'm trying to catch a glimpse of justice through the privet hedge. If I were to jump into his learned discourse with both feet, not only would I need a thesaurus, but I'd have a tough time diagramming the sentences. That won't happen here. You may not buy what I have to say about this or that judgely topic, but you won't have any trouble getting the drift.

Finally, finally, you may have heard the old saw about how you'd never want to see how sausage or laws are made. That may be true about judicial decision-making, too, and I'm not sure it represents good judgment on my part to be pulling back even my flimsy curtain on the process. After all, no pitcher ever confessed to throwing the splitter until after he retired, and this could turn out just as incriminating. Also, I've noticed that few people sound more intelligent the more they talk, which could be a serious problem here, too.

On the other hand, my retirement party (unless I blow it for good) should have occurred by the time you read this, so I'm counting on being home free. Consider, too, that I may not have time to lose, as a 39 year-old client of mine (remember, I'm only a part-timer), in apparently robust health, dropped dead not long ago for no apparent reason and without any visible risk factors (believe me, I checked), and I'm already a generation and a half older than he was. Also, my father got so he couldn't complete a full sentence, and who knows whether I've got the same gene at work. I just hope this doesn't sound too much like someone who's already missing a link, but then you'll be the judge of that, won't you?

SWORN TESTIMONY

~⌒~

So, we're off and running—er, deciding—and today we heard the tale of a young candlepin bowler who was enjoying a beer and a smoke in the parking lot during his weekly league competition when the cops pulled up to ruin the fun. They were all set to run him in for public drinking—or maybe it was for drinking while keggling—when he asked if he could return to the alley for just a moment to finish his string (New English for "game") and not leave his teammates in the lurch. The cops were moved by such commendable loyalty, so they sent him back inside and stood around chewing the fat for a few frames.

Finally, when their chat turned into more than half an hour, they went in to check on the young man's progress, only to learn he'd immediately high-tailed it out the back door and had left his string dangling. Fortunately for the red-faced officers (who were bowled over by the deception?), the combination of beer and butts diminished their guy's escapabilities and they found him huffing and puffing down the road not far away, still slipping and sliding in his bowling shoes. With his name on the back of his league shirt, a positive ID wasn't much of a challenge either. Now, instead of a minor fine for the drinking infraction, he'll be wearing an orange onesie and bowling for the "3-Squares" team for a few weeks. The moral of this skedaddle? If at first you drop the ball, pick it up and keep bowling; don't try running out the back door or you may find an even heavier ball inconveniently attached to your ankle.

~⌒~

Another big difference between Chief Justice Roberts and me is that I bet he's never had pizzas delivered to his house when someone was really ticked about a decision he'd made—and I guaranty he's ticked off a lot more people than I have. I can see why Al Gore might have considered that a few years back—sending pizzas to the CJ, that is, except that he'd probably have eaten them himself. Right, cheap shot, 'cause I like Al and he's scaled back his caloric intake since getting the inconvenient truth about his cholesterol.

For the life of me, though, I can't figure what I've done recently to get anyone ripped enough to bury me in pizzas, as well as a wide variety of ethnic meals from every other diner, bistro and café in the area. In fact, the restaurants themselves are all so pissed at me now that they're leaving opinions of their own on my home answering machine, and I doubt I could get a pizza at this point even if I showed up in person. Maybe in the face. I may have to adopt an alias and pay cash, or risk getting punched out at one of these establishments if someone spots my name on a credit card. Perhaps doing my dining out of town for a while would be a better idea. Anyhow, stick with me here and you can decide for yourself whether I deserved the pizza treatment.

Yesterday we had the typical 25 or so cases on the trial docket, many of them pretty serious drug and driving charges that might have taken hours to slog through. Amazingly, they were all eventually resolved without trials (more about how that happens later), except one—the last one. Everything came to a screeching halt at that point, as we spent more than an hour hearing how a woman's eight barking Chihuahuas had kept her neighbors up on a hot July night when their windows were open for ventilation but her air conditioner was making so much racket that she couldn't hear the yipping in her own backyard. Sounds like one of Chief Justice Roberts' 8th Amendment cases, right? You know, cruel and unusual punishment.

I eventually found her guilty—they apparently barked even longer than the trial—and then I fined her but suspended all except $25 because the neighbors said the yip fest had mercifully stopped before they lost the whole night's sleep. I should have quit right there myself, but I just couldn't keep my mouth shut. When I explained the fine, I foolishly muttered that with all those mouths to feed she probably needed to save her money for dog food.

Suddenly, it was like I was the one who'd let the dogs out. The woman indignantly launched into a doctoral discourse about how the delicate digestive systems of Chihuahuas can't handle commercial dog food and how she has to blend just the right organic ingredients and grind them all up specially for the half-pints. All the while she's talking, I'm thinking that's probably the reason she was so sound asleep and didn't hear the barking. I'm also thinking, "You idiot, you've been at this a long time but you haven't learned a damn thing"—except that maybe Chihuahuas aren't the best canine choice if you're a sound sleeper and you have neighbors within yip shot.

When I was a fresh-faced lawyer just cutting my trial molars, I was hired to defend the youngest of three teenage brothers who were [allegedly] terrorizing the area with wild drunken carousing that had the local cops careening after them from the scene of one petty crime to another. This particular time the kid was charged with disorderly conduct, resisting arrest and assaulting several of the exhausted officers, and his raucous sibs were up for similar misbehavior.

The day we arrived for trial—in this court—I huddled with the lawyers for the other young cowboys and we quickly decided that our gooses were cooked if the same judge who'd seen these guys as often as his own family was given another shot at them. Our ploy instead was to argue for a new decider, one who might not be 90% of the way toward convictions before the first testimony was uttered.

Surprisingly, the judge felt the same way, no doubt tickled to avoid wasting any more precious hours of his life on these multiple misfits. He instantly dialed up the publisher of the local newspaper who was the backup judge but who'd never seen the inside of a law school classroom (a needless frill in those days), and asked whether he could run on over to the courthouse to handle a few inconvenient tidbits.

While the newsman washed off the printer's ink and dug out his copy of the Constitution, I had second thoughts about our ploy, worrying that all his paper's headlines about our boys' prior shenanigans might make him even less sympathetic than the judge we started with. It looked grim. In a desperate move, we lawyers decided our one slim path to success lay in pointing as many fingers at each other's clients as possible, in the hope that unresolvable confusion would ensue and create reasonable doubt about who did what to whom.

When the dust finally settled, that Hail Mary play had actually landed in the end zone because, I'm embarrassed now to say, each and every one of our guilty-as-hell hoodlums totally walked. Begging the question, of course: if the person who really committed the alleged crime is found not guilty—because the state failed to prove it beyond a reasonable doubt—is he nevertheless a despicable miscreant or now pure as the driven snow? And where do we lawyers fit into that moral equation? Talk among yourselves.

The reason for mentioning this ancient history is that one of the former teenagers—not mine—was in court this week and completely stunned me when he said his name. Not only had he aged about 30 years, but he looked like he'd been going toe-to-toe with the cops every one of those roughly 10,000 days. If you know who Mickey Rourke is and you saw him first as a cocky kid in *Diner*, then saw him again in *The Wrestler*, you'll understand the basis for my alarm. The difference is that this man-child hadn't been nominated for an Oscar but was being charged yet again for more self-destructive juvenile antics.

This time the cops didn't have a witness they needed and were begging for a second chance to nail their old nemesis. I don't know what got into me—maybe it had something to do with Auld Lang Syne—but this particular rap seemed marginal even if true, so I let him walk once more—albeit with at least 50 extra pounds, a nasty limp and the posture of an early primate. As he shuffled out, I rationalized that we won't see him again no matter what; he'll either tidy up his act once and for all—though a long shot after so much chronic law-abusing—or he won't be seeing anyone anywhere much longer.

~⌐

Before wrestling with anything else down here on the bottom rung, let's punch up Google Earth, ratchet this ladder up as far as it will go, and take a nose-bleed gander at the judicial landscape here in the Granite State.

The judges of the Supreme and Superior Courts, the latter being the place where you'd get called for jury duty (my wife and son recently got notices on the same day after never being called before), are all full-timers, complete with generous pensions and lavish medical and dental plans. Some of our more urban District (now Circuit) Court judges are also in that elite fraternity/now sorority, based on the heft of their caseloads, and they get pretty much the same perks.

The rest of us are a dog's breakfast of part-timers, with our compensation based on at least three cobbled-together models I can think of. Mine actually resembles a piece-work arrangement that's determined by how many cases we push through the metal detector in a given year—a tad over 4,000 the last time I looked. Come to think of it, I guess that means we welcome as much crime and conflict as possible in these parts, 'cause if everyone suddenly became law-abiding, reasonable and responsible, we'd be out of business and looking for real jobs. Pure fantasy, I know, but I digress. Anyhow, we part-timers are pension-challenged and without any health insurance unless we pay the full tab, which is out of reach for most of us because even the basic coverage is loaded with ultra-expensive bells and whistles. Poor babies, right?

All New Hampshire judges, both full and partial, are appointed by the governor and serve until they throw in the robe or hit three score and ten, whichever arrives first. Not so fast, though, because before dispensing any justice (or approximating it) we have to be vetted (extremely?) by the Executive Council, the five-member group that provides a theoretical check on the governor's penchant for politically-motivated—and thus presumptively ill-conceived—choices. It's a partisan body itself, however, and so the Councilors give a particularly hairy eyeball to judicial nominations, trying to figure out whether a candidate will support their own agendas for, say, "throw the book at 'em" law and order, or unbridled bleeding-heartism.

Luckily, I managed to slither over the transom before dawn of the era of close nominee scrutiny. I remember just calling all the Councilors on the phone to ask for their support—the governor's office suggested I "reach out" that way—and except for telling one of them I was opposed to DWI and would "throw the book at 'em", I don't recall being tossed any hard balls. I guess they did a criminal record check somewhere in there, but they must have missed the fact that I was a [pre-Steinbrenner] Yankee fan as a clueless juvenile, and that I occasionally spanked my kids when they deserved it. (The kids would have grudgingly confirmed that they indeed deserved it.) All in all, it must have been a pretty superficial once-over. I didn't have to run the gauntlet of a public hearing—so no questions like, "Mr. Runyon, do you think someone going less than 15 over should be charged with speeding?"—or—"Have you stopped beating your children?

There may be deficiencies in this process—they used to say a New Hampshire judge was just a lawyer who knew a governor (and called a few councilors, I guess). Even so, at least we don't have to play up to the electorate, as do our brethren and sistren in the 22 or so other states where at least some judges run for office. You know, that's where lawyers and insurance companies hoping for favors bankroll judicial campaigns, and then their successful candidates assure everyone that they're not being influenced in any way by all the blatant skid-greasing.

Coincidentally, the Sunday *New York Times* recently had a front-page story about the upcoming judicial elections in Ohio and how even the Supreme Court judges there don't have any qualms about sitting on cases where the interested parties have padded their campaign coffers. Tellingly, the headline read, "Rendering Justice, With One Eye on Re-Election", and it quoted an expert on comparative legal systems as saying, "The rest of the world is stunned and amazed at what we do, and vaguely aghast." Duh.

I've never been accused of being a deep thinker, but if those Ohio judges—and their counterparts in the other justice-by-ballot states—can't spot (won't admit, is more like it) the conflicts staring them in their faces, then I sincerely hope the legal issues they're wrestling with aren't too complicated. I'm sure they want the truth and nothing but from their witnesses, yet they don't seem willing to come clean themselves. Legalized bribery may sound harsh, but if it looks like that to the party at the other table in the courtroom who didn't write a campaign check, what's the difference? I mean, really, if the robe looks like it fits, that's all that matters in this biz, where the public smells rats most of the time anyhow.

PS—As I edit this yet again for outrageously stupid comments (quite an undertaking), I note that during the 2010 mid-term elections, three Iowa Supreme Court justices were voted out of office because they had the temerity shortly beforehand to decide that same-sex marriage was legally OK in Iowa. So much for the freedom to make decisions without outside pressure. If this kind of referendum on judicial decision-making is what they crave in Iowa, why don't they just put the cases up on the court website and have everyone click the thumbs-up or thumbs-down box. The State could cut the judicial budget to the bone—all they'd need was a webmaster—and all those outraged Hawkeyes could concentrate instead on the price of pork belly futures.

But I digress once more. Our system also means we New Hampshire judges don't have to worry each time we make a hard call about how that's going to play two (or three or four) years from now when we have to face the voters again, or about whether we're making too many powerful, deeply-pocketed enemies on the losing sides of our cases. Which means that if we keep our pants on under our robes and don't fall off the wagon too badly while in street clothes, we can probably serve out our full terms without having to flinch at each well-reasoned but unpopular decision. We'll just deal with it when the pizza delivery guy shows up unexpectedly, or when the checkout kid at the grocery store works us over in front of everyone else in line as he's ringing up the peanut butter because we took his license for getting caught with a measly six-pack after the prom. (Note to self: order peanut butter online.)

Actually, it's experiences like that last one (not long ago for me) which are often cited as the key to keeping most of us as part-timers on this rung, the mantra being that if we know we may soon be standing at the public urinal next to someone we've just adjudicated, we're more likely to wield our gavels more circumspectly, i.e., without being arrogant jerks about it. Maybe that's a plausible theory to some of the State reps in Concord, but I think making the right calls just for the sake of it is more than enough motivation for most of my colleagues—so the full-time versus part-time thing is about as red a herring as they come, in my humble view. After all, even a full-time judge has to unzip the robe and take a public pee occasionally, right?

PS—A couple of weeks ago I was walking out of our local bookstore café with a cup of coffee when I made eye contact with a heavily-bearded fellow catching a few rays on a bench. I offered a hello, to which he responded, "I wasn't guilty!" I shrugged as sympathetically as possible and kept moving, perhaps picking up the pace just a little.

It was snowing pretty heavily on the way to court today, but all of us who were getting paid to be here somehow managed to slog through it, and on time at that. When the clerk handed me the docket, though, there was a note on it from a woman—whose house I can practically see from the bench—who called to say she just couldn't make it today because there was 11" at her house and she knew that because it had completely covered her cat Fluffy. I admit that I couldn't see Fluffy from where I was, but I bet she and Fluffy both could have made it if we were paying people to show up instead of preparing to take a large quantity of hers.

Back briefly to judging in New Hampshire—a nagging itch I just can't keep from scratching. When I think about the court system here, my mind always pulls up the last scene of *Davy Crockett at the Alamo*—the one with Fess Parker as Davy that Disney sent out to our massive TV armoires in the mid-'50s. The noble Davy and his little band of righteous defenders are about to be overwhelmed—and yes, killed, though Walt spared us that scene—by hordes of barely-human Mexicans. Needless to say in this daydream (nightmare?), we rag-tag group of judges are the Davys and the 400+ New Hampshire legislators are Santa Anna's blood-thirsty army.

In recent years that metaphor works because the courts here have been soldiering on in the trenches of justice as best they can, while our representatives—or at least somebody's representatives—do their best to make sure we don't have enough ammo or reinforcements to make it out alive. That means the piddling crumbs we've managed to scavenge from the State budget keep dwindling to less and less.

I haven't been around long enough—just a quarter century or so—to know whether this is a chronic feud, but in recent times the hostile attitude stems from the incongruous fact that our citizen representatives either haven't read or don't understand what the New Hampshire Constitution mandates about paying for public education. I can sense a look of bewilderment crossing your face—like, how are those things related?—so I'll try to connect the dots.

You see, the State of New Hampshire is a wonderful place to live and raise families, but its Achille's heel is that it has very little public revenue because it has no sales or income tax and so tries to finance most of State government with real estate property taxes and a bunch of niggling fees that are like death by a thousand cuts. Apart from making sure the Statehouse bathrooms get cleaned regularly, the primary expense of State government is making sure the children of the Granite State get an "adequate" education, as its Constitution requires. The trouble is, some towns have plenty of money and can handle that requirement without a lot of State help, while others are like your kid who majored in philosophy and can't pay even minimal rent without your (i.e., the State's) continuing infusion of cash, which you've never been happy about infusing.

Not surprisingly, this educational funding disparity has found its way to our Supreme Court on several occasions. And in those cases the Supremes have kept explaining those funding requirements to you (in this case, the State legislature), and yet you (they) just keep coming up with one lame plan after another about how to fund the public schools (or not to fund them, actually), which the court then swats aside like black flies in May.

So here's where the dots get connected, because all that judicial scolding makes them—the reps, now—counterpunch with a vengeance. In other words, they'll be damned if they're going to let those dress-wearing, mostly activist and probably pink, applecart upsetters get away with even a sliver more than its already microscopic 2% or so of the

State budget pie chart. Which, if my number is in the ballpark, seems a tad light for a co-equal branch of government. Which, in turn, makes it hard to pay for enough judges to defend the ramparts, especially when our funders are convinced that those of us on the front lines are dogging it most of the time, and even when working at it couldn't hit the right target [in a decision] with a laser sight.

Warning: Detour Ahead!

Don't get me wrong here; this isn't just sour grapes, and I'm not lobbying for a full-time job. If I was, I'd be taking my reps out to lunch or contributing to their campaign coffers in the time-honored way. No, I actually like the current part-time setup—it lets me keep practicing law (and I'm often reminded that even after 40 years I still need the practice), though it often proves really disconcerting to our courtroom customers.

I know that last thing because at the start of every session I make an announcement about also being a lawyer in my spare time—in order to flush out the many lurking small-town conflicts of interest. While doing so, I can see our defendants' eyes getting wider and a panicked look emerging on their already apprehensive faces as they wonder what the hell is going on here. I mean, is a real judge going to decide their cases—someone who'll be able to tell they're innocent of these bogus charges—or is this guy just some substitute teacher of a judge who's going to find them guilty because the cops wouldn't have dragged them in here otherwise? I do my darnedest to dispel that first impression by seeming to know what I'm doing, but I'm also sure the guy who walks out with a hefty fine to pay swears he's going to make sure the real judge is here the next time he's nabbed.

All this wordy wandering boils down to the fact that the State's inability or unwillingness to properly fund both public education and the court system shortchanges not only many of the State's school kids, but also the public's confidence in at least this lowest rung of its courts— where I bet people spend more time than in any other building with metal detectors.

I don't know whether this has changed since I was a kid, but the latest poll says only 15% of Americans can name the Chief Justice of the United States. Come on, quick, it's right back there a couple of paragraphs. On the other hand, 65% can name all the judges on *Dancing with the Stars*, and 59% can still identify the Three Stooges even though they've all been dead for years. (You get extra credit if you can recall who Curly took over for and a further bonus if you know how they were related.) Sadly, even though the three branches of government have been around a lot longer, only 41% of us know what they are, much less how they're related.

It's an interesting but ultimately tragic family dynamic that many juvenile delinquency cases originate where kids act out because they're distraught or angry over their parents' alcohol or drug abuse or violent split-ups. The kids don't seem to know how else to channel their feelings, and sometimes this behavior gets them yanked out of the house and placed at least temporarily in a foster or group home. Subconsciously, that may have been their goal in the first place. How do you like that analysis by someone who never crossed the threshold of Psych 101?

We had a hearing in one of those cases yesterday, and the issue was whether the 13 year-old kid was ready to go home from the therapeutic facility where he's been working on anger management and conflict resolution. After everyone else had weighed in, I asked the kid himself whether there were areas he thought he still needed to work on. He said he thought he was doing pretty well, but still needed to work on his farting.

I confess, that one totally sucker-punched me, and while I did my best to maintain a few wispy shreds of decorum, the rest of the participants, including the kid's hapless parents, collapsed in hysterics as I sputtered and harrumphed. In that couple of seconds it crossed my mind that maybe the kid meant he was still trying to perfect— not suppress—his sphincter talents, but also that this was yet another topic Chief Justice Roberts has not wrestled with. In fact, I venture that the words "fart" or "farting" or even "old fart" are not among those ever uttered in his hushed velvet chamber. By the way, I found there were other issues the kid needed to work on besides his farting, and we agreed to check on them again in a month or so. If the subject rears its ugly aroma—

er, head—again, I'll be prepared, as I wrote "This is the Farter" very prominently across my file folder.

Another thing worth knowing about us part-timers is how utterly lacking in preparation most of us were. When I came on board, the full-time judges at all court levels usually got sent to the Judicial College in Reno for a two-week cram course in all things judgely—and maybe how to shoot craps (since many cases are crap shoots). The part-timers, however, were left to dig out the sweaty old robes their predecessors left behind and then were shoved out into the courtroom with an armful of cases and an expression of sheer panic. It seemed sort of like when I was a terrified third-grader trying to play a wise man in front of all the parents at the Christmas pageant.

I'm told the process is somewhat less sadistic nowadays, and that mentors (other judges who survived their harrowing gauntlets) are assigned to new judges, so they have someone to call when the prosecutor asks for a "mittimus" and they have no idea what that means. I'm still not entirely sure myself, but I know it has nothing to do with either mittens or Christmas.

In my case, I'd blundered through all manner of District Court business for many years before being tapped as the decider, but frankly I'd never paid much attention to anything other than the facts and issues I could cobble together to save my own clients' bacon. Now, all of a sudden I was supposed to listen to both sides of the cases and try to figure out which one made the most sense, not to mention grope around for whether there was an important legal principle in there somewhere.

Wow, that was a lot harder than it ever looked, and I can remember feeling a sudden surge of respect for the guy who handed me his odorous robe, despite having rationalized many a prior defeat on his maddening failure to appreciate the elegant brilliance of my arguments. The first time I walked out of the courtroom after a session, I remember also thinking it was a good thing I was wearing that robe, because my clothes were soaked with the flop sweat of public bewilderment. Oh, so that's why the thing smelled the way it did! My street clothes have dried out a little under there since then, but I'm convinced that whoever first decided robes would be black must also have experienced my persperatory predicament and wanted to obscure the telltale signs of judicial anxiety.

Under these circumstances, one thing you pick up very quickly is what foxholes you need to dig for yourself to survive. You become adept at looking to the prosecutor for a recommendation about sentencing when you have no clue what would make sense, and if you really can't decide what to do when the last possible moment comes, you learn to put a thoughtful look on your face and take the matter under advisement for further research and consideration.

The latter practice is a minefield of its own, however, as the cases keep coming and coming—much like the mail, which may be why "going postal" has become synonymous with violent freak-outs. And if you don't stay on the crest of that wave, you soon get pounded into the sand and come up gasping for air, not knowing where you are or remembering what the cases were about when you finally get around to making the decisions several weeks hence.

My predecessor—the local dean of snappy one-liners—gave me very little advice as he handed off his stinky robe and climbed a few rungs up to Superior Court (he'd known both the governor and the governor's father), but he did offer one nugget worth crocheting onto a sampler: "If you're going to be wrong, at least be wrong fast." Since I thought he'd walked the talk himself (see above), I've taken over those words as a mantra of my own, and, if I do say so myself, I've cleared even the lofty bar he set for me. Just ask anyone.

As I waded into the swamp of judicial decision-making and started splashing around, I quickly discovered one critical exception to the "quick trigger" approach I'd been advised to take, based on another deeply profound observation on human nature: People hate to lose face more than almost anything else, including money, particularly when they don't think they deserve it (to lose face, that is), and they hate it most fiercely when it occurs in the personal presence of someone they'd just as soon strangle.

I refer to the emotionally-charged and therefore explosively-dangerous environment of our small claims cases. Think television's "People's Court" and you'll be right on. The parties file their own papers, often in handwriting unknown to the Palmer Method (ask your parents)—with bloody venom virtually gushing from their pens. Then, during hearings much like Judge Judy's (except for her made-for-ratings sarcasm), they do their best to explain—in voices quivering with rage—why their despicable opponents owe them as much money as they can conjure up. "Righteously indignant" would be an accurate descriptor of the plaintiffs, who often cite unscrupulous behavior and unwarranted disrespect among their defendants' many shortcomings. Not surprisingly, the defendants invariably see the plaintiffs as completely unreasonable in their expectations, and so rude and impatient in their demands that no response whatsoever, much less respect, is called for. The combination of these emotions is a "nuclear" concoction that routinely threatens to detonate right there in the courtroom and must be handled with hazmat gloves—like the legal equivalent of weapons-grade plutonium or ebola-laden mucous.

What all this boils down to is that no matter how clear the result appears to me—and probably to everyone else waiting their turns—no indication whatsoever can be given about the outcome of the dispute while the parties are standing so close to each other, not to mention within just a few feet of me. Any ill-timed slip on my part and the loss of face will cause God-knows-what hostilities to erupt. Instead, I assure the combatants that I've taken extensive notes—which may indeed be true—and that after considerable soul-searching, ranging from less than a minute to somewhat more than that, I will issue a thoughtful, written decision that we'll send them by mail, preferably to a destination greatly distant from the courthouse, which they'll receive after sufficient time for their molten emotions to have cooled somewhat.

When people ask me whether this is a dangerous job, I tell them, only partially in jest, that if I'm ever shot by a disgruntled customer for something I've done on the bench, it won't be for sending someone to jail—those guys know they deserve it—or even for putting someone's children in foster care—they often appreciate the respite in order to regroup. No, it will be for the temerity of telling someone who's irate over a failed (allegedly) car repair that his expectations are over the top and that he'll have to pay the disputed $50.00. And so he'll make sure, dammit, that no one else has to suffer a similarly outrageous travesty, and he'll pop me off outside the paper store, courtesy of his God-given, constitutionally-protected handgun, which, by the by, I'd have the temerity to deny him, as well, if I had the chance. Much more later on that emotionally-charged topic.

All of which is why I hate small claims more than any other slice of the court pie. The claims are mostly small—they can't exceed $10,000—but I don't mean monetarily; I mean petty. Such as, the plaintiffs are often trying to collect for something that's their own fault—like the guy who pays $1,500 for a sketchy car with 125,000 hard miles on it and doors that don't match, without having anyone get underneath it and check the thing out. Then he screams fraud when the junker needs a whole new engine after a couple of weeks. And the defendants are often worse—like the guy who takes a deposit on a roof job and then never (not even once) shows up to do the work, but doesn't think he should have to refund the money for some lame reason, like the plaintiff kept calling him every day.

If there's anything that wears through my patience faster than a teenager through a set of tires, it's people trying to pass their unreasonableness off as righteous indignation. They say, trying to hog the high road, "Judge, I didn't file this claim for the money; it's the principle of the thing." Maybe so, but a veteran lawyer in our town who was a keen observer of human nature once told me, "Phil, when someone tells you it's not the money, it's the principle of the thing; it's the money." My own experience has borne out that comment so many times it ought to be chiseled in granite over the courthouse entrance—as well as the corollary that if they say it's the principle of the thing, they often don't have much in the way of their own principles to fall back on.

So, the people who fall into this hypocritical basket may not pick it up in my demeanor—masking your personal feelings is one self-preservative skill judges work hard to cultivate—but under circumstances like the ones I've described, they can pretty much kiss goodbye any chance of a sympathetic ruling. Then, after a plaintiff gets a decision the defendant didn't count on, he's totally outraged and resolves that he's not about to pay it—ever. That means he comes back over and over again for payment hearings, with one story after another about the dog eating his checkbook or not having enough to pay for Direct TV with the NFL package, all the while showing up with a pack of $7.00 cigarettes bulging through his shirt pocket and showing $10.00 a week for trash pickup on his financial affidavit. If you can't tell, this is a topic that really gets my bald tires squealing.

In fact, sometimes I have to bite down painfully hard on my poor tongue to keep from saying, "Look, you screwed up. You trusted someone you shouldn't have and they took you to the cleaners. It's happened to all of us. Just write yourself a sticky note about how not to let it happen again, slap it on your forehead, and move on. Life's too short to get your undies in a huge bunch over this, and you're being a jerk about it yourself at this point."

Of course, even if I might have offered such a frank assessment of the situation in the old days, when there wasn't even a bailiff in the courtroom to hear it, there's no way I'd venture that much candor now, not with every word recorded digitally and stored on some cavernous hard drive for the next hundred years. There'd be a complaint lodged with the Judicial Conduct Committee before the metal detector was turned off, and there for all to hear and replay endlessly would be the incriminating (though clearly truthful) smoking handgun of judicial suicide. If I wasn't completely de-robed for such blatant lack of proper demeanor, I'd certainly be forced to endure long hours of sensitivity counseling in order to better understand the tender feelings and extreme anxiety of our hapless constituents. You could probably look me up on You Tube under "Bottom Rung Judge Goes Berserk and Blurts Truth."

I'm writing this as I continue to labor daily in the small claims trenches, and some of it is relevant to where I now find myself in this diatribe, er, this scrupulously fair and balanced discourse. At the beginning of our last small claims session, we had about a dozen cases on tap for "hearings on the merits", the judicially-verbose terminology for "trials". As always, I was hoping against hope to dodge the bullet in many—no, all—of these case studies in human shortcomings, by having our two trained mediators meet with the participants and try to work out their differences through rational discussion and negotiation. A long shot, I admit, but I make a big pitch for this process at the beginning of each session, telling people that mediation gives them a chance to hand-craft their outcomes, so they all receive a result they can live with. Otherwise, if I have to make the decision strictly on what the law is, there will be a clear winner and loser, not a compromise, and it's almost certain that at least one party will be really miffed about the result. Maybe both of them. Then, the losing party(ies) will be certain I'm an idiot and may develop homicidal ideation. Not a healthy result for me either.

The problem this day demonstrated another of the classic traits of human nature we see confirmed over and over: People are like lemmings, and once one of them heads for the precipice, they all start running for it like everything's 50% off at Walmart. Unfortunately, the first case I called involved people who didn't want to be in the same room with each other, much less try to sit across a table and work toward a consensus. Not surprisingly, they nixed mediation, and so the dike was broken, to shift my metaphor. From there on, no one in the crowd even wanted to consider working with the mediators; they all wanted a full hearing from me, whether they had to wait hours to get it and whether their cases might have been resolved quickly and reasonably by agreement. Needless to say, the results confirmed my prediction: There were six hearings, and I was an idiot a half dozen times.

For example, one of the cases was brought to collect the balance of a loan made in 1997, which the defendant probably would have paid if a reasonable schedule had been worked out, but which was now way beyond the 3-year "statute of limitations", the law that says how long you've got to sue before you can't sue any longer. I didn't say anything about that issue in the courtroom (see my trepidation above), but there was just no getting around that 500-pound gorilla when the decision was made. When he got the bad news, I'm sure the plaintiff thought I was the scum of the earth for refusing to make his deadbeat former friend (also his brother-in-law, as it turned out) pay what he owed, no matter what the reason. As a result, another black eye for the court system and the retarded judge, just because this family couldn't talk out the problem over the grill in the backyard—or over our lovely conference table.

For me, the lesson here is that when I make that first pitch for the wonders of mediation, I need to have a plant out there among the disgruntled claimants who's prepared to pop up and get the band wagon moving toward Compromise Junction right from the start. More of the parties in those cases will be happier in the long run—if indeed anything short of a pound of flesh will appease them—and I totally will be, 'cause, as I think I've said about a dozen times now, I hate those cases.

If you've managed to stick with me this far, maybe you're wondering why this guy is a judge at all, since he hates it so much. Actually, if I've given that impression, I'd better log out and reboot, because except for those pesky small claims, I really feel pretty warm and fuzzy about what I'm doing here nearly all the rest of the time.

In fact, I'll stick my neck out and allege that I was born for this work, and, without blowing my horn too loudly, that I'm right up there near the head of the class in judicial demeanor, if nothing else, despite my well-disguised and previously undisclosed inner turmoil.

That's not to say my intelligence quotient is any higher than marginally average—clinging precariously to the 50th percentile at best. However, apart from botching up the decisions half the time, I do lay claim to virtually unlimited reserves of patience, which I specialize in exhibiting even to our most obnoxious and disrespectful customers. Also, because I've had so much experience, my skin is now scarred over enough not to bleed even when flagrantly whacked and poked by all the people who think I've screwed them royally and/or ruined their very lives.

Likewise, I hold no grudges whatsoever, such that those I've convicted a peck of times in the past can take solace that they're just as likely as virgin defendants to be found not guilty the next time they do something incredibly stupid or intentionally wicked.

I view myself as a hardliner on law and order, but I don't cut the prosecutors any slack when it comes to having their ducks lined up to meet their burdens of proof—even when there's no doubt at all that the defendants really did the reprehensible deeds they're charged with.

And when I finally send people to jail, which is relatively rare, I think nearly all the budding incarcerants would agree they've finally run out the string and now fully deserve their institutional quiet time.

I'm scrupulously polite and deferential to everyone and do my darnedest not to embarrass, insult or belittle defendants, especially when I can see they already feel badly enough about screwing up and getting ensnared in the law enforcement web.

When I rule against an attorney or prosecutor, I do it as gently as I can, so they get the point but don't lose their own face in front of their peers. As I mentioned, people hate losing face more than losing to the Yankees in Boston—and that's saying something in these parts.

Even though I am indeed judging here, I try not to give the impression of judging the worth of the participants as human beings, as I've never seen that cosmic role included in my job description. After all, there but for someone's—or something's—good graces go me as well as them—or you. (I'm not making any theological judgments either.)

I don't moralize more than I can help it, except that I'm prone to deliver a mini-lecture to kids who may need a swift kick in the jeans to prevent a repeat appearance—and I try to do it in terms they can understand instead of sounding too much like an old fart (which gets harder all the time). If at first I don't succeed, I dial it up a few notches the next time around, but try to end on a note of optimism.

When I have to make decisions, I do so without delay (remember, "be wrong fast"), so the parties aren't on pins and needles wondering where the hammer is going to fall. It may fall on their noggins, but I don't whack them with it any harder than necessary.

The bottom line is that I do care about how people view me in all things, which I used to deny but have come to recognize and acknowledge, and this is particularly true while I'm sporting the dorky black dress. When I had my first judicial review a few years ago, someone sucking up big time made the comparison to Atticus Finch, which despite their ulterior motives, I nevertheless cherish more than anything anyone has ever said. By the way, today I got word that my most recent evaluation has been tabulated, and, like a kid going in to meet with the principal, I'll now have to meet with one of my colleagues to see whether I've successfully maintained my class standing. If not, I dread what my parents will say and am already calculating where to hide the report card.

Before moving on, permit me a brief reprise on the subject of part-time judging and its frequently awkward ripples. Last week, I was manning the door at home for the continuous stream of trick-or-treaters (450+ most years) who invade our neighborhood every October 31 from all over our Monadnock Region. During that tour of duty, I came face to face with several people I've sentenced recently enough for mutual recognition (note to self: wear own mask next year), including one woman whose children I could have sworn were in the protective custody of a foster home. Maybe she'd borrowed someone else's?

Then the next day at the State cross-country meet, I was taking photos of the local high school team, as I've done for the coaches for a generation now. Suddenly in my viewfinder I spied a runner's father I'd had in court just days before with another of his sons whom he'd proclaimed our juvenile system had failed miserably. I kept the camera up to my face for cover, backed up as inconspicuously as possible and snapped on my telephoto lens.

Finally, at our local theatre's benefit auction that very night, I was button-holed by the victorious plaintiffs in a recent small claims case, who didn't care who was listening as they loudly grabbed the chance to further malign their adversary to all within earshot. Actually, I'm not really sure just what they said, my only thought at that awkward moment being that at least I hadn't run into the guy on the short end of the stick or there might have been a lot of well-dressed witnesses to a murder attempt.

While we're in the neighborhood, let's hit the subject of conflicts of interest for a moment. I think it's a fair statement that most people are clueless when it comes to the kinds of situations that present even grossly blatant conflicts.

At the beginning of every session, I start with my little spiel about the pleas people can enter and the kinds of cases that would allow them to have court-appointed lawyers. I finish up with a request that they let our bailiff know if they've ever had any out-of-court business with me or other lawyers I've worked with (the part-time factor redux), so we can avoid conflicts of interest that would be taboo. Sounds straight-forward enough, right?

While the faces out there show signs of grasping the plea and lawyer parts, their eyes seem to glaze over about the conflicts warning. I know this concept isn't sinking in when I have perfectly intelligent clients and friends call me at the office for advice about cases they know I'm going to hear when they or their kids or their friend's brother-in-law comes to court the day after tomorrow.

First of all, they don't see anything at all wrong about trying to lobby me and then they seem utterly surprised when I tell them we'll now have to reschedule those contaminated cases to a day in our sister court in Keene. And when things don't end up working out for them as they were hoping I'd make it happen for them, they often let me know it in a prickly tone of voice, as though I should have made sure that judge knew they were Friends of Phil and deserved special consideration. Then, when I provide my civics clichés about blind justice being the goal, etc., I sense they're deciding to find a lawyer and/or friend who will watch their backs better than I'm obviously [not] doing. This job doesn't pay much, but there are so many intangible benefits.

Before moving into new territory, I want to jump back a couple of paragraphs to report on my current judicial evaluation, which I've now poured over in detail and reviewed with one of my full-time rung-mates.

All in all, it seems our constituents are reasonably satisfied with my benchside manner, my attentiveness (no claims of sleeping on the job at least), the promptness of my rulings (wrong but quick), and my general grasp of the subject matter, which is comforting after 20+ years. Apparently, my only serious shortcoming is leniency, or, some (prosecutors?) would say, coddling of criminals. They say I'm just not severe enough with repeat offenders and that I sometimes reduce fines for people who should be paying every nickel I could squeeze out of them.

My response to my robe-mate when this spineless liberal tendency was raised was to plead guilty, or at least *nolo contendere*, and to request forgiveness for my transgressions. On second thought—lots more than that really—I'm not apologizing for anything. My theory of judicial sentencing is this: You don't engender respect for the courts and the law by hammering people to the max just because you can.

For example, if a single mother comes in for a second charge of driving after her license was suspended because she couldn't pay a prior fine, I'm certainly not going to send her to jail, even though the offense is a serious misdemeanor and I could give her a full year off from the ill-mannered kids. I'm probably not even going to hit her with the full $500 the prosecutor recommends. Instead, if it's obvious that she drove out of desperation, either to keep her job or to take the kids to the doctor, I'll start with a pretty serious fine, but suspend a healthy chunk of it for a year, so she'll have enough incentive not to do it again. As a bonus, maybe that will help her avoid getting evicted from her apartment for an extra month or help get the kids winter coats. If that's being soft on crime, then smack me around with a wet copy of the motor vehicle code and let's move on to the next case.

Likewise, we often have people come in to fight speeding tickets or yellow line mishaps, most of them caught dead to rights but from Massachusetts where any moving violation apparently makes their insurance premiums go haywire. If the people are at all reasonable—that is, don't make complete asses of themselves by their chip-on-the-shoulder attitude toward the hapless cops who pinched them, and they don't have an embarrassing driving record of recent vintage—I'll often continue their cases for a year and dismiss their complaints at that point if they can resist other such infractions in the meantime. Probably 98% of those cases do get dismissed and we never see the people again. That experience would seem to mean people are driving safer for at least a little while—and maybe recognizing long-term that the consequences of another 15-over will get them whacked far beyond the $200 fine they might incur next time. The police often recommend these arrangements themselves, but it's indefensible coddling if I come up with the idea.

This lily-livered affliction dovetails with my penchant for letting obviously guilty criminals go free because of "technicalities" originally concocted by the "activist" Supreme Court during the Earl Warren years. Actually, no one went that far in their evaluation comments; I can just read that in the hardliners' faces when I dismiss charges based on such minor glitches as a search without probable cause or a confession without benefit of Miranda warnings. Of course, no one would blame them for raising those defenses if they or their kids or their friend's brother-in-law was suddenly tangled in the web of law enforcement, whether guilty or not, and they'd be wicked outraged if I failed to recognize the "rule of law" in their behalf.

It's funny how this works, but these attitudes always come down to whose ox is being gored and which side of the fence they're on, while the tricky challenge of my job is to make sure the shoe fits the same way each time, no matter whose foot it's being slipped onto. If I'm guilty of anything, it's of mixing my metaphors, which I do recklessly and without remorse.

This is Thanksgiving week and we're driving to Virginia to attack a turkey with our daughter and son-in-law, then make a one-day round trip from there to my hometown in North Carolina to see my aging parents who are still hanging on in their own home, if only by their arthritic, octogeneric fingernails. It's over a thousand miles in all, but we've got plenty of recorded books and we've come to look forward to the trek as an annual family reunion.

Thanksgiving always reminds me of a speeding case a few years back, when a man who was driving his own mother to visit relatives in Massachusetts wanted to plead insanity to the charge. After I quieted down the chorus of guffaws, I explained that insanity wasn't a plea option to a non-criminal charge and that nothing but a pulse and nominal mental capacity was required. He admitted those capabilities, but insisted that he wouldn't have been speeding if his mother hadn't been driving him crazy. Thinking this might be a slick ploy just to avoid the points and the fine, I asked the officer whether he made any telling observations during his time with the allegedly demented driver. The cop admitted that there was indeed a well-dressed elderly woman in the vehicle and that while he was sitting in his cruiser checking the maniac's record, the guy was pacing around and around his vehicle, waving his arms and muttering to himself in an agitated manner.

Whereupon, I filed the case in the overflowing "soft-on-crime" bin, not by reason of insanity but because it seemed that a sufficient penalty had already been paid.

I just received a memo sent out to all District Court judges by our administrative leader, asking for candidates for certification as a Family Division judge. The Family Division is the new court configuration in New Hampshire that gathers all family-related cases into one judicial basket, on the theory that one-stop shopping for family justice is likely to be more efficient and effective. Right now, you go to Superior Court for divorces and to Probate Court for adoptions and terminations of parental rights, and you come to us in District Court for domestic violence and juvenile abuse, neglect and delinquency cases. This means there are at least three judges trying to get to know the family and then undoubtedly making decisions that are at least slightly inconsistent, if not from wholly different solar systems. What this merger of family cases might mean for me is still unclear, though I'm doing my best to sort it out.

One thing it would undoubtedly mean is I'd again have to wade into the murky and treacherous waters of cases involving the dreaded "D" word—and I don't mean dolphins. That's a practice area I was eager to escape when I became a judge, on the ground that I hated divorce cases then as much as the small claims cases I hate now, and for essentially the same reasons. Namely, the people involved were too often uninterested in reasonable resolutions of their disputes, preferring instead to bludgeon their former soulmates into submission and to use me as their weapon. A steel cage death match is the mental picture I channel when I close my eyes. I'm not a psychologist (although I play one every day), but I believe the "person scorned" syndrome is often the correct clinical diagnosis.

When I took that fateful step up to the first rung here in Jaffrey, I seized the opportunity to jettison my divorce portfolio, explaining that I'd never be able to resolve the scheduling conflicts between Superior Court divorce hearings and the sessions I'd have to cover on my own bench. As a Family Division judge, I'd be tossed back into the maelstrom—and have to contend with elevated stress and blood pressure levels that could be life-threatening now that I'm so much older and weaker than when first sucked into that riptide. Hmm?

Other factors of significance are whether I'd have to give up practicing law, with its attendant social interactions and modest but necessary compensation, as well as whether I'd have to start traveling to distant and unfamiliar courts to hear cases I'd just as soon not contend with even here at home. The chief reason not to miss this opportunity for self-abuse is that if someone else slides in as the Family Division judge for our court, I'd then be relegated to the remnants of small claims, landlord and tenant, and criminal and motor vehicle cases, without even the glimmer of doing something nominally worthwhile in a juvenile case—and without enough mental stimulation to keep me from nodding off and drooling on myself, not to mention developing an uncontrollable urge to whack myself in the head with my gavel (for which I've yet to find a better use). Hmm?

OK, I filed the application, to keep my foot in the door if nothing else. Now I hope absolutely nothing is done with it until they get ready to activate the Family Division in our quiet little corner of the State. Fortunately, that won't likely happen until the bigwigs come up with a suitable location for a new courthouse in the metropolis of Keene (pop. 20,000 or so). See, they don't want to inconvenience the Keene folks by making them schlep over to lil' ole Jaffrey for their divorces, so until there's a bed for the Family Division over there, they probably won't fire up the program over here either. And judging from the glacial pace at which they settled on a new jail location for that county, which took over a decade, I may be lucky enough to retire as a Family Division judge without ever leaving any DNA on another divorce file. At least that's my goal, unless, of course, human nature morphs enough in the meantime to make reasonableness a dominant genetic trait among my fellow homosapiens. Not a chance—pigs will fly first.

I forget what time of year I started writing all this down, but now we're well into the holiday season, and with it the ubiquitous Christmas party conversations. Frequently, once the Red Sox's chances next season have been fully dissected, the desire to avoid embarrassing silences causes someone to ask whether I'm still enjoying being a judge. I don't know just why, but I always find this question mildly irritating, as though passing judgment on people who've screwed up or fallen on hard times could ever really be enjoyable. Maybe I'm being overly prickly, but it also seems to carry with it the suggestion that it's not particularly challenging to whack people with fines and occasionally have them banished from my presence in handcuffs—and that indeed it could be sort of fun. In fact, I get the feeling they'd ask the question the same way if they wanted to know whether I still liked driving my Ford Escape, with its all-wheel drive and reliable service record. Sensing they're hoping the question doesn't require a terribly prolonged or nuanced response, I usually provide the same kind of innocuous comment I'd give if they'd really asked about the Escape. If they want to know more, I figure they'll probe deeper with another question, which they rarely do. Actually, they usually excuse themselves at that point and head for the bar.

Not that everyone else has it light and breezy in their careers and never has to make critical, soul-searching decisions, but I feel like we're actually changing the trajectories of people's lives here. Maybe not roto-rooting their clogged arteries or bombarding their cancer cells, but we're definitely up to more than what got all the laughs on "Night Court".

I mean, if I take a child out of an abusive home over the parents' tearful pleas and place her in a foster home, and the surrogate parents eventually adopt the child because the abusers never get their act together, that child is going to have a much different life—and maybe even a real chance to excel. If I send a teenager with a cocaine problem to a residential treatment program, as I did twice yesterday, instead of letting the kid make more empty promises and then get high with his pals, that teenager might kick the stuff before turning 17 and avoid building an adult criminal record that could close a lot of doors—and I don't mean just in the cell block. If I give an abused woman a protective order, even after she's given up on several such attempts in the past, maybe she'll be strong enough this time to ditch the relationship for good and end up with a less bruising life after all.

On the down side, if I have to find a truck driver guilty of DWI, he's probably going to lose his livelihood and perhaps eventually his family's home. Sometimes the outcomes seem nothing but negative, but then maybe that guy's not going to kill himself or someone else on the road, which would be a net plus, right?

I think my take on the work stems from my (everyone's?) hope that I'm making some slight difference during my incredibly brief time here, and that others can [occasionally] see that, as well. It's the gizzard complex: No one wants to believe his function is completely unnecessary to the larger scheme of things and that no one would miss a beat if he suddenly failed to show up for work one day—or two days or ever again.

But maybe some people really don't care about that sort of thing or give it a moment's thought. Maybe it's plenty if they get their paychecks on Friday and then have the weekend off to enjoy them. Some of us are twitchier about it, though. For example—and no offense intended to my highly capable and committed colleagues at the bar—but being a lawyer, even if I was a really good lawyer (we all fantasize), just isn't enough for me. If I hadn't gotten this opportunity all those years ago, I'd have moved on to something else by now—politics, teaching, something where I could see a direct correlation between the work and a real difference for someone else. And I don't mean just for the people who paid me to write them a will or some other legal thingy they couldn't understand.

OK, maybe if I could come up with a contract to rid the world of tobacco, drugs and guns (I'd probably settle for assault weapons), or a treaty among nations to cool off the global atmosphere a few degrees, I'd feel differently. Don't get me wrong, you clients who may be reading this, I'm still working really, really hard and enthusiastically on your wills and all, but right now I've got a standing room-only crowd in the courtroom to deal with. For the moment they're barging in line ahead of you, and some of their lives are hanging precariously in the balance.

Today's docket exposed another side of our already acrimonious small claims business. All the people summoned in were judgment defendants who hadn't paid what I decided they owed. Most had been in at least a couple of times before, having agreed to pay something like $25 a month on a $5,000 debt but having defaulted, often within just a few weeks of having made their half-hearted promises. Some responded defiantly and indignantly, wanting to re-argue their cases from the beginning— obviously, I didn't really hear them out in the first place—and still not acknowledging that they owed their lying, no good opponents even a lousy 25 cents.

These are terribly aggravating situations because the defendants figure out very quickly that if they agree to payments, then just don't make them, it will be at least a few months before they get called back onto the carpet and then can probably start the whole process over again. Their opponents soon become indignant, too, and their outrage quickly boils over onto the court, spewing vitriol about our inability to enforce our own orders and about our spineless failure to throw the no-good scofflaws in jail.

At the other end of the spectrum are the working poor who are up to their eyeballs in debt and can't even figure out how they got there. They're unable to reliably pay much of anything and can't even come up with the funds to pay the filing fee for bankruptcy. Ironically, they suffer further losses by having to appear at these hearings, because missing time from work either causes them to lose what little they might have paid on their entailments, or to lose their jobs entirely in the extreme case. When I review their depressing financial affidavits, I can see nearly all of them could use a healthy dose of counseling about their expenses—which I should probably be more aggressive about for both parties' benefit. The problem is there's just no time for that when there're 50 more similarly hard-luck stories in the queue and everyone is not very inconspicuously looking at their watches. Given another 20 minutes with each of them, I'm sure we could whack something totally unnecessary out of their expenses that could go toward the judgments—or toward the cost of blood pressure drugs on the other side of the cases.

Finally, and the most aggravating of all, are the people who say they can't pay anything—ever—because they're disabled and living entirely on Social Security, but who look, sound, walk and act perfectly able-bodied and, pardon my jaundiced eye, appear to be malingering at everyone's expense. Of course, I can't ask what put them on the disabled list, because they have federal privacy rights that keep secret how they managed to wangle their benefits. All I can do is keep hauling them back in here every few months to reconfirm their mysterious status.

Yes, please pardon me if just a sliver of cynicism is peaking through, but don't get me wrong either. There are certainly legitimate disabilities out there, which I sympathize with and don't begrudge the recipients their rightful assistance in the least. One tip-off for me is that most of the truly disabled say they would actually prefer to be healthy enough to put in a good day's work.

As for the malingerers, though, I bet I could come up with jobs any of them could handle if, gods forbid, they didn't risk losing their freebie benefits. Indeed, they occasionally slip up and hint that they're already working "under the table," undoubtedly without paying any taxes, to boot. Still, it would take Colombo to catch them at it and—oops, I think he died recently anyhow. What's worse is that these folks rationalized away any guilt about the whole business long ago, concluding that if they could somehow finagle the benefits, then they must deserve them, this being another mutation of those "all's fair" exceptions to good citizenship. Except that this is a game we're all paying for them to play.

I have a personal testimonial about the doldrums of debt to add here. A few years before hopping up on this rung, I ventured into the murky waters of commercial real estate investment with several well-known-to-me [non-judicial] colleagues. Unfortunately, as I kept my nose to the legal grindstone and paid almost no attention to the project's financial well-being, the now-former colleague who was charged with keeping it in the black—and being paid generously to do so—wasn't acting in the best interests of the rest of us, shall we say. That's a book-length tale in itself, which won't be told here.

In very short order, and before I could say "amortization", the lender had foreclosed and was looking to me (the only solvent one left) to pony up the remaining balance, based on the personal guaranty I had blithely signed back there when everything about the project seemed fool-proof. The amount still owed, even after the property was sold, was in the mid-six-figure ballpark, which, like the balance left after the poor small claim defendant's car has been repo-ed, was way more than I could come up with, even calling upon all my lavish judicial perks.

To say the least, I saw very little promise on the horizon and was teetering on the brink of throwing in the robe before I'd even broken it in. I mean, if I had to run for the cover of bankruptcy in order to keep from losing the roof over my little family's heads, much less my children's baseball cards and Cabbage Patch Kids, how could I in good conscience hold other peoples' feet to their financial conflagrations?

I kept meeting with my creditor's posse and offering to set up the kind of long-term payment plan we do at court, but they gave the impression they'd rather just shoot me between the eyes and collect my life insurance. When the talks finally broke down because I couldn't just write them the largest check of my life, I felt sure I'd soon be visited by a sheriff bearing the necessary papers to amortize me for good. But they—the papers of death, that is—didn't come. Then they kept not coming. Eventually, I started adding up the months since their first demand for payment and I realized it was getting close to the legal deadline. As I noted back a ways, you can't wait forever to drop the hammer on someone beholden to you; the law says you've got to whack them within a certain window of years or your victim gets to move on whack-free.

In my case, the last possible day finally came and went with nary a tap, much less a whack. I couldn't believe it, so I re-counted several more times using every finger and toe I have. My math seemed right but I waited even longer, just to be safe, before starting to breathe again. Still nothing, nada. Then, a few weeks later the sheriff came huffing and puffing into the office (not the court office, fortunately) and handed me the bad news—only by that time it wasn't bad anymore.

Ironically, my pursuers' miscount led the way to a silver lining for nearly everyone. Turns out it was their red-faced lawyer who'd flunked math and missed the deadline, so it was his malpractice insurer who, after exacting monstrous premiums for years without a claim, gnashed its teeth and returned the entire amount to my creditor on my behalf. This not only got the hard-nosed and insensitive debt-demons their money a generation or more before I could have done so, but it kept me from having to slink down from my little rung in financial disgrace.

The morals of the story: Stick to what you know; don't count on someone else to mind the shop for you; and know when to be very thankful for luck you didn't really deserve.

Not all small claims expose the dark underbelly of human nature. Some are just plain wacky and have me once more looking around the room for the hidden camera.

This time a wedding DJ sued the woman who'd hired him to play at her daughter's reception. She paid him $100 up front and he was to get the other $100 at the end of the gig. He shuffled tapes and kept everyone on the dance floor for four hours, but at the end she refused to pay up, so he sued. Open and shut, right; what could be clearer? When I say that to myself, there's always a dope slap coming and this had a big one.

The mother explained that the written contract the DJ himself had insisted on specifically called for him to play *All My Life* by Linda Ronstadt when the bride and groom first took the floor, and *Through the Years* by Kenny Rogers when the bride danced with dad. A couple of really sappy numbers they were better without, if they'd asked me, but they didn't, people's taste in music being one of the most peculiar mysteries in "all my life."

Anyhow, when the big moment came, the DJ's machine gobbled the special tape, causing him to make frantic, last-minute substitutions. Let's face it, his choices were probably tremendous improvements (however, I was never able to frame a diplomatic query), but the replacements severely traumatized the entire wedding party, to hear mom tell it. As she did, the young newlywed, who was sobbing softly at her mother's side, turned up the volume enough to underscore the tragedy—and then blew her nose like a truck driver.

Observing the regular protocol of holding my fire until the parties had left the area (you know, to avoid being fired on), I promptly returned to the backroom and ruled for the defendant, actually able this time to rely on solid principles of contract law rather than my less-than-legal-but-discriminating musical judgment. Thus: The written agreement made clear the performance required of the DJ, and his technical difficulties resulted in a material breach. Moreover, the breach wasn't an unavoidable act of the music gods because the guy could have made a backup tape for just such potential, last-minute catastrophes.

For you folks not old enough to remember, those cassette tapes got tangled up all the time. The plaintiff undoubtedly planned ahead ever after—and surely converted to more reliable digital at the first opportunity. (On second thought, he probably decided on law school, too, so he'd know how to put exculpatory fine print into future contracts.)

Even though the damage done was catastrophic and irreparable—certainly warranting a pound of flesh from the plaintiff's first born—I did the best I could by denying him the final $100. Judgment *Signed, Sealed, Delivered*, with a nod to Stevie Wonder.

I'm not imaginative enough to make up stuff like this, so you'll have to take my word for it.

Christmas is less than a week away now and with it always come a number of special judicial challenges. The most critical are those that involve deciding who spends the holiday in jail, with the turkey and fixing's provided by the county. Someone with a record of being criminally naughty (after checking the list twice), or with a history of failing to show up when invited, will come in for a bail hearing on a new charge on December 23, and the prosecutor will be asking for cash to be put up to guaranty the defendant's nice behavior, or at least his return trip to court for trial.

That leaves it squarely in my lap to decide whether cash is really necessary, and so I start tossing out potential lifelines for the defendant to grab. How long has it been since the other naughtiness, and has the prior lack of niceness been cleared up? How really naughty were the former transgressions, and does the new one involve violence or other special badness? How long has the defendant lived in the area, and does (s)he have a job and/or family nearby that might ensure an interest in coming back?

Sometimes the right answers to those questions will make non-cash bail (called "personal recognizance" in legal-speak, or "PR") seem like a risk worth taking. Sometimes, though, it's just going to take some or all—or even more than all—of that Christmas bonus to be ponied up, no matter how sympathetically I try to pump up the pros and discount the cons.

Then the big job—sort of like playing *The Price is Right*—is coming up with the precise amount that will provide enough incentive for the seasonally-unlucky chap to behave or to show up for trial, but not so much that the person has no prayer of raising the funds even with family help or by cutting back on the holiday cheer. Other times it's much easier, and I make the calculated decision that spending Christmas in jail will be the best gift I can give one of our regular customers who sorely needs a punch bowl of icy eggnog in the face and some coal in the stocking. You know, sort of the gift that keeps on giving.

The same considerations often pertain to the surly teenager who's been paying lip service to my chronically ineffective efforts to drag her (yes, her in many cases), often kicking and screaming, back into the traces of marginally appropriate behavior. By the time I start thinking Christmas in a shelter facility or the juvie detention center would be a valuable life lesson, the kid has already been given enough rope to weave a hammock, and now she's used all of it.

Clearly, even though a holiday vacation may be richly deserved, the kid either doesn't think an old guy in a bowtie has the backbone to make the order, or at least can't believe I'd dare take that drastic step just before Christmas. Sometimes the kid gets away with the chronic battiness one more time, there being even a shred of improved compliance demonstrated, but sometimes even Mother Theresa would send the kid on a Christmas behavior modification pilgrimage.

Like clockwork, even the stone-coldest kid then dissolves into a sobbing mass and begs for one more chance. It's at that moment that I know I'm making my point—much like Judge Smayles in *Caddyshack* ("Danny, I've sent younger boys than you to the electric chair; I didn't want to, but felt I owed it them."). My less-than-life-threatening sentiments exactly, with a frequent concurrence by his/her beleaguered parents.

Before any of those invaluable life lessons start to sink in, however, the kid will express the sincere hope that I die choking on a turkey bone for wrecking her premeditated plan to further terrorize her exhausted family. Yes, there's nothing like the holidays to lighten our hearts and foster goodwill to all. "Say, are you still enjoying being a judge?"

This festive season also creates a surge in certain offenses that are less prevalent the rest of the year. Of course, alcohol rules the roost year-round, but even more so now because of exuberantly foolish behavior at holiday parties or as the working person's antidote to the depression that flares up like a seasonal allergy. One source of the latter is the lack of funds to produce the abundant Christmas experience we're constantly shown on television, often manifesting itself not only in binge drinking but also in a rash of desperate financial moves.

One of the worst holiday scenarios is the working poor's loan alternative. It goes like this: There's no money for toys for the kids, so the parents go to Walmart three days before Christmas and writes a bad check for several hundred dollars. They know it's dead on arrival at their bank but figure they'll have a few weeks before they get the insufficient funds notice from the store and by then they'll have another paycheck or two to cover it. The trouble is, those paychecks are already committed to the rent and lights, and the family will also need oil to get them through January without freezing solid, for which the guy who drives the truck will insist on cash because the oil company itself gets burned by scads of bad checks this time of year.

So, the family doesn't cover the check(s) after all, and along about February or March we'll see them in here when the cops finally bring the criminal charge for theft. At that point, they'll not only pick up a criminal record and have to pay the check and bank charges, but they'll get fined, making the APR on their do-it-yourself loan anywhere from 50-100%. Probably not a sound financial decision, but what's the alternative short of not buying the latest My Little Pony or PlayStation for the kids, which never seems a serious option anymore?

Despite the foregoing obstacles, I've always labored under the impression that people really do have a soft spot for each other this time of year and that at least they try to act more like they care. Today's landlord and tenant case shook that assumption to the core.

A young guy came in trying to evict an older woman from an apartment in his house. While it seemed a little harsh to be pushing for this with two weeks left before Christmas, it turned into Greek tragedy when I realized about ten minutes into the testimony that the tenant was the landlord's own mother. Apparently, the mother sold the house to the son for less than it was worth, in return for the right to live there with reduced rent for the rest of her life (query: why was any rent at all necessary, but OK). It was true she didn't pay the rent, but that was because her loving son had turned off the heat and she was going to freeze if she didn't find another place to warm up.

I started to pronounce that it's unconstitutional to evict your mother from anywhere, at any time, for any reason, but then I saw the little green light on the digital recorder and squelched my verbal disdain. When it came to making a decision, though, I found I could base it on real law after all. The ungrateful son—who acted like he'd been toilet-trained at gun point, to borrow a colleague's quip—hadn't served the eviction papers the right way. So the poor little tyke is going to have to start all over again. Awww. By that time it will be verging on Spring, and if he hasn't thought better of his treatment of mom by then, I guaranty I'll look at those landlord and tenant statutes pretty carefully before rewarding his behavior. Merry Christmas, mom. Maybe Santa will bring you a more deserving son this year.

Now it's the day after Christmas, and after four days of eating enough monstrous, albeit home-cooked and delicious, family meals to produce food coma, I'm clinging to consciousness by my fingernails as I slog through an ill-advised juvenile docket. I should have known better than to subject myself to the court's most challenging list on a day when my stress-calming exercise regimen has suffered such a devastating setback.

What's more, in the midst of all the kids came an adult fellow who was picked up on the 23rd for having an open bottle of vodka in the car—which as a house painter, he swore to the officer, was just paint thinner in a poorly chosen container. Likely untrue, but remarkably resourceful on the spur of the moment.

Unfortunately, technology being the know-it-all it has become, the computer revealed an outstanding Maine warrant for a 2001 bad check never made good. This unlucky revelation led to an unanticipated Christmas dinner with the county security staff, probably to be repeated over New Year's while the Maine authorities find someone to send down to retrieve the overdrawn chap. Perhaps he, too, fell for the do-it-yourself holiday loan option, which he'll now repay with his presence (not presents), as well as with funds he'll have to raise, no doubt in cash this time, in order to get back to painting when he arrives Down East.

Another of the eternal flames that burns higher this time of year is domestic unrest. People whose relationships are already overheated and nearing combustion are cooped up together by the weather, and then holiday family and financial issues (more loans from hell) dump gasoline on that smoldering heap.

A couple headed inexorably for divorce came in with reciprocal claims of abuse, which may have been partially founded but looked to me like attempts to establish a foothold in the marital homestead before the ponderous locomotive of divorce got rolling. He (6'6") came in first, claiming she (5'2") pushed him off a chair and grabbed him around the neck. Not to be outdone and upon being served with his temporary restraining orders, she rushed in to allege that he pushed her and bruised her knee, though she had never reported that to the cops.

When they testified at the hearing, they were both so filled with venom and rage that they were shaking like Quakers—and their versions of the incidents were so diametrically divergent that it seemed each would say whatever it took to create a living hell for the other. I thought for a moment that we were going to see the whole incident re-enacted in the courtroom.

So I cast my most jaundiced eye and dismissed both claims as lacking sufficient credibility. As unpleasant as it may be, they'll just have to co-exist under the same roof—like Michael Douglas and Kathleen Turner in *The War of the Roses*, if I recall correctly—at least until the Superior Court factors possession of the family residence into the overall termination of their marital pact.

Still, while the result feels justified legally, I'm keeping my fingers crossed that I haven't just tossed a match of my own into the tinder box. In fact, I spent all weekend waiting to hear the fire department come screaming through town, followed closely by the ambulance squad and then the medical examiner.

A much more serious domestic explosion indeed occurred over the New Year's weekend, for which I bear no responsibility this time, thankfully.

A local guy whose marriage has been crashing on the rocks for many years (I dismissed a prior assault charge some time ago after a year of non-violent behavior) got wind that his estranged wife was "with" another fellow, whom we also knew from largely alcohol-fueled indiscretions in the past but who seemed to have turned the corner toward responsible citizenship. When the distraught husband learned of the liaison, something snapped, and upon arriving at the scene he started firing like a wild man (allegedly at this point, of course).

When the smoke cleared, the wife and her new friend were on the floor with four bullet holes each, though none fatal so far, and the wigged-out husband was holed up back at his own house, with all the cops in the area surrounding the place. Fortunately, he calmed down enough after a few hours—or sobered up perhaps—and came out without further harm to anyone, particularly to his young son who was also there and must have been terrified by the experience.

When I signed search warrants for both crime scenes on New Year's Eve, all I could think of was that this had forever become a different kind of holiday for an awful lot of people. The victims will bear permanent scars and disabilities, even if they recover, as will the distraught husband who, if convicted, will spend many years in jail and whose relationship with his children may be permanently derailed. Then there are all the parents, whose anguish must be excruciating because they're helpless (as we all are) to maintain a cocoon of safety around their adult children. Likewise, all the parties' friends, some of whom had spent time with members of the ill-fated triangle earlier in the evening, will always wonder whether they might have foreseen and somehow headed off the tragedy. Finally, there's the wife of the injured man, who was probably waiting at the hospital for news of his condition at that very moment, while also surely wondering why her husband wasn't at home with her at 10:20 that New Year's Eve.

As a postscript, the trial this fall was a statewide media extravaganza. Let's face it, we don't have many cases that combine all the classic film noir elements in one incident. The gutsy defense was that despite the number of shots fired, the jilted husband had no intent to kill either of his victims—just teach them a crippling lesson, apparently—and thus he could not be guilty of attempted murder. You have to award credit for imaginative lawyering—and for massive cohones—but how you can shoot people so many times without intending to finish the job must have been an obstacle too high for the jury to clear. That is, they came back with guilty verdicts on all counts almost as soon as they'd used the potty and eaten a final lunch on the county. Sentencing is still up in the air, though the upcoming New Year's Eve will surely be the first of many the young man will be spending with a newly-extended family.

Despite the final details of the penalty to be paid, several outcomes are already certain. The young man won't be young any longer when he's finally released. Also, because I've seen both victims walking recently, they'll both need lots more surgery, or at least years of rehab, to regain anything like their pre-New Year's well-being. And there will almost certainly be long-term consequences for the boy who was witness to the violent destruction of his family. Last but no less certain, I'll be long retired by the time this tragic story is fully written.

Another domestic violence hearing from years ago comes to mind and demonstrates how even lawyers can get sucked into the powerful emotions of these cases. This one involved the still rare but rapidly breeding male plaintiff, who was bubbling over with righteous indignation when he arrived in the courtroom to describe every outrageous detail of his abuse. The ex-girlfriend defendant wasn't throwing in the towel, however, as she arrived with lawyer in tow to parry every word of the plaintiff's version of who did what to whom.

Always hopeful even in the face of an impending conflagration, I asked the plaintiff whether he was willing to speak with the defendant's lawyer before we started the hearing, on the off-chance that a settlement might be worked out to spare me the sordid details. You'd think I'd asked them all to eat worms, but they must have decided to humor me in order not to sabotage their chances.

About ten minutes later, everyone reappeared with red faces, the wounded boyfriend claiming the lawyer had completely lost his cool and had called the plaintiff a "mother-f***ing son of a bitch." The lawyer promptly objected, stating that he wanted the record to show that, in fact, he'd called the plaintiff a "mother-f***ing, c**k-s***ing son of a bitch." (I'm sure you worldly adults can read between the asterisks despite my attempt to keep this PG-rated.)

I'm not often perceptive enough to pick up on the subtleties of human behavior, but I took this exchange to mean no settlement had been reached, and so we proceeded with the hearing. Once the facts came out, it appeared the lawyer's assessment of the plaintiff was remarkably close to the mark, though clearly one he should have kept to himself if he wanted to prevent the pressure cooker (remember those?—my mother used hers for "chitlins") from blowing.

I honestly can't recall where the dust finally settled on the combatants, but I vividly remember the lawyer waiting for me in the parking lot after the session and shame-facedly apologizing for his locker room remark. While he surely remained convinced about his original opinion of the plaintiff, he no doubt hoped to forestall a complaint from me to the Professional Conduct Committee and then a public reprimand. After hearing his plea for leniency, I accepted it as well-acted if not entirely sincere, told him to wash his mouth out with Lifebuoy (you remember that, too, right?), and allowed the matter to rest benignly there, though regretting that the PCC would miss out on one of the few good chances for chuckles it probably gets.

We're off and blundering headlong into a new year now, and it's got me thinking about how much has changed about the law and law enforcement since I was the age of many of the young people we now see. Kids get brought in these days for throwing snowballs at cars, for having schoolyard fights over some pimply girl/boy, for sneaking an underage cigarette, and for exploring abandoned buildings or old quarries despite lots of "No Trespassing" signs.

No doubt about it, if I was a kid these days, I'd be packing up my baseball cards and changing my permanent address to the juvie facility, as I perped incidents like these on practically a daily basis—all the while being considered a total goody-goody by my peers. On the subject of snowballing alone, that was a true rite of passage for every '50s—'60s era kid, despite that drivers might slam on the brakes and try to catch you before you deployed your carefully-devised escape strategy. If the police cared about this stuff at all, the worst that might happen was for them to tell your parents. They'd haul you into the cruiser or meet you on the playground after school and read you the riot act. Then, you'd swear never, ever, to do it again if they just wouldn't let your parents know, and you'd either clean up your act (not likely) or be a lot more careful so as not to get caught the next time.

Telling your parents in those different days was such a frightening deterrent because that hit you where you lived and was sure to carry way more serious retribution—probably including a vigorous spanking—than a judge would dish out anyhow. Plus, nearly everyone I knew had two parents actually living together, and the mom was there all day to hold the fort and to threaten dismemberment until the dad got home to drop the hammer. Now the cops may not even be able to identify the parents, much less find them, and way too many of our court parents can't be any help because they have more serious problems of their own. Both literally and figuratively, there's no one at home.

While we're on the subject of changes in parenting styles and standards, I'll note that corporal punishment, i.e., spanking, is where the real sea change has occurred. When I was a kid, or even when my own kids were little about 30 years ago, it was considered acceptable, even recommended, to spank kids when they deserved it. "Spare the rod and spoil the child" was still the conventional mantra, the age-old theory being that if kids didn't get the right comeuppance when they needed it, they'd turn into juvenile delinquents of the James Dean in "Rebel Without a Cause" variety—and that would be worse even than being a communist in those days.

In my own pre-delinquent days, I had to go outside and pick my switch when the moment of retribution came, and if it wasn't sufficiently sturdy to produce the proper degree of painful welts, then I had to go pick another one. There was also a leather hairbrush that got called into disciplinary service when it was too cold out to pick anything and I didn't have on short pants. None of these instruments of punishment caused either serious physical injuries or lasting PTSD (that I'm aware of anyhow) and by the time my parents got to the point of resorting to this wackiness, I usually agreed that the medicine was justifiably prescribed, even if it was painful to admit.

Somewhere in the late '70's or early '80's, though, the pendulum began to swing away from the "no pain, no gain" theory of child-rearing and toward the concepts of "time-outs" and sanctions negotiated directly with the child, in order for the tyke not to feel unfairly penalized. Now, it seems, if you so much as lay a hand on the kids, even grabbing them by the scruff of the neck and shoving them into their rooms, they punch in 911 on their cell phones and text your transgressions to the juvenile authorities who'll haul you onto the courthouse carpet as a child abuser.

Don't get me wrong, I'm not in favor of child abuse in any form, and I made that clear recently when I nearly lost my own cool with a father who'd slapped his 5-year old daughter across the face several times. He started to explain what justified that appalling failure of parental responsibility, at which point I suggested he save it for his appeal, because no set of circumstances he might gin up was going to make it all better with me.

Then again, just moments ago we finished another hearing about a father charged with assaulting his 14 year-old, smart-mouth kid by smacking him on the shoulder when the kid sounded off to a cop who'd come to the house to serve some juvenile petitions—against the smart-mouth kid. Instead of thanking the father for trying to get the kid to show some respect for authority, the officer cuffed and stuffed the dad and ran him in, leaving the kid with a very mixed assortment of messages about the situation.

I mean, was the kid supposed to see that his dad had tried to teach him a valuable lesson and was now taking the punishment the kid himself should have received, or was the kid further emboldened by this turn of events, figuring he'd just threaten to call the cops the next time his father started to talk tough with him? All I know is that the kid had a smirk on his face as he testified, which disappeared entirely when I found the dad not guilty, and the youngster realized his cozy security blanket had been abruptly yanked off.

Look, there are certainly cases of child abuse resulting from disciplinary measures that boil over the top—and I'm all for making sure those people are appropriately dealt with and think thrice before it happens again. But this wasn't one of them. What's most disturbing here is not only that the officer couldn't tell the difference, but that the prosecutor also didn't exercise enough judgment to flush this ridiculous rap out of the system before it got all the way to trial. Plus, in the process the kid's charges that should have been the main focus of our rehabilitative efforts were entirely overshadowed and undertreated.

Consequently, I fear we've not seen the last of the irresponsible juvenile behavior that took the cops to the kid's house in the first place—a prediction I made sure to let the kid know, in the finest tradition of reverse psychology, about which I have received no training whatsoever.

Following fresh on the heels of that one was a 30-minute juvenile hearing, complete with lawyers making hearsay and relevancy objections, about a kid charged with assaulting his big brother during some everyday horseplay at home. The mother thought nothing of it herself, until the overly exuberant kid put a headlock on his older sibling and flipped him. That move freaked the mother enough to call 911 because the brother's neck was still recovering from surgery after a serious car accident and she wanted to make sure there hadn't been further damage done. Of course, when the EMTs respond to a situation like this, so do the police, who exercised their discretion—poorly—and brought formal charges against the brother, rather than just making sure the family had the situation under control and then clearing the scene, as they say.

I think you can see where I'm going with this. If not only every swat on the bottom but every tussle on the family room floor between a couple of testosterone-laden teenagers ended up here, there'd be no one in school or at work because the families would be lined up out the front door and all the way down the parking lot to Dunkin' Donuts waiting for me to decide who'd assaulted whom.

For that matter, most of the cops—judges, too—wouldn't have their current jobs, because their past records of juvenile violence would have made them unacceptable risks for positions of authority. Actually, I can think of a few cases where that might not have been a bad result (all current colleagues excepted, of course), but you get the point.

I whined earlier about everyone wanting to make a meaningful contribution to the human condition—or at least craving the illusion that they are. Yet even if we pull people from burning buildings or come up with a cure for Alzheimer's, nearly all of us will be forgotten anyhow once our grandchildren are gone, which is probably little more than 50 years after we ourselves implode. Until I made a point to question my own parents about their grandparents, I had no idea even what my great grandparents' names were, much less where they lived or what they did with their lives—and my parents weren't clear themselves about many of the details. I actually managed to pick up quite a few more tidbits they hadn't mentioned by some creative Googling.

I come back to this now, because during a break in the session today I started reading an article in *The Supreme Court Historical Society Quarterly* about a former justice named Henry Billings Brown. (This publication is much more interesting than new cases and statutes, which I'll have to get to eventually, but you need to do some "secondary" reading, too.) Despite my amateur efforts to learn as much as I can about the big court and its justices, I confess to knowing nothing at all about Justice Brown, not even his name. By the article's account, though, he was a "good judge", "fair minded", "willing to listen to argument", "dedicated to the ideal of doing justice", "humble", and "a genial and lovable companion". He's also the author of the infamous "separate but equal" opinion in *Plessy v. Ferguson*, the case, out of just about all of them, that the court would most like to take a mulligan on—and which it finally flat-out eviscerated in *Brown v. Board of Education*.

Alright, so Justice Brown blew that one royally, but in all other respects he seems the kind of person we'd want taking a fresh look at our case if we managed to make it all the way to the Supreme Court. And based on the little I've learned about the court, there were quite a number of others like him among the barely more a hundred men and a handful of women who've served there during our almost 250-year history. Their decisions have made dramatic changes in the course of

American life: by finally getting our schools integrated; by protecting our individual rights from over-zealous law enforcement; and by finally establishing women's rights in so many areas, just to scratch the surface. Still, hardly anyone remembers their names, even while they were doing all this life-altering deciding. Even the chief justices haven't made much of a dent in our collective consciousness—remember Melville Fuller or Edward White, or how about Fred Vinson from closer to our own time? Not exactly household names.

This collective forgetfulness doesn't bode well for my chances of achieving immortality here in Jaffrey, no matter how fairly and wisely I dole out those speeding fines—unless maybe I can get Bieber's or Miley's publicist to take me on. But then who'll really care about them either in another 25 years (or months or weeks)?

The nub of consolation for me is probably the sports concept of "staying within yourself", which is what I'm guessing Justice Oliver Wendell Holmes, Jr. (surely you've heard of him, right?) was getting at in much more judgely terms: "We are lucky enough if we can give a sample of our best, and if in our hearts we can feel that it has been nobly done." Yea, that's easy for him to say; everybody remembers his towering contributions to American jurisprudence (come on, please humor me even if you can't quite name one right this minute).

Let's keep it on the same channel for another moment, because I conducted my own empirical study the other day. Our firm's retired senior partner who just turned 90 (but who's still got his marbles and who stepped down from my very rung 20 years ago) came in to the office to pick up his mail. I asked him if he knew the guys—and they were all guys then—who'd preceded him down here on the ladder. Not surprisingly, he was able to recall the name and other vital stats of his immediate predecessor, but that's where he hit the wall. He had absolutely no idea who his grand-judge had been, though he's spent his entire life in this town.

I did some more sleuthing and learned that the now unremembered judge—my great grand-judge—spent many apparently successful years on the bench here; which means that within less than one lifetime the Honorable James Brennan's footprints have been obliterated even from the memory of his official descendants, much more from the greater public consciousness. I've stayed away from naming names here, but I feel I owe this moment of tribute to poor [undeservedly] forgotten Judge Brennan. As I feared, this isn't a state of affairs that bodes well for my own vision of an indelible legacy.

PS—I was listening to NPR between cases this morning—while the lawyers and their charges were out there mulling whether to roll the dice with me or take what they could bargain for with the prosecutor. The subject of the radio piece was how we really die three times. The first is when our old hearts finally give up the ghost and we take a sloppy nose dive into our bowl of soup. The second is when our family and friends turn away from our eternal holes in the ground and begin thinking more about the assortment of casseroles waiting for them in the grieving widow/er's dining room. And the final time is some years hence—maybe more, maybe less—when our names are uttered for the last time by a living person. That time may never come for history's true one-of-a-kinds, like presidents George, Abe, Teddy, Franklin R. [not P.] and Barack—though some of the others like Chester, Millard and Rutherford are probably on the bubble—but it's going to come shockingly soon for the rest of us. "Say, remind me, who was that judge a few years after nice old Judge Brennan who was such an incompetent nincompoop? Bunyan? Grunyon?"

It's the first Monday in October, which means baseball's regular season is over and that another nine are just taking the field to begin their season. I refer, of course, to the United States Supreme Court, which held opening day of its new term today and is scheduled to take up some real hot potato issues over the next nine months.

The one that's got my robe in a wad is whether so-called "enemy combatants" being held at Guantanamo Bay, Cuba, are entitled to use the federal courts to challenge the grounds for their detention. The present [Bush] Administration says no, because it wants the discretion to hold these potential terrorists as long as it feels the need, in order to wage its "war on terror" effectively.

As an American citizen, I find that position personally frightening, and as a member of a co-equal branch of government—the judiciary, that is, in case you've lost sight here of that pretty important constitutional fact—I find the Administration's position arrogant and insulting, not to mention in violation of the most fundamental principle that this country has stood for since its founding.

It's frightening because it's a real-life version of the dream Cathie says she frequently has, where she's accused of a crime she didn't commit but no one will listen to her or come to her rescue. Think about it: What if you were wrongly arrested for a crime, but no one would tell you what it was and you had no way for anyone else to decide whether you should continue to rot in jail or be charged and tried anytime soon?

As a judge, that scenario sounds an awful lot like an executive branch that doesn't have enough confidence in its own judgment to let anyone else review it, particularly judges whose constitutional mandate is to do just that kind of reviewing thing.

It's called the "writ of habeas corpus", and Article I, Section 9, of the Constitution makes a special point of prohibiting it from being suspended "unless when in cases of rebellion or invasion the public safety may require it." Despite everything else going on these days, there's no rebellion currently in progress, except maybe over this issue, and the only invasion was not by another country but by a group of vigilante individuals who aren't aligned with any foreign power—in fact, that's sort of the problem with fighting the "war on terror."

Yet, because it's termed the "war on terror"—and no one can look like he's soft on that and keep her political paycheck—we, the judges specifically charged to guard against trampling on individual rights, couldn't possibly be trusted to do our job responsibly because we'd undoubtedly let everyone go, and the terrorists would win, right? And it doesn't matter that the founders set up a system of checks and balances intended to prevent exactly this kind of unexamined exercise of authority, because, when it comes to those making these critical arrests, where something as vitally important as the "war on terror" is concerned, we just have to trust them to do the right thing. OK, if you say so, but what's that rotting, fishy smell blowing in over the Gulf of Florida?

My last question is this, and you can discuss it among yourselves: If there are no holds barred in such an important war, then what's to prevent an unchecked executive decider from authorizing other potentially valuable and expedient measures, including searches without warrants and confessions using torture? What, you mean they're already doing those things, too? And if the usual safeguards don't apply under these life and death circumstances, then why not also in the war on drugs or crime, each of which, by the way, kills many more people every year than all the world's terrorists holed up together in one cave?

Without getting too melodramatic about it all, I refer you to one of the culminating scenes in the play/movie *A Man for All Seasons*, where Sir Thomas More talks with a rival named Roper about the risks of heading down this appealing but treacherous road:

> **More:** Cut a road through the law to get after the Devil?
> **Roper**: Yes. I'd cut down every law in England to do that.
> **More:** And when the last law was down, and the Devil turned on you
> . . . . where would you hide, Roper, the laws all being flat? This country
> is planted with laws from coast to coast. . . . Man's laws, not God's, and
> if you cut them down. . . . and you're just the man to do it . . . . do you
> really think you could stand upright in the wind that would blow then?

And don't even get me started on the whole subject of warrantless wiretapping of the telephone conversations of American citizens. We've got a whole judicial branch here that could do this important work—issuing warrants, that is, it's sort of what we're in business for—in addition to opening all the jail cells and letting the drug dealers and sex perverts run rampant, as Presidential Administration #43 apparently thinks.

Obviously I don't have any idea what I'm talking about, because I've been reversed! No, I'm not getting younger all of a sudden, and I haven't had a sex change. I've been told by the New Hampshire Supreme Court (the Supremes, among us Motown fans) that I erred, that I got the answer wrong, and that I'll have to go back up to the blackboard and work on it until I get the answer right.

Here's the scenario: A young woman from a family that has helped pay for our new courthouse with its many generous—though involuntary—monetary contributions over the years was charged with underage possession of alcohol. As often happens, her car was initially stopped for defective equipment of some sort, which she probably couldn't afford to fix because she'd given us all her money. She claimed the open beer can they found was a dead soldier with nothing but spit backs left in it; however, the officer said it still contained a healthy gulp of cold liquid that foamed up when the officer poured it out on the ground.

That pouring-out business was the glitch, because when everyone convened for trial weeks later, the can was indeed dry as a bone and there wasn't any objective way to determine what the contents had been when the woman was stopped. Call me a stickler, but I thought that was a problem, figuring that the officer had an obligation to preserve the physical evidence, like they probably would with the roach of marijuana or the stolen X-Box or the bloody meat cleaver. Once I made that ruling and dismissed the charge, the cops, who didn't see the problem or accept my analogies, got pretty steamed and appealed.

Then it was up to the Supremes to sort it out for us, which they did without commenting on my thought-provoking analogies. If I may be so bold, I will attempt to dramatize the conversation around their conference table: "Man, if we let this decision stand, the cops are going to be drowned in half-empty cups, bottles and cans of skunky beer, wine, wine coolers, and Red Bulls with vodka (the most devastating concoction du jour, I'm told), bourbon and gingers (yuk), and 'hairy buffalos' (I threw that in 'cause it was a favorite blend of grain alcohol and fruit juices while I was underage). The containers are going to be leaking and spilling all over the cruisers, and then what happens if the cops spill the stuff while they're putting it in the evidence locker, or it dries up before the case gets to trial? We've gotta let 'em get rid of this junk or the station's gonna smell like Sunday morning at a frat house. Reversed."

Alright, so now I have a bright line to follow in the beer—and probably wine—cases: "A drop of brew means a fine for you." or "If there's a whiff of wine, there'll be a fine." This certainly makes it easier to connect the dots; I just check out the empties, take the cops' word for what was once in them, and proceed directly to guilty—yes, we accept all major credit cards. It also means I'll be washing out my own beer and wine bottles pretty carefully from now on before heading off to the recycling center—and I'll be making sure none of my vehicular equipment is on the fritz.

Case closed. But wait, what about the murkier cases, where there may be some alcohol in that cup somewhere, but there's also Fresca, Coke or other assorted liquid camouflage? Is it going to be enough for the officer just to say, "It had the faint aroma of some alcoholic beverage; I don't know what kind it was, but I know booze when I smell it, and the Supremes say that's all there is to it"? I'm not sure yet, but I'd better figure it out 'cause that case is undoubtedly waiting for me on next week's docket.

Now it's February, and after a globally-warmed January, we're finally in the deep freeze, with daytime temps struggling to reach the age of majority and wind chills well below my non-existent IQ for continuing to live here. All that frigidity has confined me to indoor exercise, and while pumping along on my elliptical device (which, by the way, I recommend to everyone with as many jarring miles on their knees as me), I've been listening to the recorded book called *The Looming Tower*, an account by Lawrence Wright of the birth of Al Qaeda and the run-up to 9/11. That, in turn, has me thinking again about how critical one vote was in the Supreme Court's decision in *Bush v. Gore*. If just one justice in that 5-4 decision had voted the other way, and if the Florida recount had been allowed to continue, then perhaps Gore, not Bush, would have been our 43rd president, and so much might be different today. For sure, we wouldn't have to worry about "nuclear" war.

Based on the book, there's no reason to think 9/11 itself would have been thwarted, because no president would have been able to cut through the ridiculous—and ultimately tragic—turf battles within our intelligence community, which in this instance had the 21st century appearance of the Keystone Cops meeting Inspector Clouseau. In other words, it sure looks to me like the blood of the 3,000 victims of those attacks is slathered all over their (FBI, CIA, NSA) hands. Still, if Gore (or nearly anyone else) had become our president by virtue of all the votes actually being counted—I know it's a radical concept—we might well have invaded and laid waste to Afghanistan, where the Taliban really was harboring Al Qaeda after all, but we most definitely would not have invaded Iraq under any circumstances. Which means the blood of the 4,000 (and counting) dead soldiers we've brought back from there wouldn't be on anyone's hands.

In the end, one vote among nine made more difference than all those Florida votes, which, I think you've gathered, it would have been my humble suggestion to count. Sure, it would have delayed the outcome by a couple of weeks perhaps—maybe even kept the "chad" counters tied up during the holidays—but there was something to be said for getting the decision right, especially when it was on the "100 most critical decisions in history" list.

Instead, by not allowing Florida to decide how to count its own ballots, the court anointed its own president, who, the tell-all books declare, promptly used 9/11 as the catalyst to get the guy who'd threatened his (43rd's) father's (41st's) life. The upside, if you will—and I'm an optimist at heart—is that we're all getting an idea what it would have been like to experience the Fillmore, Pierce (our only NH decider!) and Buchanan administrations, when some of our most competence-challenged presidents were either running wildly amok or proving that even the White House is at the mercy of the Peter Principle.

Last night about 2:30 a.m. I got a search warrant call from a distant PD and instead of making them drive all the way here to meet me at my office to review the application in person, I tried having them fax the application to me at home. The technological process worked well enough, despite that I didn't have enough paper for the printer and had to use scraps of anything I could find.

The problem was that I remained so sleepy I'm not sure my review of the facts was much better than it would have been if I'd had a six-pack first. From now on, I think I've just got to get dressed, head out into the cold night air, and do my work down the street at my office. That first wintry blast will at least wake me up before I issue a warrant likely to be bounced for some obvious screw-up I would/might have seen had I not been semi-comatose.

~⌇~

Our clerk has a habit of saying how "sad, sad" many of our cases are, particularly when they involve people who've hacked out large ugly holes for themselves by means of substance abuse, domestic violence or poor parenting, to name just a few of the implements of personal tragedy.

That lament was right-on when it came to the woman recently charged with abusing alcohol to the extent of badly neglecting her young daughter. The alcohol demon also seemed to have wrecked the woman's career as a successful lawyer and at least one marriage, not to mention her relationship with the [allegedly] neglected kid. On top of all that, I heard the woman's DWI case a few months ago, so even when she gets out of rehab, she'll be without benefit of a driver's license—a devastating setback in a rural area where you can't walk to the grocery store from most places in less than half a day.

What's the saddest part of this saga is that the woman still doesn't recognize alcohol as the culprit, telling me instead that she was in the hospital for asthma attacks. I know that because she's told the story several times now, not only in actual hearings but during calls she's made to me at home, first at 10:30 at night, then at 7:00 the next morning. There have been other attempts to call, too, but Cathie now recognizes the woman's slurred speech and is successfully running interference. Maybe the reason she felt she could dial me up is that I've known this woman, as well as her parents, for more than 30 years. Still, you'd think a lawyer who'd ever taken an ethics course would know not to call the judge hearing her case, but then alcohol's probably clouding her judgment about that, too.

In case you're wondering about the potential conflict of interest (I'm glad you were paying attention back there at the beginning), I disclosed all the past family history prior to the DWI trial, but no one seemed to think there was a conflict worth balking at, so we forged ahead. That led to a surreal experience in itself, because one of the key issues was whether the driver of the vehicle was properly identified, which, despite my super-human powers of judicial impartiality, was impossible for me to keep an open mind about, having already told them I'd known the woman since she was a teenager. Hello, if that's not a conflict I don't know what is, but having given fair warning—and gotten the go-ahead from everyone—I was damned if I was going to reboot the whole case for another judge to hear many months hence.

Next time, though, after that bizarre DWI fiasco and all the out-of-court phone chats, there's no way I'm wading back in to sort out the juvenile neglect charge, whether anyone else objects or not. Sometimes you have to bow out based on your own gut check about a situation, and this one's producing wicked acid reflux, as well as considerable sadness.

Looking back at the recent entries here, I realize they've taken on a pretty dreary tone and may be giving the impression that despair and human tragedy are daily occurrences. Alright, that's a fair assessment, but just often enough something so outright wacky happens that I find myself looking for Allen Funt (ask your parents yet again).

Such as, a kid barely old enough to have a license was stopped for DWI on the main street on one of our littlest town. That's a serious setback in a young life, so that was the "sad, sad" part, not the funny part. As often happens, the officer initially took notice because of suspicious drifting over the yellow centerline. Without blinking an eye, the kid assured me he wasn't drunk, but swerved over to avoid a huge pile of horsesh*t in the middle of his lane. When I asked him to describe the obstacle in greater detail—because I was concerned that some of it might have been tracked into the courtroom—the kid said it was about twelve inches high and as big around as a trash can lid. I conjured the image of something like the Trojan horse rolling through town, which the cop said he'd probably have encountered himself—the monstrous pile, that is—during one of his previous passes up or down the street.

So while the kid will be license-impaired for a while, the consolation is that he'll be composing successful fiction someday and will never be at a loss for an imaginative story line. He may even be persuaded by this harsh bit of non-fiction to avoid the alcohol dependence that's derailed many a great writing career. Fitzgerald comes foremost to mind, so maybe I'll refer to this as the "Gatsby Defense".

Contested speeding charges are the bane of the Court's repertoire. They clog up the docket, rarely involve a legal issue of any interest, and often boil down to the rarely-successful, "I know I wasn't going that fast." Frankly, I'm not sure why anyone would lose a day's wages to bother with that Hail Mary claim, but then I hear that the spike in our (like Massachusetts') insurance rates is the real motivator and that no matter how stiff the fine, it's just the tip of the financial iceberg. Occasionally, though, someone comes up with a story that causes me to perk up and really assess the burden of proof.

As today's pretty routine session lurched along, I could see a woman of a certain age (I think that means 50+) nervously fidgeting at the back of the courtroom and transmitting vibes of obvious discomfort. It turned out she, too, was there for a speeding charge and it soon became clear what was causing her agitation. Unlike most of her lead-footed compatriots, she didn't dispute the speed at all, but explained that the reason was a wicked attack of diarrhea and her panic to get home to avoid a serious laundry emergency. Understandably, she dropped her voice considerably when she got to the D word, which I honestly couldn't hear the first time and so made her repeat even louder.

Once I finally got the drift, I was sorry I'd asked. The officer denied hearing any of this at the time of the stop, though, which the woman claimed was due to the mortification factor, and besides she was anxious to get going before disaster struck. I was conflicted. I mean, the circumstances, if true, certainly warranted some consideration, but the woman was really flying and she failed to mention the bowel calamity either before or after the officer was running her license through the computer.

Ultimately, I flopped down on the side of guilty. Even though she seemed honest and trustworthy, I felt I needed some sliver of additional verification for her story, just some tiny detail from the time of the incident itself that would tell me, "yes, you can believe me; this passes the sniff test." (Poor choice of words—sorry.) If I didn't have that, I couldn't see how I'd draw the line between truth and bullsh*t (of any consistency) in other cases. It certainly wouldn't be a straight line in any event.

That evening at home, when Cathie asked about my day and I tried to share my troubling dilemma, she was remarkably unsympathetic, shall we say. "You insensitive pig" was about all I remember, but there was more, lots more, and to such an extent that the "Diarrhea Defense" is now an established legal maxim here in Jaffrey.

Remaining in the same vein, whenever I tell people we don't have juries in our court and that I'm the only decider, they nearly always ask me how I find any nuggets of truth while floundering in a smelly quagmire of murky muck. Actually, that's my own mental picture; they just ask how I tell whether people are lying. Many times that's a distinct challenge, but occasionally a defendant will make the process a bit easier.

Say, when a cocky teenager came in on a charge of liberating some expensive athletic shoes from a local sporting goods store but denied ever being in the store, much less taking the five-finger discount. The sales clerk thought she was pretty sure the kid was the right one, though she acknowledged she'd only seen him from behind as he sprinted from the store.

So that state of affairs probably wouldn't have tipped the scales toward conviction—until the kid's defense lawyer asked one too many questions about the weakness of the manager's ID. Once again she admitted her uncertainty about the kid himself, but then positively ID'ed the shoes the kid was wearing in court as the ones she'd seen running out the door.

When the kid's smugness suddenly evaporated and he couldn't think quickly enough to explain where else the shoes might have come from—say, from buying them—I'd received sufficient enlightenment to see my way to judgment. Which included restitution for full retail (even though the shoes were on sale), as well as a surcharge of suspended jail time that was warranted by the kid's well-established MO of shopping without benefit of cash or credit on previous occasions.

The kid's lawyer also proved the age-old maxim that you never ask a question you don't already know the answer for. That's one they don't teach in law school, but is probably way more important than all those technical hearsay rules.

Back to something serious for a moment. The young guy I mentioned who was shot a couple of months ago by the estranged husband who objected to his wife "moving on" remained in a coma for quite some time. And even when he woke up, it was still touch and go whether he'd recover. While it was the distraught husband who pulled the trigger, the culprit, in my humble view, was the handgun itself, or rather its handiness. If it hadn't been there in the glove box or on the nightstand, ready to be rushed into service at the very moment when the slightly-to-moderately intoxicated young husband's dander was up, maybe he'd have gone over there and punched the guy out—probably still a bloodletting affair—but the guy wouldn't have been fighting for his life.

Speaking of dander, I can sense it getting up on the heads of all the gun huggers out there; however, to be honest, most of them probably gave up on me during my harangue about Guantanamo anyhow. So just to be clear, I'd round up all the handguns, grind them up into BB-size morsels, and do something more useful with them, like fill the potholes that threaten to devour our cars every March. If we can't get them banned entirely, then let's regulate the hell out of them, so you'd have to check one out to blow off steam at a firing range and then have it locked back up tight when you're done.

And if the Supremes' *Keller* decision (more later on that one) says I have to concede that people can keep pistols at home for personal protection against intruders hoping to kill them in their beds, then let's make sure they keep the guns right there in the homestead and not be flaunting them every time they head to Walmart for TP and mood rings.

As for rifles and shotguns, I'm willing to be a bit more flexible if someone has no history of violent offenses, shows proof of completion of a gun safety course, and is required to keep the things unloaded and locked up except during a hunting trip.

Then, when it comes to assault weapons, just read my mind about what you can do with those.

And don't lecture me about the Second Amendment. I've read it a bunch of times just to make sure I've got the wording clear, and I've heard all the arguments the NRA keeps tazing us with.

The problem is that the Second Amendment has nothing to do with people having guns for personal sport, or for individual self-defense even. Just read the words; there are only a couple of lines. Plus, just name one instance where a guy with a .45 under his belt, who wasn't in a *Die Hard* movie, managed to save someone's life by whipping the thing out at the critical moment. Much more prevalent is the recent story about the guy who shot dead a couple of petty thieves who were running across his lawn with a neighbor's TV. Maybe they deserved to go to jail for 40 days and nights, or 80 or 160, but I doubt all but the hardest-liners would have prescribed the death penalty for a theft of electronics.

In other words, I'm convinced the legislawyers could find a way to take the action I'm describing if they had the will—really the guts—to do it. (Five guys in Washington have just opined otherwise, but more later on that front.) In the meantime, I'll keep trying to hang onto my present job, which, thankfully again, I don't have to run for—or I'd be running on empty and the gun lobby would be shooting me in the back like a flat screen thief.

Here's another PS on point. The New Hampshire House has just decided it's a good idea for everyone to be able to bring fully-loaded, concealed handguns into the Statehouse. The supporters say it's not only that Second Amendment thing but a safety measure, because if anyone starts trouble, they can all whip out their 44 magnums and blow the bad guy away.

Pardon me, but wouldn't it be a whole lot safer, especially for the school kids who regularly sit in the gallery to see their government at work, to put some metal detectors at the doors and make sure the bad guy can't come in with a handgun that needs to be blown away? Plus, if the debate was about one of these hot button issues I've been inflaming with my off-the-wall views, I'd be a little concerned about really speaking my mind if I knew the agitated guy on the other side of the debate was packing. I guess I'd better hope none of them reads this thing.

People have asked me why I've never run for office. One reason is that I got beat for town "fence viewer" (just what it indicates) 30 years ago and was traumatized by the experience. Another is that among other fatal shortcomings I've exposed, neither I nor anyone else can get elected to any office in this country on a gun platform like I've just shot off my mouth about.

A woman sent in her fine payment, claiming she had raised the funds by selling her living room furniture, which she said she no longer needed because she'd had to cancel her cable service, too. The inference to be drawn from this modern pairing of products and services is highly illuminating, and the marketing implications are apparent: If you're hoping to sell casual furniture in the 21st century, you'd be wise to offer 6 months of free cable as a promotion. A good book would be a lot cheaper, but I'm guessing, not nearly as likely to generate the same level of interest.

Today is another of our bi-weekly juvenile hearing days, which, in addition to eight hours of hazardous duty, means I'd better remember to bring a sack of bagels with me for the clerk staff or everything will come to a grinding halt while I'm sent back out to get them. I created this monster by bringing these offerings of peace and goodwill way back when I was still trying to make a favorable first impression, and now I'd totally undermine all that hard work by slipping up even once.

The docket today lists 15-20 kids in various stages of this sticky adolescent process, which is like fly paper because once you get snagged by it, it's tough to pull free. Some are making their first appearances and don't have any idea what to expect, while others are old hands and are making a concerted effort to disentangle themselves as fast as possible. A few are still paying me serious lip service and using the system to bludgeon their parents at repeated hearings and with staggering financial obligations for largely unproductive rehabilitative services. Some even seem intent on sabotaging themselves by failing to comply with any requirement, much like the kids who cut themselves when they're despondent, stressed out or angry about their young lots in life.

I must say, I've become pretty adept at reading the tea leaves of these kids, though most of the leaves read more like flashing neon signs. The ones with the "deer in the headlights" expressions are usually pretty compliant and just want to do whatever it takes to avoid having to come back again. The ones with the squint in their eyes or their lips pursed or jaws clenched, I know are going to be a challenge and will likely balk at whatever we try to do with, to or for them, at least until they see it's just ramping up their hassle quotients and prolonging the agony. Most of those will eventually toe the line enough to avoid a return trip, but some will fail forever to decipher that clue and will transition seamlessly to a life of adult crime.

Despite all the drama, I actually thrive on most of these cases. When we manage to turn some kid around and keep her from moving upstairs to the adult courtroom, there's certainly a morsel of gratification to be relished. When the process falls flat, or just gets a C+, we at least provide fair warning about what those kids can expect once they turn 17—which [prior to a recent amendment] is the age of criminal majority in New Hampshire.

With the latter kids, I confess my continuing hope for just the right moment to quote the admonition of Dean Wormer in *Animal House* that, "Son, fat, drunk and stupid is no way to go through life." Unfortunately, when that convergence of circumstances finally occurs, there either won't be anyone in the room who appreciates the cinematic reference, or I'll get called onto the carpet by the JCC for being rude, judgmental and unprofessional. Then, because it will be recorded for use at my disciplinary hearing, I'll be able to hear it played back so frequently that I'll be wishing—yet again—I'd never opened my mouth, a circumstance that occurs often enough even without the dean's prophetic words.

A pleasantly unexpected PS to this entry occurred last week when a man whose name didn't register called me at the office and said he'd like to meet briefly to "make amends" for the transgressions of his distant past.

When the guy finally came in, I didn't recognize his face either. He looked more like the sturdy construction worker he was now than the wimpy kid he said he was 17 years ago when we had him in our clutches. When I finally made the connection, I realized I knew exactly who he was and where he lived, and that his juvenile screw-up consisted of raising a crop of marijuana plants under a grow light in his bedroom closet. (Clearly, his garage would have provided better air circulation, although I doubt I offered that comment at the time.)

The fellow spent the next half hour regaling me with his tortured journey in and out of rehab, until he finally found AA and the spiritual awakening that was keeping him seat-belted to the wagon. He said he was sorry for all the trouble he'd caused, but that there just wasn't anything more we might have done at that point because he wasn't ready then to grab the lifelines we were throwing him. Fortunately, he didn't drown, though he went under a bunch of times before he washed up on Alcoholics Atoll.

In addition to completing one of the last of the guy's 12 steps, the get-together provided me with one helpful tidbit, too. The fellow said that even if someone poo-pooed the worth of AA, it was worth sending him for exposure to the stories told there. What he meant was that before long, someone would stand up and start describing the very life experience that the reluctant attendee was refusing to face. At that moment, a gaping hole would be blown in the balker's defenses, a cold sweat would break out, and perhaps a spark of self-awareness would appear that might eventually combust into a true epiphany and a meaningful change in lifestyle. Maybe that's too optimistic, but it came from the horse's mouth, so it's worth the try if nothing else has worked.

When he finished, the fellow took a deep breath and thanked me; I thanked him for thanking me; and he left for the next stop along his perilous road to recovery.

Justice John Paul Stevens announced this week that at 90 this will be his last term at the palace of supreme justice. I e-mailed my cell phone number to the White House just in case, but haven't heard anything yet—I hope I remember how to check voice mail.

If he rings me up, I'll say, "Without thumping my chest too vigorously, Mr. President, I could easily generate much of the 5-4 drivel I've seen dumped on us from the top rung of the ladder in recent years." You'd think that from such a vantage point it would be easier to spot the right result, but it may be hard to see what's going on down here near the ground because of all those trees. "Still, sir, just because others have gotten altitude sickness doesn't mean I wouldn't like to try out the view for myself. How 'bout it?"

Continuing with the day's hot button issues—let's just get 'em all out there on the table—our national love/hate relationship with the death penalty also keeps muscling its way into the headlines. Even little ole New Hampshire now has it back on the front burner because of the high-profile case of a black man who admittedly shot a Manchester police officer in the head at point-blank range.

By the way, it's just a coincidence (perhaps Freudian?) that I mention this topic shortly after yammering about uncooperative juveniles. As aggravating and outrageous as many of them are, the death penalty isn't a serious option, mostly because we know kids never think of the consequences of anything they do, so they wouldn't be deterred for a moment by worrying about lethal injections.

In fact, the death penalty's not even a momentary pause-giver for anyone here in New Hampshire, simply because no one's gotten the noose or the chair or the hypodermic, no matter how heinous the crime, since the late 1930's—which is almost a decade before my ancient self was born. We don't even have a death chamber anymore, or at least no one remembers where it is. Indeed, if I was a murderous but calculating offender, I'd figure out how to lure my victim of choice to the Granite State for a ski weekend and then knock him off in the shadow of Mount Washington. Heck, I might round up a carload of people to get even with, 'cause there have been some pretty gory multiple killings perpetrated here over the years without even one of the bad guys having to decide on his final meal. The people who still make the deterrence claim probably also think it did some good when their parents said, "If you kids don't knock it off, I'm going to turn this car around." After my father said it 10 times and my brother and I kept fighting over where the middle of the back seat was—and after he never once made a U-turn—we just started tuning him out altogether.

So we're left with the other barrel of the death penalty arsenal: Some murderous crimes are just so horrendous that people who commit them can't be adequately punished except by being killed themselves in retribution. That concept has always puzzled me, too, because of the apparent contradiction between vehemence for the death penalty and roughly the same people's supposed religious belief in all things merciful. Apparently, that irony has never troubled the Texan religious community—Texas regularly snuffs out the most people, but you can insert Florida and a number of other Southern states here, as well. They all seem to have the teachings of Jesus at their fingertips, but don't see anything inconsistent about dispatching criminal defendants at an alarming rate. I'm not a biblical scholar, but they must be concentrating a lot more on the Old Testament than the New one because I don't recall Jesus demanding to "kill those reprehensible bastards" in any of the Gospels.

The final disconnect for me is that these are the same people who adamantly oppose the murder of unborn fetuses in the abortion debate and who object to any form of stem cell research. You'd assume that because every human life is precious, even if just a glimmer in the womb or the test tube, these folks would want to preserve life at all stages of development. Not so. They don't flinch for a nano-moment before aborting other fully-formed lives if they think the bad guys deserve it.

Look, as far as I'm concerned, either human life is not for us to take away under any circumstances at any point, or we're starting to play some kind of god here ourselves. If life or death is really going to come down to who makes the best argument and gets the most votes, then the slope is starting to get pretty slippery.

Don't get me wrong, I swear I'm not mushy on crime and I don't want convicted murderers and rapists coming back to my neighborhood after a few years of confined Oprah-watching. I just say the death penalty isn't the right response, no matter what some low-life, despicable, remorseless, waste-of-food, has done. And I'll stop right there, without dipping even a toe into the swamp of whether we may be executing people who are really innocent or who are predominantly minorities and poor. When you start shooting at the death penalty with all that baggage heaped on board, it's not even a moving target any longer. I'm sure I'll come back to this later, but 'nuf said for now.

PS here, too—The New Hampshire legislature has now voted yet again not to repeal the death penalty, probably because it's working so well at this point that they don't want to upset the delicate balance. That's an attempt at [gallows?] humor, in case you didn't spot it, as is the whole subject (a joke, that is) at this point. No one's going to be executed here—even the black cop killer—and everyone knows it despite all the hullabaloo. I'd venture that the governor knows it, too, despite his hand-on-the-Bible oath to veto any repeal bill that arrives at his desk.

I'll also note here that this is largely the same knee-jerk approach as all New Hampshire governors take about any proposal to reduce our regressive property taxes with an income or sales tax: If you show any sign of weakness on the issue, you get dumped on the electoral trash heap. It doesn't matter what the merits or equities of such a tax proposal might be, no governor wants to be known forever as the spineless worm who caved on a "broad-based" tax—and being viewed as soft on crime is just as great a legacy killer. The real test, of course, is whether any New Hampshire governor is actually going to sign a death warrant. Perhaps the only way to reveal the hypocrisy of the situation is to put him/her to the test. Then, if they don't fry the guy now in the cross-hairs, I'd say there's not a prayer they'll ever divert our scarce public funds toward building another fryolator—no matter how hard the proponents clamor for justice.

We're only a few three woods—maybe Tiger's woods—from the

Massachusetts line, so we see a lot of folks from "down below" who slip up up here. One such guy recently pled guilty to aggravated DWI and received a one-year ban of his right to drive in the Granite State. That's all we could do, because New Hampshire can't take away what it didn't issue—his actual license—though you can be sure the DMV in Boston will take its shot at him once it gets the news via the national driving records hotline now keeping tabs on us all.

Anyhow, while the guy was licking his wounds at home, he got pretty thirsty but found he couldn't [at that time] buy beer on Sunday in Massachusetts. Since he was so close to the border, though, he figured he could risk a quick foray into New Hampshire to snag a 30-pack at a convenience store-slash-marina literally a half wedge—even for me— across the state line. Unfortunately, his bad luck came along for the ride and as the guy was getting into his vehicle with his ice-cold cube of Bud, the chief from a couple of towns over who had busted him in the first place was shopping for night crawlers on the same premises. Once they'd both been rung up and the fellow was pulling out for his hundred yard dash back to safety, the chief flagged him down and cuffed him for the even more serious offense of driving while still revoked for DWI— which ratchets up the stakes considerably. Not the death penalty, for sure, but still a number of Bud-free Sundays in the cooler that he won't ever get back.

This luckless nightmare called for desperate defense measures, so his resourceful counsel ran everything up the flagpole, including the kitchen sink. For example, maybe the state line ran through the parking lot, so the prohibited driving actually took place in Massachusetts—an imaginative theory but without any actual surveying to back it up. The lawyer even put the guy's poor father on the stand to say the chief must have been mistaken about spotting the contraband 'cause his son never buys Bud, only Molson—Bud apparently gives him a headache. (I was guessing the Molson would produce that effect, too, if consumed in the quantity of his alleged purchase.)

None of these strategies resonated with me, as they say, which means the son will have enough quiet time to deduce that the next time he needs a Sunday transfusion, he should either think ahead on

Saturday or make the 50-yard border crossing on foot and hike back to the Bay State with no more than he can carry that far. He'll even be able to select his preferred Molson next time, which, for what it's worth, I recommend that he buy in cans because they don't weigh as much full and the empties are easier to deliver to the recycling center.

Today's docket produced another of those Candid Camera moments that has me expecting someone to run in and expose the hoax.

A cocker spaniel rescue organization sued to get back (it's called "replevin" in medieval legal parlance), what else, an orphaned cocker it had placed in a foster home and then forgotten about for months. In the meantime, the foster folks had found a good home for the pup and the proud new parents wanted to keep him. Sounds like the ideal outcome, right? I mean the pup's got a great new family, the family loves the little guy, and the cocker savers have one less mouth to feed. One thing I've learned—and there aren't many of them—is that when it looks like that, I'm about to get dope-slapped in the back of the head.

The snag here was that the little guy was thought to be a biter and much too dangerous to be left untreated in an unsuspecting family where it might gnaw the face off an innocent child. In order for the risk to be diminished sufficiently, Sammy—I finally realized they were talking about the dog—needed a series of anger management sessions with a canine shrink at Tufts, which is apparently the Mayo Clinic for this specialty. This was the point where I started looking for the camera in the ceiling tiles.

When I finally realized this was for real—and that my expensive legal education was going to be put severely to the test in breaking this Gordian knot—I decided the whole process was seriously flawed. For me to order that a thing—Sammy—be returned, I needed to have Sammy's new family there with us in court. Otherwise, what could I do if they simply refused to part with him—I assumed he was a male but Sammy could be short for Samantha the Biter, right? There was a lot to think about, including that this was exactly the kind of arcane legal wrangling people hate.

So I dismissed the case, but not just out of spite or because I was getting a headache. What I'm counting on is that when these well-meaning people—I'll give them that much credit—see they're going to have to start again from scratch, they—or at least their lawyers (yes, there were lawyers going snout to snout over this)—will finally, mercifully, come to their senses, and Sammy will be able to stay in his/her new home.

OK, maybe Sammy needs some therapy for bad doggie issues, but surely they can arrange that with a qualified professional a little closer (cheaper, too) than Tufts, and without breaking up the whole doggone family.

At a bail hearing yesterday one of our regular customers—a young man who keeps proving that he couldn't find a clue if it was stapled to his forehead—asked me to release him on *NPR*. I started to ask why a public radio station would pony up bail for him, but then I figured the reference would be mostly for my own amusement—so I figured I'd just write it down here and hope it amuses you.

Anyhow, based on the guy's record over the last few months alone, NPR would have had to cough up a substantial portion of its PR budget to spring him. So No Personal Recognizance.

Bail was again the topic the next day, as a 20-something we've seen for alcohol and drug issues, fell off the wagon and gave the police a hard time when they responded to a noise complaint at his perennially-troubled apartment complex. The situation was complicated this time because he's produced a couple of kids since we last saw him, and they were on hand to hear the hour's worth of beer-fueled comments he used on the cops before he let them in. Incredibly, in the great tradition of families being their own worst enemies, the beer was supplied by the guy's mother, who might as well have shot him in the head instead, given his past history.

To beer guy's credit, though, he's got a responsible job now and is attending nursing school, which is what presented the dilemma at the bail hearing. Not surprisingly, the cops wanted me to jail the guy and throw away the keg, oops, key, not having appreciated all the potentially life-threatening fireworks when all they bargained for was trying to get a stereo turned down.

If I did that, however, I figured the guy would surely lose his job and then probably have to drop out of school, too, because you know the boss was paying his tuition. And where were the kids going to stay in the meantime—with their alcohol-pushing grandmother? Plus, if he had to come up with high cash bail or even to buy a bail bond for the 10% premium those guys charge, it's the kids who'd be eating peanut butter and jelly for the next six months.

As you've probably guessed by now, I incurred the wrath of the cops and released the guy, now sober again and contrite, on high PR (not NPR) bail. I tried to put the fear of the gods in him about not proving me a bigger sap than the cops already thought I was, but at least some of that speech was to show them I don't take their safety lightly, which is certainly true (that I don't take their safety lightly).

Maybe I looked at this situation the wrong way, but I couldn't help feeling a screw-up like this one, while serious enough to make the front page of the paper, shouldn't ruin a whole family's future, particularly where it was clear the kids would bear the brunt of dad's meltdown.

Once the dust settled, I realized I should have made the guy put his mom up for bail. Sadly, the pure elegance of that decision just didn't come to me fast enough, but I'm getting a stamp made for when it happens next time.

About the same time, a kid who had sped over from Vermont was stopped for just that on one of our rural byways. His testimony was that although he never saw the cruiser that zapped him, he wasn't guilty because he wasn't speeding at any time, in any speed zone, on any road, while passing through the town. Someone with that level of self-confidence isn't ever likely to take a contrary opinion well and he confirmed that theorem when I found him guilty. His feelings for me became clearer still when he mailed us the $86.40 in pennies, along with a note saying if we had to "purger" ourselves to raise money, we must need it more than he did.

Our clerk nearly ruptured a disc—at least she would have gotten some worker's comp—carrying the fine to the bank, which located one subway token among the other 8,639 Lincolns. I debated sending the kid a bill for the additional penny but decided in the end just to toss in one of my own and keep his token of appreciation as a way to remember him always.

I'm guessing that dealing with "continuances" of hearings (why not just call them postponements, for Pete's sake?) practically doubles a small court's workload, for the simple reason that they make you do the scheduling paperwork all over again—sometimes again and again. If there's any consolation at all, it's that occasionally the reason given for the request is novel and bizarre enough to make it worth the extra work.

One such was a woman who called the court to request a delay in her contested domestic violence hearing on the ground that she didn't have a bra to wear to court. She explained that she was a 38DD and that the fallout from arriving braless could be devastating—that's my dramatization. In order not to be seen as gender insensitive to this uniquely woman's issue, I granted the additional time, despite a whole lot of non-PC guffaws from our entirely female staff.

When the big day finally came, you can be sure all eyes were carefully assessing, first, whether the woman's claim of physical endowment was credible, and then, whether she had been successful in acquiring the missing support apparatus. For my part, although assessing whether there's proof beyond a reasonable doubt is often a severe challenge, this was a call that any teenage boy who'd dropped out of school at 16 could have made. As for the merits of the case, I have no recollection whatsoever.

Small claim defendants with judgments against them often come to their payment hearings with whatever crutches, back braces and slings they can muster, in order to convince me their disabilities prevent them from being able to come up with even a token contribution toward what they owe.

Today I was sure a rough-looking guy with his hand heavily bandaged would be making the same pitch, but then he promised he'd soon be able to pay off the whole amount because he'd applied for VA disability benefits and they'd be "radioactive", so there'd be plenty of money to go around.

It sounds Shakespearean but it was apparently a buddy of his named John Lyly (I Googled him so it must be true) who first observed that "all is fair in love and war." Based on a nearly 20-year statistical sample, I'm proposing that "court" be added to the list.

When I administer the truth-telling oath to witnesses, I always try to look them squarely in the eye, so perhaps they'll see I'm really, really serious about this and that somehow I'll be able to peer into their souls to detect a lie—sort of like George Bush claimed he did with Vlad Putin. Sadly, I'd say that my attempt has been largely unsuccessful—much like Bush's with Putin—and that the only factor tending to guaranty the truth is whether there's anyone else who can conclusively unmask the liar.

In other words, if witnesses feel they can get away with whatever they've concocted to say to clear themselves or their kids or their pals, they'll say it, even if there's not a kernel of truth anywhere on the cob. This is particularly true when it comes to what they view as a game of cat-and-mouse with the police in motor vehicle cases. There, they've successfully rationalized that the cops have quotas and are doing whatever they can to get convictions, so drivers are only leveling the playing field. Maybe this mindset also stems from professional sports, where the second basemen will swear he made the tag even if the replay shows he missed it by a mile. The difference is that I haven't given the ballplayer an oath to tell the truth before the game started.

You may be asking how I know—or at least why I feel—all this prevarication is occurring. The main reason is not that I take whatever the cops say at face value—if that was the case, there wouldn't be much need for trials, would there?—but because the cops keep the best notes. That is, they typically sit right there at the scene and write up their account of a vehicle stop within minutes of the event. They usually quote what the driver says about the situation and they note any other incidents of significance. If the driver has an excuse about why the speeding, say, occurred—late for work, going to the hospital, needing the bathroom (see the "Diarrhea Defense" above)—then I'm going to look askance at such a claim made months after the incident if the driver admits not having broached it on the roadside or if the officer's notes mention nothing of the kind. Stated differently, if it wasn't important— or true—enough to mention when the driver may have had a real crack at changing the cop's mind about the ticket, then absent unusual circumstances I'm going to consider it cooked up solely to feed to me.

Is it perjury? Technically so, for sure, but if we did exit interviews, I'm sure any number of drivers would say they just took their best shot, and that indeed all is fair, in their view, when the deck is so obviously stacked against them. Is this cynical on my part? Perhaps. Is it exaggerated as a comment on human nature? I really doubt it, given that millions of people are regularly cheating on their spouses or significant others or insignificant others. We see tons of that, too.

Then there are the billions in taxes that aren't paid each year because people think they can get away with under-reporting their income—or because they think the people in Washington are just going to blow it on something stupid anyhow, which is a whole 'nother story that would require several hundred pages in itself.

Just for the record, I'm of the persuasion that reporting what you owe is not only the high road, but because I was lousy at hide & seek, and because I'd also rather avoid getting one of those "boy, are you in trouble" letters from the IRS.

When I started out as a young lawyer in New Hampshire, I welcomed pretty much any legal animal that ambled in the door, and a lot of them involved minor criminal and motor vehicle charges in, surprise, then District Court. I had no trial experience at all, but I wasn't as over-matched as you'd think, because the cops who filed the charges were usually worse off. They weren't lawyers, yet even the greenest recruit was responsible for writing up his own complaints and then trying somehow to prosecute his cases. Even the best officers on the street were largely clueless when it came to making sure their complaints included all the key wording for the offenses charged. They'd leave out some critical piece of information, like where the incident took place, or they'd charge that the defendant acted recklessly when the statute required intentional behavior. My mantra was that if I hadn't found the defect in the way the complaint was written up, I hadn't looked hard enough. I'd wait for the case to be called for trial, then move to dismiss, and the panicked officer would look at the judge with eyes as big as saucers that said, "I'm drowning here, please throw me a lifeline!"

If the officer somehow made it over the charging hurdle and the trial actually got started, he'd be relying on what someone told him (who usually wasn't there to testify in person), and when the befuddled cop couldn't get past the objection that this was hearsay (Wikipedia has a good explanation), the case would fly out the window on a "technicality" he didn't understand. Why would he? Law students spend a year trying to figure out the evidence rules, and even most experienced lawyers don't have a really firm grip on them. Then, because the cop didn't pick up on what he'd done wrong, the same thing would happen to him over and over again. Great for my sketchy clients, undoubtedly, but hardly the way the system should work unless your life of crime depends on it.

I mention all this because most police departments have now hired lawyers to prosecute for them, so the legal battlefield is at least somewhat flatter than it was. I also say this because not all the departments have wised up yet, as evidenced by a nostalgic return to the old days last week.

A guy with his name engraved on our holding cell—regular customers keep us in business, just like at Home Depot—was here for trial with one of the small departments that still thinks it can handle its own cases. It charged the guy with providing beer to underage kids who were driving around on New Year's Eve from one party to another. There's no doubt that he bought a couple of 30-packs for his youthful buddies, but the cops didn't even bring the evidence with them from the station—they hadn't poured it out this time; they just schlep it over here. The defendant didn't have a lawyer either, but he'd watched enough "Law and Order" to know he was entitled to see the evidence against him.

What's more, the cops didn't even think to tell me the names and ages of the other kids in the vehicle of fun, so there was no proof they were indeed under 21. Once again, the defendant pounced, and while the officers gritted their teeth and mumbled about travesties, he sprinted through those glaring holes in the case, just like OJ, and celebrated in the not-guilty zone.

Needless to say, if this is the kind of defect a barely-finished-high-school guy could take advantage of, I shudder to think what will happen when one of the department's perps shows up with a slick lawyer on a really serious charge. What will happen is that they'll either continue to fumble cases they should have spiked in the end zone or they'll be so intimidated by the lawyer who'll threaten them with such overblown, probably incomprehensible, defenses that they'll drop the real charges down to the minimum they can salvage.

That means a guy who was plastered and should be dealing with DWI penalties, including alcohol treatment and a significant license loss, will be pleading instead to a turn signal violation, paying a $72.00 fine and figuring he can beat the charge the next time, too—so there's no good reason to clean up his MO. That puts all of us at risk that he'll drift over into our (or our kid's) lane the next night he has a snoot full.

In my humble opinion, that's reason enough for the local Selectmen to include some prosecutorial resources in their annual budgets. I mean, if the scot-free defendant ends up killing someone the next time out, it won't be much consolation that the town saved a few grand it might have spent to prevent that tragedy.

Here's a sad postscript to the small claim about the DJ who couldn't play the young couple's special song at their wedding reception: Apparently, the emotional trauma from the incident was greater than anyone could have imagined, such that the DJ's alternate selection just wasn't adequate to firmly cement the bonds of matrimony.

Tragically, the couple has now split and are at each other's throats over equitable division of the wedding loot, even down to the toaster oven and trivets that they want me to parcel out for them. Nobody asked me, and it's not much consolation at this point, but I could have told them that "Through the Years" by Kenny Rogers wasn't going to make the cheese any more binding.

With a courtroom packed with other alleged speeders, I heard the protestation of a Catholic priest in full Sunday regalia that he "couldn't have been going that fast."

Surely, I thought, a man with a pipeline straight to his god could have come up with a more inspired revelation than that. Though being careful to point out that the holy father's honesty and truthfulness were not being impugned—which would call for a trunkful of rosaries—but that his powers of foot-control and speed limit observation were subject to the frailties of all poor mortals, I found him guilty.

Not surprisingly, this lack of compassion melted the resolution of many of the priest's followers, causing a stampede of guilty confessions and monetary penance. Had I not maintained the bright line between church and state, I would surely have been deluged with similar speeding supplications, without any slings or arrows to stem the tide against the evil of unrepentant driving infractions.

I've worn bow ties for longer than I can remember, in fact so long that I don't recall making a purposeful decision to do so. Now, apart from the fact that I like their snappy appearance, the reasons I wear them are that few other people can tie the knot and that it's one of the few lawyerly-acceptable ways of setting myself apart from everyone else—and doing it cheaper, too, because they tie up less raw material. If everyone started wearing bow ties—and I admit to getting a little miffed about their Johnny-come-lately popularity—I'd probably switch to ascots or string ties, or maybe to pearls. For the same reasons, I still play tennis with a wood racket and golf with wooden woods, neither of which is likely to become a mass phenomenon. Call me a stubborn curmudgeon, but don't relate it to being a certain age, because there's been a lifetime of such character flaws.

Despite the calculated non-conformism, it took me a long time to wear bow ties on the bench. On juvenile days I didn't wear them because I was afraid the kids would take me for an old fart who, like their parents and teachers, couldn't possibly understand their issues or have anything even remotely relevant to tell them. I didn't wear them on days when we had civil and small claims cases either, because I figured they seemed too jaunty and sporty (the ties, not the cases) for occasions usually marked by one financial catastrophe after another. And I didn't wear them on regular criminal docket days, because they seemed to convey a mood of informality that I thought undermined the serious message I was trying to dole out to some college kid in here on his second or third possession of alcohol.

Then, after maybe five years, I just decided, WTF. Nobody was going to care about the tie I was wearing if the rest of what I did was worth a damn. The kids weren't going to think I was [any more] out of touch in a bow tie if I could come up with something to say that made sense to them, which isn't easily accomplished with or without a tie of any kind, much less the Zorro outfit. The fact I was wearing a bow tie wasn't going to register with anyone else either if I gave them reason to take the process seriously and to think I was actually listening to their woes and cutting them the right amount of slack. It's been about 20 years since that moment of epiphany and I haven't looked back. Now I even wear bow ties to funerals, which I seem to be attending at this time in life almost as often as court.

A landlord was suing his former tenant for an unpaid electric bill that the tenant owed but which was in the landlord's name. The landlord was incensed and he railed on and on that his good name had been brutally "deflamed" by the delinquency. When the tenant said he shouldn't have to pay because he had no hot water, I thought the landlord was going to spontaneously combust. Maybe deflamation was what he needed after all, along with a portable defibrillator.

I promised the parties an early decision and asked the bailiff not to let the tenant leave until the landlord had smoked out of the parking lot. I better get this one right or I may have to call the fire department to deflame my own house. I'm still right there in the book, after all.

I mentioned a few blurbs back that cops who try to prosecute their own cases are throwing their defendants a lifeline, particularly where there are lawyers at the defendants' table. That's not always the case, though, and it was never more apparent than when a college kid came in on a DWI charge with his high-paid defense specialist. The kid had blown a .17 on the breath alcohol machine (the "breath of death", they say)— more than twice the legal limit—so the lawyer knew he wasn't going to win an attack on that front. Instead, he decided to challenge the basis for stopping the vehicle in the first place, because if he could show there was no good reason to do so—no "probable cause"—he could get the rest of the evidence thrown out, and his young man would be out the legal bill but home free on one of the most serious charges we've got.

The cop's report said he'd pulled the car over because he saw the passenger drinking from a Busch beer can as the car passed where the officer was parked. The lawyer was skeptical of such keen powers of observation, so his cross-examination lasered in on this potential chink in the case. Then, to make his point most dramatically, he decided to conduct a demonstration.

First, the lawyer held up a Busch can, with his large hand wrapped around most of it, and the cop correctly ID'd it as just like the one he'd seen. Everything was going great so far. The crafty lawyer next held up another can in the same manner, which looked to my untrained eyes to be yet another Busch. Clearly, the lawyer was counting on the cop to see it that way, too, on the theory that he'd taken a shot in the dark but couldn't really have known it was beer, particularly when all but the colors at the top were covered up by an adolescent paw.

Not a bad ploy, I thought, until the officer quickly chirped that this was instead a Lemon Fresca can. You could have knocked the ruggedly-built lawyer over with a cocktail napkin, as he removed his hand and revealed the Lemon Fresca for all to see.

After stammering for a few moments, the red-faced lawyer sarcastically asked the cop how he managed such a lucky guess. The cop cheerfully replied that although he didn't drink beer himself, he made a point to know what the different beverage cans look like—oh and he loved Lemon Fresca!

Not surprisingly, the defense's express to success ran out of gas at that point, and while the lawyer did his best to show he was still full of fight, the outcome was never again in question.

I'm sure once in a million swings, even a Little Leaguer might hit a 90-mile an hour fastball out of the park, but I actually got to see it.

Just after the start of another depressing day of trying to collect civil judgments and with the courtroom thronged with down-trodden defendants facing hopelessly large obligations, the solemn mood was broken by the entrance of a swarthy man in cuffs surrounded by a gaggle of armed law-enforcement types. OK, we're all thinking, some guy stole "Grand Theft Auto" for his X-Box at Ocean State Job Lots or smacked his girlfriend during a drunken tirade over whether he'd cheated with her sister. But when the clerk handed me the complaint, we all learned that our sights were set way too low: "The charge is that you are a fugitive from justice in the Commonwealth of Massachusetts and are wanted there for the crime of murder."

You'd think everyone was stuck with a cattle prod. Financial affidavits fell to the floor, mouths hung agape, and eyes bugged like I'd just taken off all my clothes. When the commotion settled down a few moments later and the guy had agreed to go back to Massachusetts to face the music there (it's called "waiving extradition"), our defendants were suddenly intimidated or terrorized to such extent that a new record was set for establishing voluntary payment orders.

As the last shaken defendant left the courtroom, it occurred to me that all the banks, credit card companies and collection agencies might do well to forget lawyers and instead to finance a similar one-act performance every payment day from now on. Unfortunately, the

Massachusetts guy probably won't be available for a while.

I sometimes get the impression from defense attorneys, prosecutors, police officers, and the public in general, that they think I'd have a tough time walking and chewing gum at the same time, much less coming down on the right side in their cases.

Often it's as subtle as a raised eyebrow or a barely audible huffing sound at a ruling I've made. Other times they stomp out of the courtroom in obvious disgust at my blatant incompetence or they file an extensive motion to reconsider the obviously bonehead decision I've blundered into. If I'm correctly reading those vibes, I do hope they're only first impressions and that eventually I'll manage to do something to dispel them. On the other hand, after almost two decades of disappointment they've probably given up the ghost by now.

One DWI defendant who must also have thought my gullibility quotient was off the charts gave the following explanation for his predicament: He admitted being totally blotto at a party somewhere out in the boondocks but said that instead of trying to drive home, which his good judgment warned him would be irresponsible and dangerous, he curled up on the passenger side of his pickup and dozed off. Then while he slept soundly, confident in the knowledge that he'd made the correct decision, a mysterious truck-napper jumped in next to him, drove the vehicle several miles over washboard roads and ran it aground up a roadside embankment, all without waking him. And when he finally came to, the driver's side door was open and the night rider was long gone. Thus, he'd been totally framed and I was the only one who could rescue him from this blatant case of Driving While Incomprehensible.

My innate faith in the goodness of human nature caused me to deliberate a respectful moment, though ultimately I declined to adopt the young man's version of the evening's events, concluding instead that I'd have to be drunk and incomprehensible myself to choke down that much complete horsesh*t. Even so, I think the prosecutor was worried, because I'm sure I heard a distinct sigh of relief as I announced my ruling, though I exercised sufficient restraint to avoid putting on the permanent record the part about the horse. Still, it's a discouraging commentary on my decision-making that the prosecutor felt the outcome so seriously in doubt—and that my reputation was such that the kid thought he could toss his junk ball past me without so much as a foul tip.

Let the word go forth that even a judge with no more brains than a chimp (chump?) will eventually reach the correct conclusion if given enough opportunities.

It could be my mother calling to say my father, who's just struggled to his 91st birthday, has finally given up the fight. It could be one of the kids—or a rescue worker—calling about a serious accident coming home from a party where everyone's keys should have been confiscated. Instead, mercifully, it's a cop from one of our towns reporting a disaster affecting someone else's life, which is heartless and insensitive, I know, but which is the unavoidable human response.

In most such cases the officers say there's a woman with them whose husband or boyfriend or former boyfriend or obsessive co-worker has smacked or choked or threatened her while the male involved was stupid with drink or jealousy, and they want me to order him out of the house and away from her, at least until he sobers up the next day. That usually makes sense, and so I do, and then I go back to sleep hoping I won't get one of those closer-to-home calls during the rest of that night at least. In fact, this is the very last thing that crosses my mind every single night before my brain waves crash on sleepy beach.

Some cases couldn't have occurred before the age of technology.

At a domestic violence hearing the woman who filed that petition a couple of weeks ago claimed her husband had hit her with the television remote during an argument over what they were going to watch. Despite that she needed emergency room treatment at the time—those things have gotten as large as billy clubs and the space-age plastic could probably stop armor-piercing ammunition—she denied there were any other problems with the couple's relationship or that anything like this had happened before. In fact, she wanted to drop the case because she said she loves her husband, presumably even more than what her favorite cable show had been (*Breaking Bad?*).

I couldn't help thinking this was a situation likely to recur as soon as *Lost* was up against *Boston Legal* again (substitute your own viewing dilemmas here), and that this was a situation where "thinking outside the box" was called for, if you see where I'm heading.

I told the sedentary couple I'd continue the case for 60 days to see whether the wife's risky assessment was accurate, but that they'd have to do more reading or take more walks because the trouble-making tube— and remote—were banished to the garage during that period. I had no idea how that order would be enforced ("If the cops see a purple glow coming from your place, you guys are in trouble!"), but you'd think I'd just doomed them to 20 years on a frozen rock pile. Actually, if I had, they could have watched a state-of-the-art flat screen in jail, so maybe this really was worse than incarceration.

Happily, the time went by without a blip on the screen and the couple showed up on the appointed day to get their dismissal—so they wouldn't miss the final episode of *Survivor Fiji*. I neglected to ask what had been on their interim reading lists, but I'm guessing maybe *TV Guide* and *Soap Opera Digest* were involved.

We don't have many real, irreversible tragedies in our work here. If I convict an innocent person, they're certainly not going to the gas chamber—I'd have to order someone to build one first (see above), which I probably couldn't get away with. Then there's the snag that if I think the book really needs throwing, I can only prescribe a year in jail anyhow and she'd be out much sooner with credit for good time. No, it's our juveniles who are the most likely to risk life-threatening harm, and they're much more likely to self-inflict it than I am to create it for them.

The reason I bring this up now is that word just arrived about one of our 15 year-olds who took her parents' car while they were away and killed herself by crashing it on her way to the beach. The girl was an enigma, one of those free spirits who doesn't understand why parents are still relevant at her age, except to finance whatever expensive entertainment she cares to engage in and to come get her at the police station when the frequent need arises. She was involved with all manner of drugs and alcohol, without apology or remorse, and every time we had a hearing about it, her eyes seemed so vacant and distant that I wondered whether my voice was even registering on her eardrums as it shot through one and then immediately out the other.

The sense I have is that despite all the fun, she was depressed to the point of being dangerously reckless about her own safety, so the fact that she didn't really know how to drive and was going to be in a lot of trouble even if she returned safely from her joy ride, made no real difference to her. If we'd spoken about all this before she left home, I doubt those factors would have caused even a momentary pause in her decision-making, and I'd have been blown off as just a parental clone. She'd probably have figured she had little to live for anyhow—especially if it meant ending up like any of us—and that this was only another adult attempt to throw cold water on what promised to be a good time, albeit life-threatening.

For sure, I'm rationalizing my butt off here and trying hard to convince myself there was nothing I could have done to divert this self-destructive train onto a safer track. I mean, I only spent a few minutes with this young woman every few months and never established any meaningful bond with her. Still, I can't help feeling there must have been some combination of words, even one magic sentence that might have struck a chord or that she might have remembered afterwards to shift the course she was on just enough to keep her alive. I'm still working on what it might have been. If I come up with something promising, I'll run it through some clinical tests in future cases, like a new cancer drug, and compare its effectiveness with the worthless placebos I seem to be dispensing at this point.

The saddest part is that whether anyone says anything life-saving or not, most kids who fit this train-wreck profile at 15 manage somehow to run the adolescent gauntlet without dying, and end up with a healthier take on life by 20 or 25. I was way too goody-goody to have personal testimony to offer, but we all at least knew people like that, who now just shake their own heads in disbelief when we remind them of their nearly fatal shenanigans.

All in all, maybe the best I can do for our young woman—and for my own sense of inadequacy—is to ensure her tragedy wasn't totally in vain and that others seemingly on the same course hear enough about it to make them pause for just that critical moment.

A human drama of a different fabric was played out today when a nervous young woman arrived for her small claim hearing against the seamstress who had failed to return some clothes entrusted to her for alterations—and this was despite a family relationship between them and repeated pleas for cooperation.

Sounds pretty tame, right, and I was caught off-guard, too. Something about the plaintiff, though, told me I was dealing with one of life's chronic victims, which was confirmed when she choked up while describing the special place in her world that the missing garments occupied.

Luckily, the unresponsive seamstress had brought the renovated items with her, leading to the bizarre scene of the young woman trying on (getting reacquainted with?) all her old friends just outside the courtroom and parading the whole wardrobe back and forth past the open door.

Once we'd finished dealing with a number of less colorful disputes, I called the women back in for a status report. They were both overcome with emotion, seeming almost to have undergone a religious experience here in our little chapel of justice. The plaintiff effused that her clothes had been so lovingly and meticulously treated that they had taken on a spectacular new life, while the seamstress confessed it had been so long and she'd grown so attached to the mystical items that she just couldn't bring herself to part with them.

The case ended with the plaintiff paying a gratuity for the unexpectedly remarkable workmanship and promising the thankful seamstress that she wouldn't consider allowing anyone else to minister to her garments from then on. I had never seen parties leave the courtroom so deliriously happy, having repaired their family ties and forged a life-long wardrobe alliance—all without any misguided alterations from me.

~⌣~

I crossed the Rubicon into senior citizenship last week, as my long-dreaded 60th birthday passed me like I was standing on the interstate with my thumb out. There were cakes at some friends' houses, at my law office, here at the court, in Virginia with my daughter and son-in-law where I had taken refuge from any other attempts at celebration, and then back home again with my son and his family.

I sincerely appreciate all their thoughtfulness but can't help also sensing just a touch of perverse gloating by them at my arrival at this milestone of mortality. Some older cronies are relieved to have me finally on their side of the river (Styx?), while the youngsters are still smug that this geriatric tragedy remains far over the horizon for them. The latter group had better watch their steps, though, because I'm planning to live long enough that my bodily functions break down entirely and they have to spend their golden years attending to my lapses in personal hygiene.

The relevance of this to the judicial process is not only that I may be dozing and drooling more often on the bench, but that I'm even older now than nearly all the people who parade through here. I know this because all our court paperwork includes the birth date of the person in question, no matter what the charge, and because I'm now paying closer attention to those numbers than ever before.

In fact, I routinely play a version of the carnival game where someone bets they can guess your age within two years—which I'm lousy at—and it seems like I get worse the older the people get. I'll call the name of someone who looks like they got a ride to court on the retirement home shuttle, and after deciding they must be at least four score and seven, I'm horrified to see they're only 57 and that I was already babbling in complete sentences when they were born.

Some of these folks have clearly beaten themselves up pretty badly by abusing all manner of legal and illegal substances, but others just look a lot older than I'm prepared to acknowledge when I look in the mirror. I find myself speaking louder, more distinctly and even deferentially to those demi-codgers because they must be nearly blind and deaf, and if I was too harsh with them they might have a stroke or a coronary. I want to be uniformly firm with everyone, but I'm not looking to kill anyone in my presence if I can help it.

Then again, I don't want to get so agitated myself that I end up grabbing my chest and disappearing behind the bench in front of a bunch of strangers, which is getting statistically more likely all the time—though at least I'd be wearing the right color for the occasion.

Honestly, tragedy isn't a regular occurrence here but it's struck us again before we've even picked ourselves up from the last blow. Another of our teenage girls just couldn't see the way through her present predicament and hung herself while at one of the group homes we often turn to when everything at home has broken down.

At first I couldn't even place her face with the name, which worried me because maybe I'd sent her off without trying hard enough to understand what was going on there, or without enough concern about what might crush her spirit. Only now am I recalling a girl who seemed backed into a corner with a huge chip on her shoulder because no one was willing to accept her wildly unrealistic version of the truth.

Sound familiar? Even knowing the outcome, I still can't figure what more we might have done for this young woman. She couldn't go home because we'd tried that and she'd proved she wouldn't stay there. She insisted on the right to come and go as she pleased, sometimes without a trace and for days at a time, and we just couldn't allow a 15 year-old to keep that up.

Maybe we should have tried to find her a mentor, one of our alumna who could have made a dent in that impervious exterior with something like, "Look, I know what you're going through because I've been there myself. No matter what anyone said to me, I could only see the world from my own self-centered perspective. It may look hopeless, but I made it through and you can, too. Just cool it enough so you're not freaking out your family, and you'll be able to stay home, probably even getting most of what you want because they'll be so thankful for any improvement. And home is where you need to be, no matter how bad it seems right now."

I guess I should have seen that a guy 45 years older, in a role that represented everything she was pulling away from—and wearing a bow tie—just wasn't going to cut it with her. My voice must have sounded like the adults in the Charlie Brown shows—too garbled even for those goodie-goodie characters to understand.

Speaking of mentors for our kids, I made a pitch for more of them to the local Rotarians several years ago. They'd asked me to give them some ideas about what their club could do to help with our work at the court.

As I spoke, they stared at me like I was proposing higher taxes, and so the mentor suggestion went nowhere. That was probably because those largely older (than me even), white-bread, business people didn't fit the right profile at all, and they recognized that better than I did. They certainly wouldn't have gotten anywhere with the girls I've described—or with our whole cadre of 15 year-old boys. You know, the multi-pierced, baggy-jeans-barely-clinging-to-their-asses ones who stay up all night on websites too disturbing to imagine, then can't get up to go to school, or if they do get that far, get suspended for cussing out the teacher for telling them to cinch up their pants. Ships passing unnoticed in the night is the image that comes to mind.

Maybe it's a total cop-out, but cancer kills a lot of people, too, even though the doctors know what they're dealing with and throw everything they've got at it. Maybe a small percentage of our self-destructive kids are like, say, pancreatic cancer: resistant to treatment that's been effective on other strains but inevitably fatal. I'm hoping now that we don't have a third such tragedy, like the superstition, but the only chance of preventing it is to try even harder to diagnose those high-risk, particularly toxic, cases before they go fatally mutant. Then to try to prescribe the most effective and aggressive treatment and keep our fingers crossed that we—really, I—haven't somehow made an inaccurate diagnosis and tipped a precarious situation into a truly life-threatening zone.

Back to the mundane, which I've decided I like better than I thought. I'm at our annual Town Meeting today, and as the droning goes on and on about the winter road salt budget, I'm trying not to fall asleep in public, in order not to give people the impression that this is a chronic judicial occurrence, as well. I'm currently listening to the bloviation of a local guy who comes out of the woodwork once a year, like Punxatawny Phil, and who feels it's his civic responsibility to make sure we all know where he stands on each and every issue before we vote.

The reason this is in here is that the guy reminds me of the self-assured lawyer who was in court last week representing a logger charged with having gotten his log-laden truck up to a speed far in excess of the posted limit—or as Cathie refers to it, the "suggested limit". This scenario always sets off an alarm, because whenever I see so much lawyerly effort and expense going into fighting a speeding charge, it's almost a lock that the driver is no stranger to law enforcement and that this otherwise innocuous ticket may be the camel's back-breaker for his driving privileges.

The logger's proximity to license disaster must have come to light only after the stop, however, because the officer testified to the logger's relaxed and cavalier attitude at the scene of the incident, including his sincere apology for going so fast. Then, once the fellow added the new points to his existing total or saw what another conviction would do to his insurance rates, he put his truck in reverse and tried to roll back his speedometer. By the time everyone got to court, the newly-hired lawyer was confidently loaded for bear, having somehow tracked down the drivers both in front of and behind the logger's truck, although he never let on how he might have done that.

I managed to stay remarkably alert during all this, even to the point of taking way more notes than usual about how fast everyone was going, to make sure I didn't mix up the numbers. When it was all said and done, I checked over my scribbling several times, but couldn't locate any reference, by anyone but the cop, to even the ballpark speed the logger himself thought he may have been doing. Maybe that was intentional hiding of the incriminating ball, but when I pronounced the guilty verdict and explained my reasoning, there was a lot of bluster and stammering coming from the defense table.

Remarkably, I could see the logger's sense of outrage directed at the lawyer, not at me for a change. As for the lawyer, maybe he thought I'd be so impressed with his array of witnesses that I wouldn't notice the radar reading standing like the quarter-ton gorilla in the corner. Or maybe he just fanned on that element of his defense and paid for it by eating the balance of his fee, as well as a little crow—a delicacy all lawyers, present company definitely included, have tasted many times.

Then the lawyer was either so embarrassed or so pissed at me that he sent an associate in to handle the next couple of weeks' cases. Eventually, of course, he wandered back in here himself and we moved on like nothing had happened, which is the way it has to be.

Unemployment is climbing dramatically as the economy slides into the tank. When that happens, the DWI cases start arriving like holiday mail at the post office, no matter how much media attention is focused on the tragic consequences of drinking and driving. So while I'm never looking to trade on others' expense, that's the very nature of this job. If people suddenly stopped acting like brainless high school freshmen, I'd gladly file for unemployment—but I'm not losing any sleep over job security.

Today's "deewee", as they're known in the biz, was another no-brainer—and I'm not referring to my brain for a change. The driver and his vehicle left the road and meandered down a steep embankment before plunging into some trees at the bottom. The normally laconic officer, whom I'd never seen resort to hyperbole in 20 years, declared that "this young man was just about the drunkest driver I've ever seen." Based on that dramatic assessment, I was pretty much cruising on this one until the defendant took his turn on the stand.

The guy said he'd had to take an "awful pee" and thought he'd better get his car as far off the road as possible, in order not to be a traffic hazard. When he found himself a little too far afield—that is, over the shoulder and into the woods (and halfway to grandmother's house)—he was pretty bummed and decided he might as well start drinking to take the edge off. After just two beers, in combination with the Prozac and the cocktail of other allegedly prescription drugs he was taking, he was in the totally sh*t-faced condition that the officer observed. Unfortunately, he neglected to mention any of this to the officer, due to his extreme stupor on the night in question, no doubt, and then also forgot to bring along any evidence of the prescriptions that were the purported culprits.

As I weighed the facts and circumstances, the only things certain in my mind were that I must look way more stupid than I feared, having suffered untold brain damage when I fell off the turnip truck. So, when I found the heavily-medicated, depressed soul, with the weak bladder and poor driving skills, guilty, this was either the worst miscarriage of justice in our parts in a generation, or righteous retribution for the most pungent pile of bullsh*t (not horsesh*t this time) ever shoveled into a courtroom in southern New Hampshire.

General stores have been the focal point of New Hampshire villages since colonial times. In the early days they housed the pharmacy, post office, and occasionally the local court, with the aproned storekeeper dispensing both justice and a pound of ground chuck to his customers. As I reported early on, even as recently as the '80s—the 1980's—the well-intentioned but non-lawyer newspaper editor of the local paper served as our own court's backup judge, literally creating the news for himself to cover as he worked his way through the docket. (He was known to impose a fine and then ask the defendant whether it was too much—there'd be no reason to bother asking these days.) Today general stores offer fax and copy machines, too, and frequently the ATM machine of a nearby bank.

This sociological buildup is to help explain the theft charge brought against a youthful resident of one of our outlying towns, who allegedly ran off with a pedestal ashtray standing next to the store's new ATM. The store owner had thoughtfully provided the ashtray, which the young man (a smoker, I'm guessing) apparently thought was there for withdrawal as much as his cash—in multiples of $20, please, and for a modest service charge, of course.

The detail the fellow overlooked was that even in this outpost of technology, with nary a security guard for ten miles, the machine was equipped with a continuously vigilant surveillance camera. After recording furtive glances in each direction, the camera dutifully picked up the guy grabbing and making off with something beyond his Jacksons.

The young man initially pled not guilty, because, in his haplessness, he thought he was all alone at the time—it was after midnight, for Pete's sake—and so there was no way they could PIN this on him (see the theory above about habits of truthfulness). Once shown his incriminating transaction in high definition, however, he quickly fessed up, ironically having to return to the scene of the crime to come up with his fine money. No ashtray anymore, though, so he'll have to pocket his butts, or big brother will nab him for littering next time.

Federal judges get paid more and deal with weightier legal issues, but they miss out on the quirkiness that meanders through our dockets on a daily basis. If that hasn't become apparent yet, I need to work harder on my writing skills.

As further support for this hypothesis, I offer the case of a seemingly ordinary resident of our county jail who came in with his public defender to argue for early release. His theory was that as a cross-dresser who wears women's undergarments beneath his mandatory pumpkin suit (the vernacular for our incarcerants' flashy orange coveralls), he was being accosted cruelly and unusually in the insensitive jail environment. Thus, what was a run-of-the-mill six-month sentence for most defendants seemed like considerably more for this sexually-vulnerable soul.

It was a close call for me—they never covered this issue in law school—but I finally decided that the young man's choice of an alternative lifestyle couldn't be used for a leg-up on the system. I mean, if it was a condition or illness that was involuntary or unavoidable, OK, I'd have taken another peak, but he chose to put on the bra and panties and he could either revert to some man-briefs for a few months or go totally commando, which I'm told is a liberating experience in itself. One thing the hearing clarified for me was why the shoplifted contraband was a 34B brassiere.

Take that, you straight-laced federal guys.

The predicament of one of our 13 year-old girls just became way more complicated than she realizes, as she arrived for her hearing in an extremely pre-maternal state that had developed since the last time I saw her. She's "pretty sure" who the father is, which suggests there may have been several occasions when better information about birth control would have come in handy.

The putative father is himself only 15 years old, which puts a further damper on things, because he's chargeable with statutory rape if anyone goes to the trouble of a paternity test. It also means that even though these two profess to "love each other" and want to "be together", I can't let them have so much as a face-to-face chat unless closely supervised, for fear they'll put other things together again.

The most frightening part, aside from the fact that at least one young life has been dramatically accelerated into adulthood, is that the girl has been with us for kicking her mother in the stomach and generally resorting to severe temper tantrums when things don't go her way. That doesn't bode well for the safety of her child, as I recall having anger management issues myself when our screaming kids wouldn't go to sleep for what seemed like days at a time—and I was 26, not 13.

We've already had one kid who shook his baby to death a few years ago, ruining two lives in the space of a couple seconds, and I fear the same risk here. If the authorities are smart, they'll scoop this kid right out of the nursery and put it in a relatives or foster home for a few years, until this mom gets her training wheels off and earns at least an associates degree in early childhood parenting.

I'll be interested to see, too, whether the young couple really does get together once it's no longer a criminal offense.

The police called today to let us know that a mean-spirited, vaguely dangerous character—Bob Ewell of *To Kill a Mockingbird* would be an accurate mental picture—who had kept us in the small claims business for many years as both plaintiff and defendant, had walked out to his field, put the butt end of his shotgun in the ground, and blown a large hole through his chest.

They said the fellow left a long suicide note revealing depression on many fronts, and though he didn't mention the court in so many words, the note was found atop many of the hearing notices we'd sent him. What's more, his son, who alternates between abusing woman and alcohol and was even charged with abuse by his father, reportedly told the cops that his father's death was all "Judge Runyon's fault."

I fail to see how the kid's assessment is even remotely plausible, but it does make you wonder whether some small, seemingly inconsequential, disappointment at the court's—my—hands finally caused the fatal meltdown. If so, it never presented itself with any kind of fair warning notice attached.

None of the cases by or against him ever involved any serious money and no ruling I made ever threatened to ruin his way of life, such as it was. Though I rarely found him on the right side of any issue, I recall being polite to a fault, even when he wasn't reciprocating, which was frequently. My mantra, after all, is, "often wrong, always polite," but I guess that's not enough consolation for some people, and if you recall, Bob Ewell spit in Atticus's face without any provocation either.

Ever wonder why just about the tallest building in every major city has an insurance company's name on it? Boston's got the Prudential and Hancock towers—I see them looming over the bleachers at Fenway every time I'm there—New York's got MetLife atop Grand Central, and San Francisco's skyline is dominated by the Transamerica pyramid, to name just the ones I've seen in person. There's even a pint-sized version in lil' ole Manchester, New Hampshire, that's visible from the top of Mount Monadnock about 40 miles away. Many theories may account for this architectural phenomenon, but one of them is not that they voluntarily make good on claims they can avoid. Indeed a highly plausible postulate is that they have unmitigated gall, which they exposed recently before my very eyes.

The company in question—which shall remain nameless lest I never be able to hear another of their frequent cases—sent a big-time lawyer in a dark suit all the way from Manchester to Jaffrey to get back the $400 it paid out for damage to one of its customer's vehicles. I bet it paid him—the lawyer, that is—more than that just for the ride over, but that's often what the companies do: They pay their customer's claim and then they file suit to get back each and every one of those nickels from whatever third party they think was actually responsible for causing the damage. Not a bad MO in itself, and one they'd argue helps keep their premiums low—well, lower anyhow.

My whiff of sarcasm here stems from the fact that the vehicular damage in our case occurred when the insured's car ran over and killed a little boy's dog that had pulled away from him just as the car went by. The 10 year-old himself was even here to tearfully explain how he'd tried his best to hold the dog, but how its leash had snapped at the last fateful second.

Apparently, though, this real-life version of *Old Yeller* was not a sufficient excuse for the business-is-business folks in the tower of insurance, as the lawyer matter-of-factly hammered away about the kid's negligence in failing to maintain reasonable control of his dog and about how such irresponsible negligence was the "proximate cause" (law school lingo again) of the resulting damage to the vehicle. The young hotshot even dotted the "i" by pointing me to a statute that makes dog owners absolutely liable when something like this happens. "Slam dunk," I may actually have heard him say in his best George Tenet voice (remember him?).

As usual, I took the case under advisement (remember why?), but there seemed like little reason to do so from a legal standpoint, given the heavy artillery that had pounded the kid, like Davy by all those Mexican cannons at the Alamo. Then, as I was starting to compose a reluctant "judgment for the plaintiff", I glanced to see who should be listed in the decision as the plaintiff. I was surprised to see the insurance company itself shown on the papers, rather than its customer whose car needed the repair. Gee, I thought, in his zeal to prove the kid negligent, the lawyer himself had negligently failed to establish the company's right to jump into the driver's seat of the damaged vehicle and sue in the dog-squasher's behalf—it's called "subrogation" in obfuscating legal parlance, and nearly all policies provide for it somewhere in the maze of fine print.

The problem was that the lawyer just assumed that crucial fact, which courts aren't allowed to do no matter how common the practice may be—and besides we all know what happens when we assume, right? So, if the company—or rather its budding Clarence Darrow—hadn't proved it could sue, I wasn't going to be able to slam its dunk.

I could dismiss its case, however, and that's what I wrote instead, hoping as I did that maybe the lawyer's firm itself would cough up $400 for the miscue and that no one would bother the youngster again. He'll learn life's hard lessons soon enough, but in the meantime he'll probably need to save his cash for a new dog. I hope he has something left over for a more substantial leash, too.

Today was a truly red-letter day, although black ink is what I'm really talking about.

In my long career of dispensing orders to pony up the fines for all manner of transgressions, we've never before experienced a day when every single person has actually come up with the cash without broaching the subject of an installment plan. We usually give people two weeks to pay when they need it, and if they insist they won't be able to do it even then, because of some perfectly good reason like needing a new battery for their iPod or not having finished paying for their last tattoo—OK, maybe they just don't have a job—I offer the option of going to work for the House of Correction where they'll get credit at an unbelievably generous $150 a day. There have been more than a few takers of this opportunity over the years, but when faced with that prospect, most folks put the two weeks to good use and somehow find a way to settle up in the conventional manner.

Today's haul was over $4,000, which may not sound like much, but I bet it's more than it costs to run this place for eight hours. I was so moved by the outpouring of financial support that I wrote our head judge to crow a little, but also to forestall his next memo about being too lenient and taking too long to collect our fines.

PS—This must have been the legal equivalent of a perfect game in baseball, because it's never happened again in 20+ years—not even close.

PPS—We've now got the option, too, of letting people do community service in payment of their fines. They can empty bed pans at a nursing home, dust the shelves at the library, or feed the kitties at the local animal shelter (a popular choice). The statute says they get credit at $10 per hour for their efforts, but the minimum wage these days is just $7.25 and I'm damned if I going to make it any easier to pay fines this way than by slinging burgers over a hot grill at McDonald's across the street. The public defenders give me a jaundiced look when I size it up this way, but then I remind them that their clients can get a way better hourly rate at the House. That never fails to settle the issue.

Contested domestic violence cases are actually quite rare. Usually, either the guy (still the defendant most times) doesn't show up at all, or if he does, he admits he was a jerk and promises that it won't ever, ever happen again. Today, though, was a different story. It wasn't about who did what to whom, or about who gets the children or possession of the house. No, it was about the return of the woman's personal effects, chief among them her pink vibrator, some X-rated videotapes the defendant had taken of her, and, I'm not kidding, her two goats.

For a fleeting moment, I thought maybe I had dozed off and drifted into the midst of a bad SNL skit. Unfortunately, that moment quickly passed and I realized this was a real-life nightmare from which I wouldn't wake up at the crucial moment when everyone suddenly turned to me for a decision. The goats were one thing—certainly no farther out into the solar system than those yipping Chihuahuas—and even the unseen videotapes weren't beyond the pale. I mean, somebody has to be recording that stuff you see on YouTube.

The vibrator, on the other hand, clearly shot way over the top, particularly in front of a courtroom of other unfortunates barely able to control their snickering despite their own train wrecks yet to come. I don't have a handle on what vibrators cost, but they'd have to be more than a fully-loaded Lexus for me to raise the subject in front of a bunch of smirking strangers. As we went on, it appeared that the woman simply wasn't about to give the guy the satisfaction of keeping such an intimate memento of their love life, and she figured all vestiges of her privacy and dignity had already gone up in smoke.

In the end, she got what she was willing to fight for. He didn't want the goats or even the videotapes, and I wasn't about to add further insult to injury by denying her the one item which will not be mentioned again. If I ever get nominated to the Supreme Court—and I keep refreshing my resume—this case may rank with Clarence Thomas' Coke can embarrassment. Maybe at least they'll let me tour the building before kicking me back down to the rung where I belong.

We don't often have a regular court session on Monday, but it's inevitable that someone ends up in jail over the weekend and I have to come in to decide whether he (though increasingly she) stays there. This time it was a brazen guy from "down below" (what we call Massachusetts when we're being snooty) who pushed a shopping cart full of cigarettes and dog food out of Walmart without benefit of a sales receipt. He pled not guilty—maybe he'll say he thought the checkout counter was in the parking lot—so I was left in the dark about whether he was going to eat the dog food or maybe had a bunch of dogs who couldn't lick their butts.

The guy was originally held on cash bail, not because he was a danger to others (although we now know secondhand smoke can be fatal), but due to vagueness about his name and address, which is not the way to impress your bail commissioner. Even after I probed further for this information, he kept bobbing and weaving all over the place, convincing me, too, that $1,000 in cash was about right to ensure he'd come back for trial. It got even more interesting when I asked him to sign the bail form and the clerk noticed that his signature was entirely different than any name he'd mentioned so far. When this was pointed out to him, he realized his cover was blown for sure and he attempted to scratch out the name and ball up the form. I actually thought he was going to try to eat it, but he couldn't get it to his mouth with handcuffs hooked to his ankles. Our clerk managed to wrestle the paper away—the guy was messing with the wrong person there—and then it took three large officers to escort him back to the holding cell.

When the new name was run through the national gallery of rogues, it produced outstanding (that is, active) warrants in several other states, as well as an increase in bail to $10,000. I suspect it will now be considerably longer before Mr. Mysterious will be pushing a cart of anything unless it's dirty pumpkin suits on the way to the laundry. On the way home two things occurred to me: (1) if you were really trying to camo your identity, wouldn't you scribble out a name that no one could read, and (2) I hoped someone was available to feed his passel of hungry, chain-smoking dogs.

Murder cases are the rock stars of criminal justice, but, like U2, we rarely see them here in Jaffrey. Occasionally, though, they pass through on their way to Superior Court, to test whether there's enough evidence to bother the folks up the ladder with a full jury trial. We call it a "probable cause" hearing 'cause it has to be probable that the defendant did the deed. These are usually pretty quick and uneventful, but this one would have made a good episode of *Cold Case* because it happened more than a decade ago and had gone completely frigid by the time it warmed back up.

Back then, a woman was found lying in her bathtub after being raped and then strangled with a vacuum cleaner cord. Understandably—and without intending any disrespect to the family—the case made quite a splash when it hit the papers back then, not only due to the gruesome details, but also because no clear culprit emerged. Of course, the hubby is always suspect number one in these cases—remember *The Fugitive*?—but there was nothing tangible linking her guy to the crime and there was no inkling that the couple's love boat was on the rocks. Still, all the gossip was about him and how he'd gotten away with it, which eventually hounded him out of town to escape all the hairy eyeballs at the Post Office.

Finally, when no arrests were made and nothing more happened to suggest the presence of a serial bathtub killer in our midst, the cops all but closed their file. I say "all but" because recently a New Hampshire officer dusted it off for a real-life cold case conference in Florida. Without much hope, of course, he talked it up to cops from all over the country to see if anyone anywhere else might toss him a lead. Incredibly, a Florida officer said the details of the crime closely mirrored one they'd had, and what's more, the guilty guy was cooling his heels right there in jail. When they investigated further, they were shocked to discover that the Florida felon had been working up here when the crime was committed, and for the same company as the beleaguered husband, less than a mile from the deadly bathtub.

All this came out in dramatic fashion at our probable cause hearing. As the relentlessly-determined cop recounted the unlikely scenario, you could hear mouths dropping all over the courtroom, which was packed to standing room capacity. In addition to family members of the victim who were still looking for answers, there were lots of the same local busy-bodies who'd never gotten their fill of the sordid details, as well as stringers from every tabloid who could find the courthouse. Only the husband was conspicuously absent—after all, he knew he hadn't done it—though he might have taken some satisfaction at seeing so much crow being eaten at one sitting.

It turned out that the Florida guy had known his victim for some time, in the Biblical sense, and he'd slipped out of the shop that day to pay her a visit. Clearly, the husband had nary a whiff of the tryst or he might have spared himself a world of grief. What we never learned was what went bad between the secretive couple to have it end the way it did. On the other hand, if the guy reprised his crime in Florida, maybe there was no explanation except that he's a brutal murderer with an unconventional MO.

Anyhow, it didn't take much of a leap for me to get over the probable cause hurdle, and to decide that *Cold Case* may be a show I'll want to check out from now on. Maybe they'll give me CLE credit if I put them onto our case.

~⌇

While we're on the subject of brutality between romantic partners, I'll mention the sentencing hearing we had the other day for a swarthy-looking hubby who'd pled guilty to clubbing his wife with a three-pound ham. Fortunately, she wasn't seriously injured, but that didn't mean the guy wasn't a pig. Pardon my flippant attitude, but there's a fair amount of dark humor in this line of work, particularly when you're always wearing black.

Anyhow, a critical factor when you're working up a sentence is the defendant's prior record. If it's a first screw-up, you generally cut some slack—depending on the severity of the offense, of course—but if the guy's past history with law enforcement is a mess, then the slack has been played out and the rope is probably tight enough to hang the defendant. In this case I was not only interested in bad behavior in general, but particularly as to any other attacks with meat products. I also wanted to know, but was chicken to ask, whether the ham was bone-in or bone-out, or even canned. After all, some of those configurations could have made the difference between a sloppy slap with a hunk of Spam or a vicious attack with a deadly metallic weapon.

In the end it didn't really matter because the guy's extensive resume cooked his bacon and he ended up going away for the full year I could dole out, not happily I might add. I guess he figured that if you can eat the weapon, you shouldn't have the cookbook thrown at you. If I haven't become a vegetarian by the time the guy's released, I may have to watch my back at the meat counter for a while.

So far, my account of bizarre behavior here on our altitude-challenged rung of justice has kept yours truly out of the starring role, which is the way most judges want it. We all try to make the right decisions, but even when we blow one, we don't want it to appear we're loose cannons who are drunk on the sound of our own voices. Then along comes a judge in D.C. who's suing the dry cleaner that misplaced his really extra special favorite pants, for $65,462,500. He cites pain and suffering, mental anguish and litigation expenses, and he wouldn't even take the $10,000 the poor Asian laundry owners were intimidated into offering just to make him get out of their faces.

So now we're all power-crazed egomaniacs yet again, even though I buy my pants at Sam's Club for $19.95, which is less than it costs to clean them. I can only assume that this guy let the pressure of his caseload get the best of him and decided that instead of sending in a discrete letter of resignation, he'd opt for going down in flames on national TV—sort of like the postal worker who can't deal with all that new mail arriving every day and starts shooting up the place before blowing out his own brains. Ironically, the judge is up for a re-certification hearing soon, which, if the authorities were smart, would be held in the psych ward at Walter Reed. Of course, that doesn't help the rest of us who have to deal with the fallout. And if I was ruling on his case, the guy would have been awarded just enough to buy himself a comfy pair of jeans with the extra room he needs for his enlarged a**hole. I mean, what was his Honor gonna do when the sacred britches eventually wore out?

Back to five finger discounts for a moment. A Massachusetts shopper at our Walmart store, which is located temptingly close to the State line, pled guilty to shoplifting 96 separate items and then begged for leniency because she was taking so much medication that she didn't know what she was doing.

As an aside, I've always wondered why the influence of alcohol or drugs is never a good one—they never seem to cause anyone to do the right thing, the smart thing or the nice thing. In fact, if those substances suddenly disappeared from our cases, most of the cases would disappear, too, and I'd be asking whether you want fries with that Whopper.

Anyhow, the woman claimed her medication was for a seizure disorder (no one else appeared to appreciate the irony), which seemed totally ineffective if you consider how hard she fell off the wagon. I suspended a good chunk of the pretty substantial fine, 'cause boosting 96 of anything means she'll have a cartful of restitution to pay. She'll also need to renew her prescription for that seizure medication or we'll be seeing her again pretty soon. Come to think of it, there's a pharmacy at Walmart. Let's hope it's near the front door, so she's not tempted by all that defenseless merchandise on her way to and from. Plus, I hope she takes some water with her to wash down a few capsules right there at the counter, because I'd hate for her to get into trouble again by walking out without paying for the new prescription.

I don't even know how to describe this next case in a book that's supposed to be suitable for the entire family. Let's just put it that the old saying about "screwing the pooch" has become a reality for a young man so discouraged by his unsuccessful efforts to attract females of the human variety that he looked for love in all the wrong places. Unbelievably, his defense was that the victim consented, although I was too timid to ask how he determined that fact. 'Nuf said, and even that's probably TMI.

The phone rang about 1:30 in the morning, but there was no one on the other end when Cathie picked it up. Then the same thing happened about five minutes later, and again about five minutes after that. When we finally disconnected the phone in the bedroom, we heard the downstairs phone ring several times before whoever was calling finally gave up. The caller's mission had been accomplished by then, however, as we stayed awake 'til dawn trying to figure out who might have been sufficiently put out by something I'd done to sacrifice their own night's sleep. If they'd said something, even as a threat, I'd have picked up some hint of the person or problem and known whether I needed to call for help or just to take it with a grain of salt, of which I have enough for winter road work at this point.

After mulling it for a couple of hours, all that came to mind was a child neglect case a couple of days earlier, where the volatile combination of alcoholism and poor parenting skills convinced me the child wouldn't be safe staying at home, and where even the grandparents got into it in the courthouse over who should have the child. None of them seemed as good as a foster home without further investigation, which was the decision they would have received in the mail about the day before the calls were made. If it was them, they must have figured they'd be shooting themselves in the foot to have me know who they were, so they settled for keeping us up all night. Then again, maybe it was only a glitch at the phone company.

Coincidentally, one of our storm windows facing the street was broken by a rock this winter. Was it another irate customer or something hard that was kicked up by a speeding plow truck? When you live and judge in the same fishbowl, with your name and address in the phone book, you never really know about these things. It's good that paranoia and suspicion aren't among my character flaws or I'd never be able to make a decision about anything, even which bow tie to wear.

This time there was no doubt who was making the calls. There was also no doubt, yet again, that small claims are the gaping hole in my boat as I attempt to stay afloat in our frequently treacherous judicial waters—alright, so that's a little melodramatic.

Anyhow, for the past month or two I've been getting voice mail harangues on my law office phone from a woman I've never laid eyes on, but who says she's the sister of a woman I ruled against last year in some kind of case. Honestly, I can't remember the issues involved or why her sister lost out, but I do vaguely recall that it had something to do with landlords and tenants, and there were firearms involved. I'm not telling Cathie about that aspect of the rants. Oops!

Whatever it was, this caller has picked up the case like it was *Roe v. Wade* and I was the abortion king. Who knows, maybe I totally blew the decision—that's happened more times than I've got fingers and toes—but if so, she's now gotten me back for it many times over. The messages go on for as long as the system will allow, then she calls back again, goes off on a different tangent, and eventually fills up my mailbox to the point where no one else with a bone to pick can get through. Of course, that rankles them, too, some of whom might actually be clients I'd like to hear from. When she's finished with that filibuster, she calls my partner's extension and does the same to him, on the theory, I guess, that he'll also dump on me for causing his mailbox to clog up like a bad septic system.

Lately, the messages have wandered off the original subject almost entirely and are becoming more about the caller's historical problems dealing with the local cops—what a surprise—but eventually the rants meander back to my collusion with her sister's abusers and to how I should be yanked off the bench in cuffs during mid-session.

The challenge is what to do about the whole business, and though lawyers are supposed to be good at strategizing and developing clever plans of action, I'm without a clue on this one. The woman is clearly looking for validation of her paranoid delusions, so if I report the calls—which I've recorded just in case I suffer a suspicious comeuppance (probably from the firearms)—she'll go totally viral and start screaming about judicial abuse to all the media outlets she can punch up on her laptop.

So I'm trying to ride it out. The discouraging part is that it's now been 9 months or so, and that just about when I figure the calls have run their course, I come in to find the message light blinking furiously and a whole new spate of middle-of-the-night tirades to ramp up the venom yet again. Do I have to say I hate these cases another time or are we crystal clear by now?

A ways back I confessed (albeit without Miranda warnings) to convicting a woman for speeding despite impending diarrhea. On the upside, the experience (with an assist from Cathie) forever sensitized me to the urgent demands of bodily functions. Today I was presented with my opportunity to atone when a dour woman about my age took the stand to explain why she was going 58 in a 35. I had seen her sitting in the back of the courtroom all morning and I could tell by her constant fidgeting that she was even more uncomfortable than our usual clientele. From her demeanor—she looked quickly away whenever I glanced in her direction—I guessed her charge was something pretty dire.

When I finally came to her name on the docket, I was surprised to see that it was just a garden variety speeding summons. After the officer's perfunctory spiel about calibrating his radar gun and getting an accurate read on the woman's velocity, she took the stand and started crying even before getting out her name and address. Eventually, she managed to choke out that menopause had hit her prematurely and left her with sudden, uncontrollable incontinence which had struck only moments before she'd been caught racing for home. The officer indeed confirmed that she'd dashed for the woods immediately on stopping her vehicle—even before producing her vital papers—but that she'd failed to share all the sensitive details with him upon her return.

Never you mind, I thought, having learned my lesson well and fearing further retribution at home. I quickly continued the case for a year, deciding to take the distraught woman up on her claim that she's not a scofflaw and wouldn't let this happen again no matter how loud nature called. I didn't ask for specifics on how she could make good on the latter promise, figuring, though, that she'd do anything to avoid further self-mortification and would surely pay the next ticket without a whimper if another bladder emergency occurred while in motion. I also made sure to get full credit from Cathie for my enlightened and newly-sensitized decision-making. You've got to rack up the points where you can, although I think I'm still showing a negative balance.

I returned to the bench after a recess to find a folded note addressed to me by one of the officers in court that day. It said the registration of my car out in the parking lot had expired, and by more than just a couple of days. I knew I'd gotten the car inspected when I took it in for its 15,000 mile checkup, but it had totally escaped me that I still needed to get it registered—yea, right, pal, ignorance may be bliss, but it's not a defense! Now here I was, seven miles from home, with expired plates, and with every officer in the region alerted to nail me on the way to the motor vehicle office.

At the next recess, I called Cathie, and after she finished laughing for longer than I thought was really necessary, she agreed to go into the local office during her lunch break to make it safe for me to leave the courthouse. As I did so after the session, I had visions that a BOL (Be On the Lookout, dudes) had gone out to all the local departments; that patrol cars would come screaming in from all directions; that cops would yank me out of the car and slam my face against the hood; that my hands would be splayed and my legs spread while they patted me down for weapons and drugs; and that countless others would be drawing a bead on my head.

I was relieved when none of this happened, which I hope is a sign that local law enforcement doesn't feel too badly abused by me or too motivated to "get even with that rat bastard," though it may only mean that the cops had made one last check of the records before swooping in and had learned, to their great disappointment, no doubt, that Cathie had bailed me out once again.

Today we had a short docket of cases from Peterborough, the town where we live—the address and phone number are in the book, but please don't throw rocks at my windows or send pizzas. One of our customers was a guy who said he's a professional driver for a daily newspaper. So, like many people who fear losing their licenses, he vigorously fought the charge of passing a stopped school bus, not denying that he did so but claiming, unconvincingly, that he acted defensively to avoid being rear-ended. After I found him guilty and imposed a modest fine that I thought fit the circumstances, he announced that he's the guy who delivers our newspaper and that in light of my ruling, we would never see another dry one.

Everyone else seemed to think this threat was pretty funny, but I doubt Cathie will be pleased to learn of this further unanticipated drawback of cohabiting with the local judge. The unkindest cut is that I send in a tip for the carrier with each renewal of my subscription, which I guess I'll have to increase considerably now, despite the soaked papers, until I've paid enough to cover the guy's fine and any license restoration fees. I thought about calling the newspaper office to complain, but I decided I'd rather have a soggy paper than one tossed through the window.

PS—Reference is made to the preceding entry—and to the fact that my irate bus-passer has thus far made good on his delivery threat. In fact, he's even found a way to get the papers wet when the weather's dry. None of them have gone through the windows, however, so I've got that going for me.

It's been about a month now since the Virginia Tech campus was rocked by a lonely and troubled young man who killed more students and teachers than in any other prior outbreak of academic terrorism. This incident reminded me of the Columbine disaster almost exactly eight years ago, when two high school students armed with guns and bombs randomly killed or wounded about 25 of their fellow students and teachers, and then did themselves in before anyone could ask why. Unfortunately, we learned too late in both cases that these young people were seriously disaffected, for reasons only dimly understood, and that they'd carefully planned their attacks, over considerable time periods, in order to produce maximum devastation.

What makes this relevant for my purposes is that the Columbine guys had both been in juvenile court about six weeks earlier on petty charges and that NPR had played the tape of their final hearing with the judge. Both students were polite and respectful and gave no indication whatever of the murderous rampage they must have been planning even then. It made me realize anew how little we actually know about the young people we're dealing with—even our own children, when you come right down to it. We have absolutely no clue what's really brewing inside any of them or whether we're responding effectively to alter some tragic or self-destructive course they're secretly embarked on. And it's pretty unsettling to realize that any of our court kids, who sit about four feet away from me during our cozy little hearings, could also be saying whatever is necessary to get themselves out of the system, just like the Columbiners, in order to get back to the arsenal they're readying in the basement.

Time responded with a cover story about how to spot troubled kids, and I agree there are signs that may be visible in some cases. The problem is that anyone can spot the flashing neon billboards. The kids that end up doing most of the damage, though, are careful to mask any obvious signs. And they've figured correctly that maximum devastation depends on non-existent security coupled with the element of total surprise.

None of this is a reason to throw up our hands, but—here I go again—it suggests to me that getting better control of the guns would be easier than reading minds. The kid at Tech was able to buy guns and ammo like they were a new set of woods and irons, and no one raised an eyebrow, much less an alarm. He might still have been able to get the weapons he needed, but requiring a siren to go off at the point of acquisition, like a warning shot, might have sent up a flare, raised a red flag, caught someone's attention, pushed the panic button, whatever, before it was too late. Even whispering about greater—hell, any—gun control, however, sends the Second Amendment posse down to their basements for assault rifles and ammo belts, all the better to blow me to bits. I'm the real threat in their minds.

It's been four years now since we moved into our shiny new palace of justice, as Cathie calls it. That's one area where we can compete with the big boys, and a day doesn't pass that I don't thank the facilities gods for how much better we have it now than in the former industrial plant we shared with a couple of loud manufacturing companies for about 15 years. I recently found a note I'd made during an August session of those days, complaining to no one in particular that without any air conditioning I was having a hard time keeping the sweat from dripping onto the paperwork and making a real mess of everything. It was not only dropping off the end of my nose, but dripping down the inside of my shirt, and from my knees down into my socks. Not a pretty picture.

Although I didn't find any written record of what happened during the winter, I remember often using one of those little hand warmers where you light the fuel rod and clamp it into the fireproof case. Our clerk even knitted me some black mittens with a cord between them so I could wear them under my robe. The trouble was, it was too hard to write "guilty", much less "not guilty", to use them during a real session. Plus, I may sound like a kindergartner, but I didn't want to look like one if I could help it—and it's hard to pick your nose very discreetly while wearing mittens.

Without doubt, the courthouse amenity that's improved the most is the bathroom. The old building had just one of them and it was in the public area where our customers came and went throughout the day. Consequently, despite how much coffee I may have had, I had to hold onto it until we'd finished with the docket and I could head for the head without fear of getting punched out by someone who'd just had an unfortunate experience in the courtroom. This kind of bladder restraint was a real challenge at first; however, it's amazing what a motivator the fear of physical violence can be.

Lawyers seem to gravitate to areas of the law where they feel most effective and comfortable with their skills, or at least where they can make a living. Specialized needs also give rise to specialized services. Because auto insurance companies are hiking the premiums of drivers who get any sort of moving violation, lawyers have cropped up as specialists even in speeding cases. When I used to practice in this court, I urged clients charged with speeding to take their best shot themselves, but to save their money to pay the almost inevitable fines, instead of me. Now the premium increases may be even greater than the lawyer's fee (is that even possible?), and once jacked up, the premiums aren't likely to settle back down for years and years—and probably more years.

The problem is that speeding charges are tough to beat if you're really speeding, so the lawyers have had to come up with a number of innovative defenses. One tack is to have a radar specialist standing by to testify about how unreliable the equipment is and how its readings can be distorted by everything from rain, wind or darkness, all the way to curvature of the earth, phases of the moon, and bad karma. They may also claim that an LED radar reading can't be used as evidence if there's no printout made to verify it. In other words, the speed shown on the LED screen becomes a sort of document at the moment it appears, so under the rules of evidence, the only way that kind of radar reading can be used is by producing the document itself, so to speak—which vanishes as soon as the car pulls over.

So far, none of those claims has gained any traction with me, for the simple reason that if the State authorizes the use of this kind of equipment, even certifying annually that it's working accurately, it must intend that the results are reliable enough to be taken seriously. Add to it the main rap against judges these days that they legislate from the bench, and our legion of critics would have live ammunition for that claim if I started tossing out all those certified radar readings. If the speed lawyers want to pitch someone about radar [un]reliability, they can do it in front of our 400-plus elected representatives in Concord or they can appeal one of my convictions to the Supremes just up the hill from the State House. Then we can see whether any of them will take the bait.

The defense raised today bypassed the radar roadblock entirely and came at the charge from another angle. It latched onto the exception in our law that permits police officers and fire personnel on emergency business to exceed speed limits—we've all gotten out of the way as the cruiser or fire truck goes roaring by as fast as it can, with lights pulsing and sirens blaring. Thus, the lawyer argued, since the prosecutor failed to prove the driver wasn't on one of those protected missions, there must be reasonable doubt in my feeble mind about the reason for the defendant's speed in this case. The prosecutor stammered around about how desperate and ridiculous this claim was, but I had to give the lawyer an A for creativity—or at least for creative Googling.

Where I finally came out on this novel theory was that reasonable inferences could be drawn from the inconsequential conversation the driver had with the officer at the time of the stop. I mean, if there'd been a real emergency in progress, wouldn't the driver likely have spoken up or mentioned his destination instead of sitting there calmly while the cop took 20 minutes to run his record through the computer? The lawyer must have counted on this reaction, because he protested indignantly that his client didn't need to say anything when confronted by the police, but was entitled by the Fifth Amendment to remain silent. I agreed that the lawyer and his client might really be onto something there—which they could also take up with the Supremes when they appealed the $72.00 fine.

PS—Since it's been awhile now and I haven't heard about being reversed again, I'll make another inference, that my ruling wasn't as outrageously unconstitutional as the lawyer implied when he sped indignantly out of the courtroom.

After spending years in the trenches of divorce law, then hearing the intimate details of hundreds (thousands?) more domestic violence cases here, I thought I had exhausted the spectrum of bizarre behavior.

Then today a woman came in to file a request for protective orders against her husband because he had told his co-workers that she'd died of cancer. Not only had she not died but she was symptom-free of all other ailments, to the best of her knowledge, unless you consider fear of being mysteriously rubbed out by your husband a legitimate neurosis.

It turns out the husband had also traded on his co-workers' sympathy by accepting $7,000 of their contributions toward his staggering medical expenses—I guess it costs quite a lot to have a perfectly healthy young woman declared dead. Unfortunately for the husband, his wife wasn't in on the faked death scam and totally freaked when she opened the card of heart-felt condolences from all the husband's fellow employees.

The wife brought the card with her, and as I issued the temporary protective orders, it occurred to me that we should all have such caring and concerned people to share our working lives. Of course, now that her cancer has so dramatically vanished, from some miracle of biblical proportions, the only thing those co-workers may care about is how to get their hard-earned sympathy funds returned. That may require another miracle.

We do a lot of business in underage possession of alcohol—some days as many as half the cases on the docket are soaked in one adult beverage or another. The law used to be that you had to find the actual 30-pack or bottle of cheap liquor—that's probably a condescending comment, but it's based on my own youthful experience with stuff like Thunderbird or Double Barrel that were less than a buck. Now, though, intoxication can be used to prove internal possession of alcohol, even if the cops can't find the actual source of that condition.

My question is why intoxication makes any difference if the real issue is whether the underage person had any degree of alcohol possession. See, if you're under 21 and have the unmistakable aroma of some alcoholic contraband on your breath, it doesn't seem like much of a leap to figure you've had the bottle or can in your hand at some point, right? Plus, isn't it a bit like being a little pregnant—either you did what it takes to get that way or you didn't, and the number of times you did it—or the number of drinks you gulped down—is really immaterial? The logic seems unassailable, but . . . .

Not according to the college freshman who showed up today. When questioned about how the odor of some alcoholic concoction materialized in his mouth, the smug young man denied ever putting the offending substance to his lips. (Please refer back to my "all is fair" theorem.) Thinking faster than usual, I suggested that it must have been a case of "immaculate consumption". I waited . . . and waited some more, but no one even raised an eyebrow, much less pronounced me a modern-day Dorothy Parker.

So, after my rapier-like riposte drifted into nothingness and an awkward silence pervaded the courtroom, I decided I had to move on. I postponed further action on the complaint for a year, with an ominous admonition to the kid about trying to play such cutesy games again. In other words, immaculate conception has allegedly happened only once, to anyone's knowledge, and immaculate consumption isn't likely to repeat itself either, at least not in Jaffrey. I'm just not a believer.

The other day I was doing some legal research on a case—hard as it is to believe based on what you've read so far. In the course of floundering my way to an answer I probably should have known anyhow, I was referred to a 1938 case that I found in a calfskin volume coincidentally printed by the commercial press of our local newspaper. (The press gave up the ghost once people could print their own stuff online, and the paper has since merged with a competitor that's itself available online.)

Anyhow, the book's cover was still soft as butter and the spine was so stiff that I suspect it's never been opened in its roughly 70 years on the shelf. Before replacing it for another 70 years of repose, I happened to check the flyleaf to see who made up our Supreme Court way back then. I was shocked that the names meant absolutely nothing to me; in fact, if they'd been written in Chinese, I wouldn't know any less about these guys—and they were all definitely guys in those days, old white guys.

Way back, I wrote about a now long-forgotten U.S. Supreme Court

Justice—I'm blanking on his name myself—whose disappearance into the fog of history made me question anew my own shot at a Holmesian legacy. As ironic as it seems, if you do your job every day, keeping the balls mostly in the air, never embarrassing yourself like a Spitzer, Edwards or Weiner (remember them?), and then retiring with the appreciation of your colleagues after [in my case] more than a quarter century as the decider in these parts, you have a better chance of being forgotten so much sooner than if you do something outrageous enough to keep the oral history of your exploits forever on the lips of your [embarrassed] descendants.

For instance, if I pulled out a gun and shot some really guilty, despicable and unrepentant defendant right there in the courtroom, my place in history would likely be secure—though I'd also be securely detained for the rest of my days. I've never gotten quite that worked up yet, and before doing anything nearly that drastic, I promise to fish around for other non-life-threatening alternatives—maybe mooning a full courtroom and having it go viral on YouTube. That wouldn't jeopardize anyone's health except my own, which would be seriously at risk when Cathie got hold of me. Drifting quietly into anonymity is looking better after all.

Jim, my law partner of ten years, came into my office last Friday afternoon with a peculiar look on his face. After some small talk about our Red Sox—who are currently leading the vaunted Yankees by more than ten games, I might add—he closed the door and announced that he's about 95% set on joining a big Worcester, Massachusetts, firm that's been courting him with more money—probably a lot more—than he's been making at our little popsicle stand. They're also promising more challenging business deals to work on, or at least fewer of the yard sale-variety projects that are often aggravating but are the bread and butter of a small town practice.

Jim's a very enjoyable guy, a fellow connoisseur of vintage rock 'n roll and classic movies, and a good lawyer, and he's surely been carrying me to some [considerable] extent in the last couple of years as I've spent more and more time dubbing around over here at court. I started to push back like the lawyer I am, but it was quickly clear that this deal was nearly done and that too much water was already under the bridge and over the dam before I was even aware it had started raining.

Two days hence, and yep, he's completely over the fence now and I'm going to have to figure out where that leaves me. On the upside, he said the big firm is willing to talk to me about an "of counsel" relationship, but that usually means you get little or no benefits and you eat only what you kill, which may leave me a hungry lawyer. I guess I'll find out what they've got in mind first, then consider whether it beats what may be realistic for me as a loner (maybe an orphan is more like it) or what might be offered by one of the other equally microscopic firms around the area.

I'm guessing this whole issue wouldn't have surfaced if I'd been pulling my oar more vigorously, which I would have been doing, because I always did, if the court's demands hadn't kept growing like Audrey's appetite in *Little Shop of Horrors*. This may be a part-time job in the State's caseload formula, but it sure seems like full-time, and that's with me getting the work done as efficiently as seems responsible. Most notably, that includes no breaking for lunch (as opposed to braking for moose, which can save your life), so I can get through the docket as quickly as possible and then head back to the office by early afternoon. If we took an hour or more for lunch, as every other court I've been to does, there'd be no office time left at the end of the day unless I worked until midnight, which clients might find an inconvenient time to return their calls.

Believe me, it causes serious agida at least a couple of times a week when I can't resolve the cases any faster—because lawyers haven't shown up yet or the sheriff isn't here with a prisoner or some landlord wants to show me 37 blurry photos of the marks his tenant left on the walls. And I'm sweating about clients showing up at the office in 45 minutes. What's more, I spend almost no time reading new cases and statutes—because there's just no time—figuring that if I need to know about them, I'll get a communique from the home office or some sharp young lawyer will point me in the right direction. I could also be going to conferences on domestic violence or alternative juvenile sentencing, which might make me a better judge for those critical situations. But there's just no time. So, like a marriage where the wife finds someone new because the husband spends too much time at the office, Jim's eyes are wandering because I'm not giving our practice relationship its worthy props. I'm sure the separation will be cordial and civilized, but rejection is still hard to swallow even when it's called irreconcilable differences.

While the future of my private practice hangs in the balance, life goes on here at the court. Two late teens from one of our outlying towns pled guilty to snatching a neighbor's digital camera. The camera was recovered undamaged and when the cops checked it out, they came across some photos the kids had taken—of themselves—before ditching it. Clueless is the word that comes to mind and the clue they should take from this self-inflicted wound is that if you steal an electronic device, you'd better at least brush up on the technology involved. Maybe they should have stolen the owner's manual, too. On the other hand, I'm not sure these two would have been able to decipher it.

This may not be a high-paying job, but if unanticipated variety is worth anything, the compensation is probably more than fair. I was supposed to be reviewing the ability of a man named Peter to pay a judgment he owed; however, when the defendant came forward, he was awash in bling, fully tressed and coiffed, wearing a flashy skirt, and asking that I call him Tammi. I couldn't tell whether the others waiting their turns were picking up on this dramatic 180, but I was doing my best to cover for him/her by choosing my pronouns as carefully as possible.

All this tiptoeing around the issue was unnecessary, however, because when I asked how much the payments could be, Tammi responded with unladylike vehemence that she had no ability to pay, due to appalling and outrageous lifestyle discrimination in the workplace that had kept her from landing any job at all. I might have inquired where the trendy wardrobe and accessories had come from without a paycheck, but I chickened out and said we'd come back in a few months to see whether the marketplace had become more tolerant in the meantime. I should have suggested eBay or Craig's List as a way to turn all that hardware into cash, though that might have been considered sexist, as I've never suggested to a guy that he put up his gun rack or bobhouse (Google "ice fishing"—no, that's not a typo).

The judge of a nearby "municipal" court has retired after 42 years on the bench there, and the court itself will head out to pasture with him. Nearly every town in New Hampshire used to have its own municipal court, probably because people weren't as mobile as they are now, but also so the judge would know everyone who showed up there and could give them just what they deserved—alright, maybe that last part is more result than purpose. When the court consolidation law was passed in the '60's and district courts like ours were created, all the municipal courts were grandparented (I have to be PC in this job) until their current judges died, retired or ran screaming from the premises.

For instance, there used to be a municipal court in another nearby hamlet, until [I always heard] the judge got miffed one day about some administrative requirement and abruptly disrobed. I thought I'd dialed the wrong number when I called to inquire about a case there and heard the message that the phone had been disconnected. That judge was a volatile character on the best of days, once quipping when I stood up to make my final argument in a DWI case, "This better be good!" As I feared, it wasn't nearly up to his standards.

Anyhow, the retiring judge was the youngest in the State when the law went into effect, having been appointed by a long dead and largely forgotten governor even before the budding judge had passed the bar exam. Those were the days! Now, some 35 years after our court opened for business, he was finally turning 70 and his municipal court was the last one standing. By the way, the judge lived right next door to the courthouse, as did both his father and grandfather who also rode that bench. I can only imagine the things he found in his yard or written on his fence when a disgruntled customer was heading home.

A surprise reception for the judge was held in the town hall, just upstairs from the courtroom, and when he came in after wrapping up his last session, there were more than a hundred friends, extended family members, judicial and legal colleagues, police officers, and interested passersby, all there to heap on accolades, share their war stories of cases past, and thank him for a career of historic length and dignified equanimity. In other words, the kind of send-off the rest of us hope for at the sunset of our modest efforts.

One thought crossing my mind during the festivities was that the next day all those municipal court cases would be making the journey over to our court, where they had been assigned more than a generation ago when our district was laid out. It was not a happy thought, as that town had earned a reputation for spawning some of the area's—even the State's—most troubling domestic violence and child abuse and neglect cases, as well as a cadre of eccentric court customers committed to a wide range of petty offenses.

Case in point: When I was sitting in for the retiring judge a few years ago, I called the name of one of the regulars, who sauntered up like he owned the place and propped his elbows on the bench like we were there for an intimate chat. That caused the rest of the courtroom to erupt in laughter, which I first thought was directed at my bow tie. It turned out the guy's pants had fallen down when he raised his arms and he was standing there without benefit of either briefs or boxers, in effect mooning the entire docket. I couldn't see any of this over the bench, but the bailiff didn't miss a beat. He hiked up the guy's pants and stood there cinching them from behind, as if this was the guy's shtick for unsuspecting substitute judges and the bailiff was his straight man. Now I was to have regular performances from this contemporary cast of Dickensian characters.

PS—That was eight years ago and my prediction of the nature and extent of the town's gene of bizarro behavior has been confirmed repeatedly. If Dickens came back from the dead, he would do well to settle there 'cause he'd never have to worry about writer's block.

After generations of bloodshed, lasting peace has been achieved in

Northern Ireland and the Balkans, and Vietnam has become a tourist destination. Yet my small claims cases remain struggles to the death, almost entirely without hope of a cease fire.

Today a roofer and his home-owning customer insisted on a full hearing over a $20 box of roofing nails. That's no typo—$20.00. The customer's defense was that the roofer quoted him a price per square of roofing shingles, but said nothing about an extra charge for the nails necessary to affix the shingles to the roof. I guess the roofer should have had a lawyer draft a more thorough and detailed written contract which the parties could have signed in blood, but really.

I won't dignify the dispute by disclosing my ruling, which I wrote once to blow off the steam that was threatening my aortic tributaries, and then again for the official record. When I'd finished, we sent out the latter (at least I hope it was that one) and I folded the former into a paper airplane and chucked it into the shredder. Doing it this way is cheaper than beta blockers.

Juvenile cases are conducted in a much smaller and more confined room than our adult docket, in order to sell the proposition that this is a warm and nurturing atmosphere with the focus on protecting the child's still tender interests. Those logistics present their own special concerns, however, to which even our bailiff is sensitized.

As one recent case was about to start and in view of the intimate quarters involved, the bailiff, who typically gets everyone seated and then beckons me, came to warn me that someone had farted really badly in there and that perhaps I might find some paperwork to attend to for a few minutes first. I thanked him for the tip, and by the time I'd counted up how many more cases were on the docket, sorted my paper clips, and rearranged my pens, the aroma in the courtroom had returned to the usual mélange of nervous teenage perspiration and failing parental deodorant.

In order to fully justify the compensation the legislature grudgingly allocates to my judicial responsibilities, or to trade dockets with another judge so we can resolve each other's conflicts of interest—it won't fly anymore to hear one of your client's cases (remember that part-time factor)—I'm occasionally sent packing to another court, where I try my best not to botch things up for a fellow decider.

One of my frequent assignments during these away games is to hear DWI cases defended by an attorney whose abrasively aggressive tactics have pissed off nearly every judge in southern New Hampshire, some to the point where they're no longer able to see his name on the docket without rupturing an artery. Somehow I've avoided this potentially life-threatening reaction, largely, I think, by sidestepping the almost overwhelming temptation to go toe-to-toe with him and by nodding appreciatively as he attempts to get me back on the straight-and-narrow when it appears I might stray toward a ruling his client wouldn't like. Still, I've blundered into finding a bunch of his clients guilty, which I sense this fellow hates more than most, if only because his ability to command the rumored $5,000 he exacts from his desperate clients depends on preserving a league-leading batting average.

I will digress here—though everything I've said may seem such— to comment on the widely varying courtroom styles of the lawyers who wage DWI defenses for my consideration. The fellow I've been describing bases his reputation on all-out warfare—which is what rankles my colleagues most—not to mention intimidating many of the local prosecutors, even those who are attorneys but don't have the same facile command of the evidence rules and the DWI-friendly judicial decisions. What this means is that nearly all the prosecutor's questions provoke an objection of some kind, right down to whether the cop actually raised his hand to swear to the summons when he signed it, and whether the road where the client was swerving dangerously was really a "public way" even though it's a numbered highway.

This approach makes the trial process akin to having your wisdom teeth removed without benefit of anesthesia, and I confess that it also takes every bit of balanced judicial temperament I can muster not to hold the client responsible for this pain-in-the-ass style of lawyering. While it does occasionally trip up the prosecution, it also gives the client the impression that all stops are being pulled out to save his bacon (even if his bacon is crispy). More likely, though, it persuades the prosecutor to reduce the charge to something like littering in order not to suffer the dental procedure I described.

The other prevalent lawyering MO among the DWI pros, which sits at the opposite end of the spectrum, is based on the "less is more" theory of defensiveness. The concept here is that the trial should be about what really matters to the outcome and that everything else is just chaff that isn't worth objecting to. What this means is that plainly objectionable evidence won't be challenged unless it's important to the decision I need to make. So, we'll be hearing about whether the client was really swerving on the road, not about whether the road was really a road. And I'll be deciding whether the driver really had two beers or six beers, not whether the beer cans really contained beer or some other mysterious liquid substance.

From the way I've painted these portraits, I'm sure the latter comes across as more attractive—like my preference for the clarity of a Hopper or Homer over the two heads and three eyes of a Picasso. If nothing else, it lets me focus on the real "merits" of the case, as lawyers say, not on whether I can keep from clobbering the client with the club I'd rather use to bludgeon his lawyer.

The perils of the part-time judgeship keep blindsiding me when I least expect it. This time I granted a request by our social service agency to remove a child from her home due to potential sexual abuse by her step-father. Straight-forward enough, I thought. The rub was that, unknown to me at the time, the step-father in question also happens to be cleaning my law office every night, when he's not [allegedly] abusing his step-daughter.

So now what do I do? I can't fire him; he works for the cleaning company hired by our landlord. Plus, it won't do to tell his employer about the pending case, as it might get him fired even though the case hasn't been heard yet—innocent until proven guilty and all that—and juvenile cases are confidential by law anyhow.

In the meantime, though, do I just erect a kind of Chinese wall between what happens at the court and what's taking place at the office, maybe pretending I don't recognize that our step-dad is the same guy trying to Hoover up the sand under my desk? Or do I disqualify myself from hearing the guy's case in light of his custodial duties?

Either of these moves might deal with the conflict of interest, but it doesn't do anything about having a twice-charged (as it turns out) sex offender cleaning our office—where, by the way, we have my partners' teenage daughters coming in after hours to use the computers for their term papers. And what about the other women who work in the office who may have an objection to being exposed to this guy, literally, when they're working late?

For now I'm sorting it out by bowing out of the case, because my judgment can't help but be influenced by the fact that this guy has a key to my office and could sabotage all sorts of things there if the situation doesn't go his way. I'm also giving the office folks the ominous warning that there's a [mysterious unidentified] person regularly under our noses who's charged with child sexual abuse and that they should avoid being alone there—or letting their children come in unattended. That should put all the female minds completely at ease.

Of course, if the guy's found chargeable, I'll have to figure out what else to do from there. Maybe I'll suggest that he request a transfer to another cleaning detail, so I won't have to make that request myself. I suspect that veiled threat would work, but it wouldn't do anything for the unsuspecting people at his next assignment. If the guy was convicted criminally, he'd have to register with the police as a sex offender. Otherwise, though, if the whole thing remains closeted in juvenile court, the law makes it a crime in itself to disclose anything to anybody. So while I'm whining about my dilemma, the real crisis results from this latter state of affairs, which probably means we're all unwittingly bumping up against a lot of people we'd just as soon be crossing the street to avoid.

Another postscript—The guy was indeed found chargeable, but managed to get out from under my nose all by himself. Where he went and under what circumstances I've not investigated, although I'm not sure what I'd do—or be able to do—even if I knew.

∾☙

Yesterday I agonized through one of the most aggravating DWI trials in recent memory. Not only did it involve the lawyer I accused of beating every horse to death, but it was a case the cops could have won pretty easily if they'd just followed the bouncing ball.

The young woman defendant had already been convicted of two previous DWIs, which couldn't be used as proof she was guilty this time (we all get a fresh chance at stupidity each time out), but which certainly meant there was a lot on the line, the most dire consequences being mandatory jail time, followed by years without a license and then enormous insurance premiums if she ever wants to drive [legally] again.

The problems began when the woman refused a breath alcohol test, which most people with DWI experience do because they know a failing result will likely be the breath of death. That left the prosecutor with trying to bring in the blood alcohol reading the hospital got when it treated the woman for injuries after she drove her car off the road. The snag was that the prosecutor failed to tell the lawyer she planned to call the hospital personnel to testify, which the court rules require to be done at least 14 days before trial. It got worse when the prosecutor wanted to use what I'm guessing were incriminating statements made by the driver to a witness at the scene, which are also required to be disclosed ahead of time, but weren't.

This may all sound like those "technicalities" people blame on slippery lawyers, but think about that for a minute. If you were the defendant and you'd worked with your lawyer to prepare your defense, you'd want to count on what you expected to be the evidence against you at trial. You certainly wouldn't want the cops springing something new on you at the last minute that might undermine all your planning or keep you from thinking ahead about how to counter it. In other words, technicalities, like beauty and obscenity, are in the eye of the beholder.

Anyhow, I said no dice to those last minute revelations, which meant no blood test results and no statements about how (I'm guessing here) the young woman didn't want the witness to call the police because she'd (the woman, not the witness) had way too much to drink. That made the "beyond a reasonable doubt" bar a lot harder to get over— sort of like trying to get the 747 safely to the tarmac on one out of four engines. It might be possible, but it takes an awful lot more work from the pilot.

Right now, I've got the case under advisement, and as I think about how to sort it all out, I'm waffling back and forth. With those other key pieces of evidence, I doubt I'd be having this much trouble. More to come once I figure it out.

Despite considerable exposure to the workings of the criminal mind, I continue to get lost in that bizarre maze of malignant neurons. This time the overnight clerk at our 24-hour convenience store invited her pals to help themselves to all the beer, cigarettes and lottery tickets they could carry out. Of course, the whole shopping spree was recorded on the store's candid camera, which it's hard to believe the clerk wasn't shown during her orientation session, but there go some more of those crazy neurons.

The kid on trial was one of the lucky shoppers, his defense being that the officer who testified against him was lying because he (the kid) wasn't the one on video-left in the hooded sweatshirt, but the one in video-middle in the baseball cap holding a cube of Bud. Once again, I guess I missed the subtlety of the argument, which was unfortunate for the kid because he's now doing 90 days in another 24-hour establishment, having, it turns out, also had starring roles in several previous surveillance videos.

I've dropped a couple of my favorite malapropisms already, but they come so fast and furiously that I probably forget more than I remember. What made me go back to my list today was that before sentencing a guy convicted of assault, I asked him if he'd ever been convicted of anything else I should know about. I had his record in front of me, but I wanted to hear what he thought was worthy of note. Apparently, there wasn't much there to worry about because he only mentioned a "negligible homicide" and he said that was quite a number of years ago. I'm not sure what made it negligible—I was too busy writing that one down—but I doubt the victim felt that way about it while he still had the chance to do so.

Other verbal faux pas include the woman who admitted needing a "psychic evaluation" before having her children returned, presumably to make sure her stars were lined up the right way for the big reunion; and another mother who acknowledged her need to "therapize" in order to get control of her "substitute problem" with drugs and alcohol.

We also had another guy whose reputation had been "deflamed" by the incendiary claims his ex-girlfriend was making, while on the other side the woman claimed her ex's attitude was so bad, it always "exuberated" the situation.

Another fellow claimed his ex made up "factitious" stories about him just to get him in trouble. I guess they seemed like facts, but weren't really.

On a positive note, we were proud to have the guy who saved his friend by giving him "CPI", though that might have killed the victim if he was an economist. I could go on, and perhaps I will, but now at least I know where Norm Crosby (ask your parents) might have gotten much of his material.

Back a ways, I noted my periodic trips to other courts to ensure I'm earning my judicial keep. Most of them turn out to be business as usual, but every now and then there's a diamond in the rough. During a recent session at the Keene court, I hit the mother lode.

A distinguished-looking 70 year-old who was dressed like an investment banker with a bad comb-over was charged with trespassing at an upscale shopping mall. Most places like that want to attract as many customers as possible, but this gent had been banned from the premises for chatting up other shoppers within what they felt was their personal space, a harmless enough indiscretion, really, but one that seems to freak people out during this skittish age of fearing that every stranger might be a convicted pervert ready to snatch their children.

The reason the gent was in court now was that he'd returned to the scene of his close-talking conversations to take in an Octoberfest promotion by the brewpub located in the mall. When I asked the fellow why he'd violated the ban, which he readily admitted—in fact, he said he'd called 911 on himself because he wanted to see how long it took the cops to get there (and he wasn't impressed)—he explained that the pub had some of the finest bratwurst he'd found anywhere and that "a good bratwurst is worth going to jail for."

I'm afraid I didn't see that one coming, so it took all the lip biting I could muster not to dissolve in laughter like nearly the whole Keene PD, who'd gotten word of the case and were apparently primed to expect some colorful entertainment. Since you may have gathered that this was not a first offense, the only real issue was sentencing. The prosecutor wanted some jail time, to "send a message once and for all," even though he'd been laughing as hard as anyone. I said OK, but suspended it for the time being and settled for a fine for now. In doing so, I emphasized that the gent would have to eat his bratwurst in jail if he went back to the mall again, which he assured me he would consider very carefully but couldn't make any commitments about at that particular moment. Right now, though, he said he was happy to pay the fine, which he calculated was less than it would have cost him to hire a lawyer, who wouldn't have let him say what he wanted to anyhow. I think we were all grateful he'd reached that conclusion or we wouldn't have had nearly as much fun.

The reason I called that session a bonanza—to maintain the gold rush metaphor—was because of the case that followed on the heels of Mr. Bratwurst. Two sisters, both of them looking like they could defend themselves, were charged with assaulting a guy over a vacuum cleaner. One of the sisters, whom I'll call Melissa because I think that was her name, had been living with the victim's family and had let them keep her Hoover for the time being when she moved out. Now Melissa wanted it back, so while she stayed outside with the truck running, her sister Margaret allegedly barged into the house, without knocking, to complete the recovery mission.

At that moment the man of the house was parked on the sofa in the midst of a PlayStation session, while another guy, who it turned out used to live there with Melissa and still owed her $120, was dozing in the recliner. Margaret made a beeline for the rug sucker, but as she headed for the door with it, the homeowner refused to let her leave with what I gathered was the family's only vestige of civilized housekeeping.

Margaret said the man of the house "belted" her in the head and grabbed her by the hair to toss her out the door without the vacuum, which confirmed the appliance's critical importance because these people all seemed to have been friends before being sucked into this maelstrom. Not to be lost in the scuffle, the lady of the house then jumped in, too, claiming the vacuum had to stay until theirs got fixed, even though Margaret said they'd only gotten that one at the dump. About here, Melissa tagged in to Margaret's rescue, allegedly kicking and scratching the husband to get him off Margaret; thus the assault charge.

As is nearly always the case with so many people involved, all the stories were wildly inconsistent about who did what to whom, although it was clear no one got hurt no matter how many punches were thrown. Perhaps it helped that all the participants in this melee were—I'm trying to be as delicate as possible—fully adult.

I never heard who ended up with the ubiquitous appliance, but everyone must have been satisfied with its final resting place because no one wanted my help to get it back. The whole process took about 90 minutes, dragged in several cops from their regular beats, and tied up two public defenders because M & M both needed lawyers to vindicate themselves. No one quipped that the whole case sucked, but the thought crossed my mind (and stayed there until right now).

If this isn't justice at the most primal level, I challenge anyone anywhere to come up with a more deserving entry. I guaranty it won't have occurred in a building with marble anywhere on the premises.

Bi-polarity is a serious mental illness that is the root cause of many domestic assaults and other emotional aberrations we see in court. I don't suffer from that malady, which is at least one shortcoming our customers don't have to worry about, but I do admit to being bi-political. That is, I'm a registered Independent—like the majority of voters in New Hampshire, it seems—and I waffle back and forth between the Democrats and Republicans based on where their candidates stand on the issues.

I say this as a preface to the critical remarks I'm about to make about President Bush's commutation of the jail sentence of Scooter

Libby, the Uriah Heepish aide to Vice President Cheney. You'll recall [perhaps] that Libby was convicted by a federal jury of four counts of perjury, obstruction of justice, and making false statements to federal investigators, all of which got him sentenced by the judge to 30 months in jail. Then, just as he was about to start packing his toothbrush, the president decided it was "excessive" and commuted it before Libby had even spent a weekend away from home.

Bad call . . . no, really bad call, in my humble view, because like *Bush v. Gore* it confirmed the people's sneaking suspicion that justice isn't a half-dressed blind lady holding a scale, but a good ole boy in cowboy boots who takes care of his posse with a wink and a nod. Without having any of the stats at my fingertips, I can pretty much guaranty that there have been lots of convicted felons, first in Texas and then in the federal courts, where the defendants got way more excessive sentences than Libby. Take the biggest enchilada of all sentences they regularly dispense in Texas—and then consider that former Governor Bush thought letting those sentences get carried out without interruption was a fine idea.

Don't start with "they all do it", like President Clinton did with rich guy Mark Rich, because that was wrong, too; it just wasn't quite as big and loud a splash of cronyism and so didn't blow as gaping a hole in the public's respect for the rule of law. For me, apart from the righteous indignation I'm feeling right now, there's also a depressing sense of sadness and disappointment, not unlike the bottom half of that bi-polar thing after all.

I make a point of paying attention to what people are saying in the courtroom, which, no doubt, will come as a surprise to many of the participants. What's more, to the best of my recollection, I've never dozed off during the festivities, which on quite a number of occasions has taken all the will power I can muster and which doesn't mean I haven't drifted into the breakdown lane a couple of times before snapping the wheels back into line. Believe me, it's not my iron will power that keeps me from snoozing; it's just that there's so much colorful scenery to hold my attention most of the time—sort of like those shiny objects they hang over the baby's crib.

When even that won't do the trick, though, one method I've found helpful for maintaining consciousness during those periodic bouts of excruciating boredom is to try to reconstruct exactly where I was and what I was doing at the time of the alleged offense I'm trying to sort out. Many times nothing memorable at all comes to mind, but sometimes I can recall a particularly enjoyable trip to the islands, or a night at the theatre, or a ballgame with the grandkids, or maybe a weekend with the family at the lake up north. It's at that point that I have to be careful, because if I miss even a few sentences of someone's tale, er, testimony, I may miss the microscopic kernel of relevancy hidden in the pile of sleep-inducing chaff.

A slight variation on this exercise is to check the birth date of the defendant, then try to place that date on my own timeline. As I drift toward my dotage, and as more and more of our customers are even younger than my own children, it gets easier to place those dates of birth somewhere in my adulthood but harder to make sense of the blurry outlines I manage to conjure up. One of my favorite authors, William Maxwell, called his master work *Time Will Darken It*, and I can relate to that observation.

I was doing my date association thing the other day when a very young woman and her son came in for protective orders, asking that her live-in, the child's father, become a live-out due to alleged chronic abuse, the camel's back-breaker being the purported pulling of a knife on the four year-old boy when he (the four year-old, that is) wouldn't stop acting his age.

As I looked to see when the woman said the incident happened, it occurred to me that the boy looked about the age of my own grandson. She continued with the sad account of her partner's—though with partners like that . . .—frightening and demeaning misdeeds while I checked the petition for the child's birth date. When I saw that the child was born the same exact day as my grandson, I admit the shock of that discovery kept me from registering much more of what she said.

Instead, I began wool-gathering about how very different the lives of those two children have been and will likely be. My grandson's no lily-white angel—he taunts his sister, throws tantrums when he doesn't get his way, and wouldn't eat a vegetable unless it was dipped in chocolate—he just acts his age, too. What he doesn't do is get threatened with deadly weapons because of those age-appropriate developmental shortcomings. He also lives with both his mother and father, who may get into it verbally once in a while but who haven't resorted to martial law yet, as far as I know anyhow.

So that's at least the crux of the present disparity, and the chasm between these kids is only likely to widen and deepen as time goes on. The other kid will probably start out with some kind of trouble in school—because his home life is so screwed up that he can't concentrate—or maybe he'll be bullying other kids in the footsteps of the male role model who's been terrorizing (allegedly, for now) the household. That means the boy himself may be back in here in 6 to 8 years, perhaps suspended from school, and, because of the hassles there, wanting to quit as soon as he can. Then, he'll spend the rest of his life trying to make ends meet—not that we all don't find ourselves in that boat occasionally—but maybe having explosive and violent arguments over money with his girlfriend and her kids, and reprising the whole cycle of abuse for another generation.

Unduly pessimistic and alarmist, you say, but I've seen it repeated through three generations during my time—after I finished walking five miles to and from school, in my bare feet, uphill both ways, carrying buckets of water for the outhouse. The kids I represented on petty juvenile stuff back in the '70's have become unprepared and dysfunctional parents themselves, with kids I had here on similar charges during the early '90's. Now their grandkids are starting to surface, too.

How is this possible, you say, when generations take about 25 years to run their course? The simple answer is that kids don't have to walk five miles to school anymore or carry water for the outhouse, so they get through with the whole growing up thing much faster. Or maybe it's that the folks who fit my profile are severely compressing the generational timeline by having children while they're still children themselves. As authority, I refer you back to the pregnant 13 year-old I mentioned, whose mother isn't much over 30 even though you could only prove she wasn't 50 by looking at the birth date on her complaint.

If it hasn't become apparent yet, I'm convinced lack of education is the root cause here, not because the 13 year-old didn't learn how babies are made, but because when kids drop out of school as soon as they can, they're starting to live adult lives immediately. So they're living together and having children at 15 or 16 instead of playing on the soccer team and touring Washington with their classes—or maybe going on to college or technical school and working at a career for a few years before ever thinking seriously about pairing up for good at 25 or 30. At that point, at least theoretically, they have considerably more experience and maturity, not to mention 401k plans, under their belts.

It's a terribly vicious cycle—and really a chicken-and-egg conundrum—because while lack of education is the most visible obstacle, the problems of abuse at home that got me started on this rant are what sabotage the educational process. If we could stop the abuse, I'm convinced the problems at school would take care of themselves within just a couple of semesters. On the other side of the equation, if the abuse continues, it doesn't matter what award-winning efforts the schools are making to keep their kids engaged, 'cause the kids have got other, more distracting—and dangerous—things on their minds.

I've already pled guilty to playing the "how old is the defendant" game, and now, in the interest of further disclosure of my judicial dalliance, I need to fess up again. What I nearly always do before going into the courtroom is to scan the docket to see whether any of my friends, neighbors or clients are likely to be staring me in the face when I walk out there. If so, I try to alert the bailiff, so he can send them down to the clerk's office for a new date—when another judge will be here to make sure they don't get the special treatment they're hoping for.

While I'm checking for conflicts, I also look for distinctive names I might butcher if I haven't tried to sound them out ahead of time, and I survey what people have gotten themselves charged with. Then, when I get into the courtroom and I'm regurgitating my introductory remarks about what the different pleading options mean, I'm also sizing up the faces and body language of the unfortunate souls staring back at me and trying to match up the names and charges with the faces.

Let's play here. I bet the middle-aged fellow sitting there with a flushed face, a Rudolph shnoz, and a woman with pursed lips next to him is probably the one charged with a second DWI. He looks like his years of low-grade alcoholism have finally caught up with him, and his wife's expression reveals her total disgust at the prospect of paying his fines and his inflated insurance premiums, much less chauffeuring him around for the next couple of years.

That whole row of kids in the 18-21 age group is undoubtedly the carload of college students who bought a couple of cubes of Bud at a convenience store near campus and thought they were in the clear because the guy who went in for the stuff was 21. Not true, which they should have learned from the carload of their party buds who came in last month.

The ones holding charts or sorting through photos are getting ready to fight their speeding charges—"I was already in the 50 zone when the cop radared me"—and the people with a fistful of letters and forms will be trying to convince me their licenses weren't really suspended or shouldn't have been suspended or have now been unsuspended.

Likewise, I can tell from the various facial expressions and body language whether they plan to submit voluntarily or to fight to the death (like I used to do with Mom's spoon of Pepto Bismal). If they have a softly apologetic look in their eyes or appear embarrassed to be here at all, they'll be pleading guilty or "nolo" in order to get the whole experience behind them as quickly as possible; they may even say they're sorry for taking up the court's time. If their eyes have a narrow squint to them, though, or their chins are raised and thrust out, then I know righteous indignation is coursing through their veins and there's no way they're taking this lying down, baby.

I may never have taken a psych course in school, but I've had lots of what's now called "clinical" training and I'd put my skills at reading the human tea leaves up against any ivory tower PhD. By the way, you look guilty.

When I first started out as a lawyer, none of the courts I went to even had a bailiff, and the situation hadn't changed much 16 years later when I started making the decisions in our new palace of justice. Oh, we had a "security officer" by then, but the guy I inherited, who was supposed to put his life on the line for our safety, was close to 70 (as I am now!), didn't have a weapon of any sort, and certainly didn't have any kind of metal detector to use in figuring out whether one of our customers was up to no good. In fact, if we'd had a scuffle break out, I'd have needed to jump over the bench and keep someone from knocking the elderly chap into assisted living.

Boy, have times changed. Now, with one of my colleagues having been shot dead a few years ago, not to mention many similar occurrences in other states, we have a walk-through metal detector that can tell whether someone has a pierced navel as well as a 357 magnum in his pocket. When we started using it, our clientele was clearly unprepared for that degree of sensitivity, and for how far into their personal space we were probing.

For example, that first day a high school girl charged with underage possession of cigarettes was charged with a second offense when the detector picked up the foil wrapper on the pack of Marlboros she had tucked away in her purse. Another young man who came in with his mother was mortified when he had to disgorge the pack of foil-wrapped condoms in his pocket, as was the guy whose similar stash was exposed to his girlfriend, who was visibly pissed either that his overly optimistic plans for her had become apparent or that the extent of their relationship had been exposed to public view.

But by far the most bizarre and disturbing discovery of the day was the pack of Polaroid snapshots (which also have a foil layer to them, it turns out) we found on a goofy-looking teenager that showed an older woman who was hiding nothing from the camera. That was bad enough, but then a closer look revealed that the subject of this expose was the kid's mother, who had come to court with him, and who, mercifully for all of us, was now fully clothed. Sex education apparently begins at home in more ways than we had anticipated, or perhaps this was the family's strange attempt at reverse psychology. I mean, if these snapshots didn't shock their young son into total abstinence, then he certainly wasn't going to "just say no" when his health sciences teacher said so.

In any event, the trauma of this last experience caused the security staff to turn the detector's sensitivity way down. Sure, we may be missing some things, but it turns out that ignorance can be mercifully blissful in courthouse security, too.

Reading back over some of this, I'm concerned about implying that we have nothing but cranks, wackos and pathetically dysfunctional socioblobs passing through our recently-modulated metal detector. That's a distortion. Most of them are just regular folks like you and me. OK, maybe that's not a helpful comparison, but there are indeed many days when all we do is hear that plain old people didn't realize what speed zone they were in, or that their '92 Toyotas couldn't possibly go 46, or that they never got the notices that their licenses were expiring.

Today went about like that, too, with the exception of a Massachusetts man also charged with speeding, who said he couldn't have been going 46 in a 30 either, but offered another explanation, as well. He said he had just passed Thomas Road and that it made him think of his son Thomas who had died. Despite the late hour, he said he could still make out the profile of Mount Monadnock (our signature landmark that dominates the horizon from practically everywhere here) and that he and his son used to climb the mountain together. All this distracted him, he believed, which was why he may not have been paying enough attention to his speed and which was why I should cut him some slack.

This kind of pitch is always troubling for me, because there's no easy way to know whether the guy even had a son, or a son who died, or a son who died named Thomas, or, taking a jaundiced view, whether this was just a ploy by a guy with a driving record as long as your arm who'd say anything not to lose his license in Massachusetts for yet another moving violation. Then, too, while this explanation for distracted speeding tugs at the heart strings, is it really more slack-worthy than a woman who's pre-occupied about an abusive partner, or a guy who's lost his job and is frantic about losing the family home to foreclosure—or any other of life's perpetual challenges that might make the mind wander while driving? Most of those people don't spill their guts about their private lives, either because they don't think it will help or because they don't want their personal laundry washed on the public record.

All this was going through my mind during about 20 seconds while I had my pen poised over the complaint. In the end, I found the guy guilty but expressed my concern for his loss and reduced the fine some to show I wasn't a completely heartless bastard. I was afraid the guy might burst into tears at my total lack of humanity, but surprisingly, the guy seemed happy with the result and he headed downstairs to pay the clerk. Maybe he felt like he got away with something or maybe he just needed to know someone had listened to him and given some validation to his memory of Thomas. Who knows whether I got it right. Maybe we should have our bailiff do exit interviews like on the People's Court. Then he could report back to me and I could adjust my own sensitivity meter.

I've written most of this during the ten or fifteen minute recesses the prosecutors want during every session to try to make as many deals as they can so they don't have to go the full trial route on 30 or 40 cases a day. This time, though, I'm sitting in the little gazebo—we've always called it the "summer house"—at the cottage on Lake Winnipesaukee that my wife's family built about 1935. This is a memorable occasion for two reasons, the first being that it's the only time in my 40 years of coming here that I'm entirely alone on the premises. I don't mean just Cathie and me without kids or grandkids; I mean all by myself. Cathie is in San Antonio at a conference her company is running, and our son and his family left me here a couple of hours ago to drive the 90 miles home to Peterborough to go to his company's summer picnic. Usually when we're here, there are at least a half dozen other adult relatives, plus three or four of their kids and about as many dogs. But today it's just me, the diving loons that keep coming up for air nearby, and a few beers I don't have to worry about because I'm not going anywhere.

It's also a memorable moment because it's within a few weeks of the first time I visited Cathie and her parents here 40 years ago on Labor Day weekend. That first weekend set the bar for merry-making pretty high, because the weather was rainy and windy the whole time, and the dozen or so of my fraternity brothers and their dates who'd also been invited spent the time indoors doing what you might expect of 20 year-olds. No, not that—well, maybe some of that—but mostly it was drinking gin and tonics and beer and playing sophomoric drinking games of the day like Thumper and Cardinal Puff. We'd stay up until 5:00 in the morning doing all that stuff and listening to music very loudly— on vinyl in those days, of course—while Cathie's parents tried to sleep in the next room so they could get up early and brave the elements to play in an annual golf tournament they never missed. Of course, while they were dragging themselves around a soggy golf course all day, we were sound asleep so we could party-hearty the next night the same way. When we finally pulled out to head for school on Labor Day, we were relaxed and rested, but Cathie's parents looked like they'd just been sprung from a prisoner of war camp.

Actually, it was our great time together that weekend that put Cathie and me on the path to eventual lifetime partnership—39 years now and counting—and led to our move to New Hampshire more than 33 years ago. We'd been living in Atlanta where I'd been practicing with a big downtown firm and we'd been trying to get up here for vacations as often as possible. With no direct flights in the those days, though, it always took at least 24 agonizing hours in the car at each end of the trip to travel back and forth, and it was always such a bummer returning to the daily rat race that I ended up resentful and stressed when I got home, which was about a 180 from what you hope for from a vacation.

Finally, while complaining about that unpleasant phenomenon on one of those trips, my father-in-law must have had enough and suggested I go talk with one of his golf buddies who was a local lawyer with a small-town practice. I was desperate, so after hemming and hawing for a couple of days, I decided, what the hell, it couldn't hurt, and I called the office. I was surprised when the lawyer answered his own phone, and after working around his golf schedule and Rotary lunches, we made a date. When I arrived at his office, which was a walk-up over the local paper store, I found him wearing a golf shirt and reading the morning paper. I'd never seen that sort of thing before, because at my white-shoe firm on the 14th floors of three adjoining bank buildings you'd have gotten a closed-door meeting with the senior partner if you showed up wearing a sport coat, much less going tie-less altogether. In fact, I recall people wearing dark suits even when they punched in for a couple of hours on a Saturday morning.

Anyhow, once Gerry regaled me for a couple of hours about the virtues of his uncluttered way of lawyerly life, I was ready to go back to Atlanta and give my notice whether I'd found another job or not. Cathie was all for it, too, but she wisely pointed out that we had one toddler already and were about to make it two, and that perhaps I'd better approach this plan with a little more analytical discipline than a drunk college student might bring to the task.

So, I buckled down and spent the next couple of weeks writing the definitive "give me a job" letter, then another couple trying to figure out where to send it. I had access in our vast firm library to the national directory of lawyers, but I had no idea whether the firms I was applying to were in places where we might want to live. This was worrisome, because we'd already surveyed all the small towns outside Atlanta in order not to have to make too drastic a move, but found most of the inhabitants we'd met severely lacking in dental hygiene and post-primary education, and we weren't eager to be the first residents with toothbrushes and diplomas—sorry about the aspersions, folks, but as a native of one of those towns in North Carolina, I figure I'm licensed to express myself freely on the realities of Southern culture at that time. And there was no Google in those days, if you can imagine it.

In the end, I just sent the letter to practically every member of the New Hampshire Bar, of whom there were fewer than were working in the conjoined buildings where my Atlanta firm was located. Then I waited expectantly for the offers to pour in by return mail. Shockingly, there wasn't even a trickle, and most of those who did respond weren't interested. In fact, they often sounding like I must be crazy or on the lam to want to move all the way from the bright lights of an up-and-coming place like Atlanta to their measly one-horse towns.

I'd pretty much given up hope and was resigning myself to the rest of my Thoreauvian life of quiet desperation when the phone rang one night just after I'd gotten home from that day's race. It was a guy calling from Peterborough, New Hampshire, and although I was having a really hard time translating the unfamiliar Yankee dialect, I eventually discerned that he was indeed a lawyer and that he was calling about my letter. He said he thought I was exactly what they were looking for and he wanted me to come see them as soon as possible. I made like Peterborough was our first choice, too, but once he hung up and I finally located it on the map (B4, I believe, were the Rand McNally coordinates), I realized we'd never even passed through that part of New Hampshire. A few days later, however, I called in sick and made a whirlwind trip up north and back, during which I took photos to show Cathie, who'd never been there either. Over Thanksgiving she visited with me to see for herself, liked it, too, and the rest is our personal history.

Despite a few anxious months while I sweated out the New Hampshire bar exam results—that multiple choice part was a killer— and questioned the wisdom of buying a house (where we still live) before finding out I'd passed, we've never looked back. My colleagues at the Atlanta firm did a lot of eyeball rolling at the news, probably wondering among themselves how they could have so misjudged the sanity and lawyerly judgment of someone they thought they knew. By the way, the old firm's now got more than ten times as many law people as it did then, and the directory they sent me of just its alumni is larger than our local phone book.

I'm not sure how I got this far afield, but I must now mention that the sun is setting over the lake, the hills on the horizon have taken on that purple hue of the famous song, and the sky is flaming orange to such an extent that I need to run get my camera so the family will believe my inarticulate yammering about it when I get home. OK, now the mosquitoes have found me, so I'm shutting down this trip along memory lane and going inside to see whether the Red Sox have managed to hold off their white-stockinged rivals.

∼〇

It's Sunday morning this time and I'm repositioned in the summer house, having had my hit of coffee and the *Sunday Times* and watched the lake wake up on a day as nearly perfect as it gets. It's like a mirror and the air is so clear I can see cars driving over the Long Island bridge probably three miles down the lake. Yea, not the one about 250 miles south of here—the air's not quite that clear, at least not once you get to Metro NYC, which is one more reason (of the hundreds) for being here instead of there or someplace like it. Looking north, though, Mount Washington is more than 50 miles up that way and it's cutting a razor-sharp profile today.

Anyhow, being here like this reminds me of the weekend two years ago when I was also parked in the same spot and trying to do a bit more than gathering scraps of wool. I had one eye on the laptop and on my piles of papers that were doing their best to blow into the lake, and I had the other eye watching to make sure I didn't miss any loons that might be popping up nearby. I was also doing my best to make heads or tails of the case that put our little court on the map for its 12 1/2 minutes of notoriety—to say fame would be a little self-indulgent, but now you be the judge.

The case began innocuously enough with a Hispanic kid charged for criminal trespass by the New Ipswich PD, but it was the legal theory they'd cooked up that eventually got everyone excited. The kid hadn't trespassed anywhere in the traditional sense—he'd only been stopped for speeding—and in the course of running the kid's record, the cops found absolutely nothing. That is, they found he had no driver's license (so that charge was added) and no record of having entered the country legally from his native land [somewhere in Central America].

Yet when the cops got back to the station and breathlessly let the federal immigration folks know they'd bagged what used to be called a "wetback" in non-PC days (before undocumented aliens had advocacy groups), the feds in Boston were completely unimpressed and had no interest whatever in taking custody of the kid, even if he was gift-wrapped and dropped on their doorstep by a police escort.

That's when the chief in New Ipswich got his dander up and decided he wasn't going to look the other way just because the big boys weren't interested in doing their job. So, whether on his own or with some creative prosecuting from the police chief's association, the charge became more existential. That is, the kid was criminally trespassing in the town as a whole by virtue of having no legal right to be there—or anywhere else in the United States of America, for that matter.

I confess that when the kid first came in for arraignment, I gave little thought to such novel charging, because the courtroom was full of people and he just pled guilty and accepted his modest fine. At that point I think even the chief was just planning to let the kid's friend (probably with no papers either) pick him up and deliver him to wherever his home away from home was.

It was a few days later when the pot started to boil. A firm of immigration lawyers who'd somehow glommed onto the case filed a motion to take back the guilty plea and undo the conviction, then to dismiss the charge as being in violation of federal immigration law. Not surprisingly, the New Ipswich chief took offense at that un-American affront to the sanctity of our borders and objected. I thought the case was still fresh enough to give it another look and that the kid probably didn't really understand what he was doing in the first place anyhow—despite my [maybe not quite] thorough review with him of his waiver of rights form—and that the legal issue being raised was way more interesting than whether yet another pimply teenager "couldn't have been going that fast."

About that time I also got wind that another eight likewise undocumented chapistas had been similarly charged by the Hudson chief in the Nashua District Court. That coincidence prompted me to call our chief judge about maybe having one judge hear all the cases, so as not to embarrass our little judicial fraternity/sorority with inconsistent results, thereby confirming the public inkling that we really don't know what we're doing on these unpaved and dusty backroads and low rungs of judicial decision-making. The chief (ours, that is) thought the suggestion made modest sense and asked whether I'd take on the whole ball of wax if the people in Nashua didn't want it clogging up their docket. I volunteered, but mostly because I never thought for a moment that the big city guys would pass on the chance to weigh in on this cutting-edge issue of national law enforcement. Besides they had 8 times as many irons in the fire as we did. Five minutes later, the CJ called back to say they were all my babies. Gulp.

We heard the New Ipswich case first, all by itself, and by that time the national media had sniffed out a quirky story in the making. It was not only the novelty of the charge in general, but also that we had non-Caucasian people of any kind in New Hampshire. The day of the hearing the parking lot was full of trucks with satellite dishes pointed at the heavens—like someone was going to launch the shuttle from the Dunkin Donuts next door—and our courtroom's jury box (I'll explain that sometime later) was full of reporters with cameras and recorders, not only from our local high schools but also the *Associated Press, The New York Times, The Boston Globe,* and even the San Antonio whatever-it-is. There hadn't been this much interest in us even when our nearly-finished courthouse suspiciously burned to the ground about a month before we were supposed to move in. (Turned out it wasn't a pissed-off small claimer, but the plumber whose solder smoldered until everyone had left the premises; then whoosh.)

The lawyers engaged in a spirited debate about the legal issues, and I chimed in with questions designed to show I was not only paying appropriate attention but wasn't too stupid to be wrestling with matters so momentous to our national security. I must admit, it was an out-of-body experience to be moderating a debate about federal immigration policy when I could look out the window and see people lining up for their Big Macs with cheese at the McDonald's drive-through across the street.

After the hearing I announced solemnly that I would withhold my ruling until we heard what the people involved in the Hudson cases had to say. Then I promptly put the whole thing out of mind and headed down to see my folks in North Carolina, where the tobacco crop would rot in the fields were it not for legions of unquestionably non-credentialed pickers.

During the roughly 30 days between hearings, there were stories about the cases in papers all over the country, even a profile of me personally (angle: who is this dorky, bow tie-wearing, part-time judge attempting to set the standard for state enforcement of federal immigration law?). The conservative talk show circuit made a darling out of the New Ipswich chief, who proved an articulate spokesman for all people who want to solve the immigration problem by shipping (and I quote) "all those wetbacks back where they came from."

Friends all over the place were forwarding AP photos of myself from their local papers, and observant waitresses were recognizing me at diners between here and NC. By the time of the Hudson hearing, you'd think we were reprising the Scopes trial for a new generation, which I guess we were in terms of the lightning rod aspect of the issue—though it's ironic that the Scopes trial itself would make an even bigger splash today than it did the first time 80 years ago. There are certainly more vocal evangelicals these days.

Anyhow, once the cases were finally in my lap, I swallowed hard and fired up the laptop right here at the summer house, hoping to cobble together some words I wouldn't cringe about seeing reprinted in every paper across the country. I made a few false starts, but by midweek after the last hearing I thought I had my arms pretty well around the issues and had expressed myself about as well as I was capable. I must confess to being helped in that effort by so-called "friend-of-the-court" memos submitted by everyone from the NH Civil Liberties Union to the Mexican American Immigration Rights Association. At the eleventh hour, the whole Government of Mexico even hired a big firm from Boston to kick in its two cents, but by that time I'd been directed to most of the cases and statutes that had anything important to say on the subject.

Finally, a week after the Hudson hearing, I e-mailed the finished product to the public information director at the New Hampshire Supreme Court who posted it on the court system website for everyone to take their shots at in unison. Then, I held my breath.

Surprisingly, the feedback was mostly not unfavorable. By the way, I dismissed all the charges on the ground that federal immigration law and its sanctions preempted local police departments from using state statutes to achieve the same result. Most people who said anything to me said they liked the call. At least no one called me a jerk to my face. It was only the hard-nosed, law-and-order-at-all-cost conservatives who reamed me out on the internet for being just another liberal, good-for-nothing, soft-on-crime, judicial activist who's undermining everything that's good and true about our fair land.

The following Saturday Cathie and I were having breakfast at a little place we go to in Wolfeboro, up near the lake. The waitress came over and whispered that she knew who I was, but that she wouldn't tell the big guy sitting at the counter, because he didn't like me. I was puzzled; I'd never seen the guy before and didn't realize I could make enemies even without an introduction, until she told me his name. Turns out he was the most vicious of my critics among the Boston radio mouthpieces and had spent the past 24 hours ripping me a new one and making sure everyone knew what a brainless, spineless, nincompoop I was. I kept my face in my pancakes until he lumbered out and then sent Cathie out to start the car before we left.

Seriously, my colleagues around the state sent many nice words of appreciation (relief may be more like it) for not making them look like idiots by association. Even our chief decider congratulated me on not making him look stupid for entrusting such a hefty matter to one of his part-timers.

While wrestling with the decision, I'd taken some consolation from the assumption that no matter where I came out, the losing side would appeal and some other court would eventually draw the lasting heat. I even envisioned the cases going all the way to the Supremes in Washington and sitting in the gallery for oral argument while the justices tried to come up with questions as penetrating as my own. In the end, though, the State's Attorney General announced that she saw no reason to pursue the cases any further—I took that as a concurring opinion—and she went so far as to order local PD's not to continue busting people on trespass charges like these.

The postscript is that the New Hampshire Nine were free and apparently able to resume their prior lives of undisturbed illegality. All in all, our moment in the sun turned out about as well as I could have hoped, including (I can't resist noting) the really gratifying article in the Concord paper that called me a "gentleman" (actually in quotes) in a banner headline, which, after all, is what General Lee advised us all to aspire to when I was undergradding at Washington and Lee back in the '60's—no, not the 1860's. Then it was back to "I couldn't have been going that fast."

Now that our time in the crosshairs of public scrutiny is over—although I still avert my gaze from the talk show guy when our breakfasts at the lake coincide—I want to comment generally on the issue of our national immigration conundrum, being the widely-known expert I have become. If you don't give a rip about my weigh-in on that topic, however insightful it may be, just skip ahead to another amusing story of bizarre defendants engaging in quirky high-jinx.

Based entirely on the immigration decision, people assume I'm a bleeding-heart liberal who'd send someone for anger management instead of frying them to a crisp even if they laid waste to my whole family. That's not true (although they're right that I wouldn't fry them no matter what). I do, however, line up with the Kennedys and their ilk behind the view that the country was built on the backs of hard-working immigrants and that our ancestors were all boat people unless they were standing on shore when the Vikings or the Spaniards or the Pilgrims came over the horizon. It's just a matter of when your family's particular boat arrived.

So, yes, I do think we should keep the official ports of entry open to new generations coming here to pursue the American dream. Unlike some, though, I'm not handing out free passes to all those whose backs are still wet or shirts are ripped from swimming or crawling in and trying to put down roots without following the prescribed path to lawful citizenship.

The dilemma is that there are now twelve million or more swimmer/crawlers without proper papers and there aren't enough planes, trains or automobiles on the planet to take them all back where they came from, even if you could determine that. Plus, if we did that, all the restaurants we like would have to close or we'd have to bus our own tables. And even the most hard-line Republican isn't going to do that.

Some have been here 20 or more years, with good work records and no run-ins with the law, while many other recent arrivals are still out of breath from being chased around the New Mexico desert by INS cops. The former may not be entitled to moral high ground, but they at least arrived before the current spotlight was cranked up to high on preventing illegal entries, and their established records of law-abidingness should count for something.

OK, here's the Runyon plan: I say, let anyone who's been here longer than 5 or 10 years (I'll negotiate), with a good record of employment, tax payments and civic responsibility, register with the immigration authorities within a prescribed period of time and pay an appropriate fine, the latter being used to offset the inflated bureaucratic expense this immigrant round-up will generate if it's like any other government undertaking. Those people would be funneled to the end of the road to citizenship without having to go back home and start from square one—and we'd still be able to enjoy their fine service at our favorite urban bistros.

Anyone here less than the minimum time (once it's properly tweaked) should have to go home and get at the end of the immigration queue with everyone else trying to do it by the book. Sorry for the inconvenience there, folks, but you were pretty clear about our hang-up with people crawling under/climbing over the fence when you made your decision to try it, and the line in the sand has to be drawn somewhere. Also, and I believe this is a very important component, anyone who doesn't register within the prescribed period gets sent home no matter how long they've been here, and employers who hire or retain people who aren't buying into the program get to contribute generously to the budget for the enforcement program, as well.

There need to be other bells and whistles added, and the details are often what get Congress' undies bunched up, but everything would follow from this basic plan. And let's hang onto the money we were going to throw at the Great Wall of Mexico, which anyone really serious about tunneling under it, climbing over it or blasting through it could do anyhow.

If this all amounts to what the hard-noses are calling "amnesty", then that's what I'm in favor of. Amazing, isn't it, how somebody hears one lousy, bottom-rung immigration case, reads a few briefs that other people wrote, gets some ink about the bizarre nature of the whole scene, and thinks he's become such an expert in the field that he can expound with a straight face on how this Gordian knot should be untangled. Must be an a**hole for sure.

～⌒

If all the public attention we got gave me an inflated sense of importance, all it took was another day or so to pop that balloon. In fact, both of the parties ended up stomping out of the courtroom muttering about the "system" and how they don't understand it and don't know why it doesn't try to help them.

The gist is that a landlord representing himself [poorly] gave his young woman tenant, who was here with her very cranky baby, a notice to vacate within 7 days because she hadn't paid her rent. As often happens, the woman claimed she had withheld rent due to problems with a leaky roof, which she had lots of photos to document.

The problem for the unsophisticated landlord was that his notice gave no amount that the tenant could pay to avoid eviction, as the law requires. That shortcoming rendered the notice ineffective and meant the landlord had to reboot the whole process from scratch. The problem for the tenant was that in an eviction case, the court can tell the tenant to vamoose or let her hang in there (with rent in escrow) until the repairs are made, but it can't order the landlord to make the repairs.

In light of all those pesky legal snags, I suggested the parties might want to chat about how each of them might get at least some of what they wanted without having to come back here, but they looked at me like I had three heads and not a brain in any of them. "Talk to that scumbag—are you kidding me—I'd rather eat the rent money!"

So, the landlord was sent away for a do-over, without much of a clue about how to do it any righter the next time, and the tenant likewise departed with no satisfaction about getting her leaks patched. Of course, if the parties could talk to each other—even the Israelis and Arabs occasionally do that—they might not have to leave it to me to screw things up for them, which is the only part they'll remember about their foray into the legal wilderness.

On the other hand, with their emotions so laden with venom, a face-to-face encounter might have led quickly to mutual combat, making a criminal case out of a civil beef. I'll just wait for notification of both parties' complaints to the Judicial Conduct Committee, which won't give a hoot about my nationally-famous immigration decision. How soon they forget.

Speaking of things turning criminal, not long after that fiasco, we had a small claim where an antique car obsessionist alleged that his repair guy had not shown the appropriate standard of care in replacing a convertible top. The photos actually showed a shocking failure of workmanship—like I had done the work—but the repairman was incensed at having his good reputation (perhaps among the blind) publicly impugned and he wanted his top dollars.

The two quit listening to me almost as soon as the hearing started, so I quickly announced my "under advisement" dodge and told the combatants to take anything further they had to say out to the parking lot. That had the same effect as throwing a lit match into a box of cherry bombs and the fireworks that erupted outside were just as explosive. The top guy was still pissed about his customer's vicious aspersions and not only took a poke at him but also pummeled another of his (the obsessionist's) vehicles to the point of needing professional services itself.

All the parking lot shenanigans led to criminal charges against both guys—all the cops had to do was look out the window. When the two came back in for a different kind of court appearance about 15 minutes later, they both claimed they were immune from prosecution because I had told them it was OK to settle things outside. I said I was glad to see they had finally agreed on something, but I suggested they'd better work together on another defense (like temporary insanity) before their trial date, as I was pretty sure I'd never given them literal carte blanche to duke it out.

In the meantime, I guess we'd better preserve the transcript of my poorly worded recommendation, this being the first time I can recall providing evidence in a case I'm also hearing. I wonder whether I'll be a credible witness.

~⌇⌇

I ranted way back there about people who fail to tell the truth in court—alright, they lie—and we had a perfect example yesterday. Two young women who had been friends—though with friends like this . . .—were standing in front of me, under oath, the plaintiff assuring me she had loaned her defendant ex-pal $4,500 in cash, and the defendant swearing she'd never been given any money at all. That is, not just less money, or that it was a gift, not a loan, just no money at all. Simple as that.

One of the combatants was obviously committing perjury, and yet when I made sure they were aware of the serious criminal consequences such an offense carried—and then gave the culprit the chance to fess up with no strings attached—neither of them even blinked.

The problem was that cash was the medium of [alleged] exchange, and that since they were such good friends, no one had signed anything documenting a loan or detailing how and when it was to be paid back. Still, a decision had to be made, and so I made one. How was that possible, you ask?

Well, for starters, the plaintiff had a look of outrage and righteous indignation on her face throughout the hearing, while the defendant seemed almost smug, even briefly slipping over into a smirk, I thought. The curl of her lip almost seemed to say, we all know I got the money, but she can't prove it. Also, the plaintiff had brought her father with her, and he testified he'd taken the money out of his own account for his daughter and was standing right there when she gave the defendant the bulging envelope. He no longer had a record of the banking transaction, of course—that would have made it too easy for me—but his corroboration did tip the scales in my mind.

Maybe there was undisclosed bitterness between the ex-friends that might have led to risking a perjury charge, but I couldn't see attributing the same ulterior motivation to the dad, who appeared to take his oath seriously and seemed much less worked up than the estranged friends. If the defendant really never got the money in the first place, then I was way off base in making her pay it back and a terrible injustice was done. On the flip side, if I'd blown the decision the other way, there would have been a similar miscarriage. It wouldn't be my first miscarriage either way, and it won't be the last. I'm certain of that much, if nothing else.

No court for me this week—a couple of visiting judges are weathering the dockets and cleaning up my conflicts—while I'm rebonding with my aged parents who retired to my hometown in North Carolina. I started out there, where my father worked at the cigarette plant of a large tobacco company—he smoked them, my mother smoked them, and they offered them to me, for free, when I hit about 14. I declined—my friends were incredulous, but the thrill of sneaking around was so cruelly denied me—however, I probably inhaled more than a lethal dose of their second-hand smoke.

After a few years at the butt plant—it actually had brass spittoons in those days, along with black people to empty and polish them—he must have done well enough to get noticed by the home office because he was kicked up to the executive enclave on Park Avenue in New York City. That was the early '50's and those were the salad days for big tobacco—think *Mad Men*—before it had to start sparring with the Surgeon General and defending itself against dying/suing smokers all over the country.

Anyhow, we packed up like the Beverly Hillbillies and moved to the Jersey suburbs, from which Pop took the train, ferry and subway to get to and from the company's tony address just two blocks south of the Waldorf. I remember Pop walking the couple of blocks to the train station at 7:15 every morning, complete with briefcase and *Herald Tribune*, topped off by the de rigueur winter felt or summer straw hat and with a frequent nod to fellow traveler Bobby Thompson, of *Shot Heard 'Round the World* fame. He'd plop down at his desk about 9:00, and after a long lunch (in those three martini days) and probably a drowsy afternoon, he'd reverse the whole process about 4:30, this time with the *World-Telegram* to pass the time.

That trek was repeated thousands of times over the years, all having now merged into a single foggy blur—as I feared would also be the fate of all my time perched on this little rung of justice unless I tried to single out a few memorable moments here.

Anyhow, the mind-numbing grind of Pop's daily ritual is probably why he cashed out at the first opportunity and raced back to within a mile of where he and Mom (and I, too) started, picking up seamlessly with the friends they'd waited 25 years to get back to.

Pop is 91 now and losing it on all fronts, and though Mom still seems as sharp as ever, her lifetime of avoidance of any flicker of aerobic exercise has taken a crippling toll on her mobility. We went out to a local place for dinner last night and it took longer to get the folks in and out of the car than to eat a big slab of fried catfish, which I did.

I may seize up with cardiac arrest (in the hospital where I was born) while running in the 90-degree heat and humidity down here, but I'm damned if I'll be as dependent as the folks are on other people, especially when it comes to the basics of personal hygiene—like getting into my pants and then out again in time to avoid needing help with something even more embarrassing.

Speaking of running, I've seen some surprising things while pounding the pavement, but this morning as I was clomping past the referenced hospital, there was a woman standing out on the sidewalk in nothing but her johnnie and paper slippers, holding her IV tower with one hand and what looked like an unfiltered Lucky with her other. If there was any doubt about it, this is still a hard-core tobacco town. In fact, I tell people back home that the restaurants all have two sections: the smoking section and the heavy smoking section. You can even smoke in retail stores, which always comes as a shock when you go to buy, say, underwear and it smells like someone's been smoking them like a pork shoulder.

While with the folks, I managed to take in a minor league ballgame in Winston-Salem—where it seemed like there were enough smokers for a chemo convention—but most of the time we all just sat around the kitchen table talking about family history and watching CNN belabor every story into the ground. It's amazing how when I'm with my folks, no matter what kind of shape they're in, I still feel more like an irresponsible teenager than a judge or lawyer.

I don't know whether Chief Justice Roberts still has any parents left, but I bet he'd say the same thing. As a matter of fact, in the biography I'm now reading about our own Justice Souter, the author quotes a call President Bush [the Elder] made to the justice's mother in a Concord nursing home, promising that he'd "take good care of her boy" once he was confirmed for his new job. At that moment the justice probably felt a lot like the homesick kid in short pants whose camp counselor was calling to reassure his mother that she wouldn't have to come get him after all.

All carefree vacations must come to an end and I hit the brick wall of mine yesterday. The most substantial brick was the stalking petition of one grandmother against her counterpart on the other side of the family, but that was just a smokescreen for the real issue, which was the visitation rights of their divorced children with the pre-school grandson. I say pre-school because the plaintiff grandmum claimed the defendant nana was taking photos of the grandmum from the woods outside the tyke's day care center, where the grandmum had gone to pick him up for some time with her son. The nana admitted also using her car to block the grandmum from leaving the parking lot with the kid, which is when the "f***ing this" and "f***ing that" started and the kindergarten cops had to step in to avoid a menopausal girl fight on the playground.

(As a lengthy aside, girl fights were everyone's favorites when I was in school, because there were no holds barred and the girls fought like banshees—probably over some pimply boy with bad breath. Now, that kind of thing gets you dragged in here, but it used to be just one of those dramatic rites of passage that made school tolerable. In fact, I can't honestly remember much of anything about the classes I took back then, but I can tell you who the combatants were in several of the championship bouts I witnessed.)

All in all, there was little dispute over what happened; the only issue was whether all this juvenile behavior amounted to stalking. I said no. The grandmum was clearly unafraid of the nana and could probably have knocked her block off if I'd suggested they settle it that way, as I'm apparently wont to do. Plus, I sensed she was mainly looking for a way to get a leg up on her rivals when they all returned to the divorce court for another sordid dust-up over what visitation rights would be in the poor little guy's "best interests".

Ironically, the kid would be better off if he didn't have to see either of these harpies until he was 16 and then could decide for himself whether he wanted anything to do with them. Fortunately, I bit my tongue on that editorial perspective—noting out of the corner of my eye that the red light of the recording equipment was still on—but I did mention in the last sentence of my order that the ladies (using the term expansively) would do well to avoid situations where their precious little fellow was likely to be permanently traumatized.

Someday, many years hence, the young man will either be lying on a couch in some therapist's office talking about how the incident keeps him from being able to trust any female relationship or he'll be in jail for abusing older women, probably under the influence of alcohol and drugs. Because the parents themselves were also here to endorse their respective moms' petty and destructive behavior, the guy may also knock off one or both of them someday and then claim PTSD. If I'm not yet drooling in a nursing home, I may testify for him on the subject of justifiable homicide.

PS—While reading this through a second time—it was painful, but I did—I was faced with a 10 year-old charged with assaulting a chaperone during an evening roller-skating session in the school gym (they say he pushed her and she hurt her knee when she fell down). Rather than come up with an out-of-court diversion plan for the kid, which would have made too much sense, the cops are going full-bore, presumably to teach this kid a lesson neither he nor his lifelong series of therapists will ever forget. The defense lawyer (oh, yes) has now moved for a competency evaluation to determine whether the 10 year-old understands the difference between the "recklessly" and "knowingly" states of mind being charged—so he can assist in his own defense and make an intelligent assessment of how to proceed.

I told them I'd order the evaluation, but more to give them time to work something out than to seriously consider the competency issues, which I told them I could take a pretty good whack at right now if they wanted me to. I assured them I wasn't prejudging the situation—no one likes judges, but they hate pre-judges—however I said I'd be surprised if it took much serious professional analysis to sort this one out. Admittedly, my 8 ½ year-old grandson hasn't had the benefit of another year and a half in the classroom, but if he could tell me the difference between "recklessly" and "knowingly" at twice that age, I'd lick the bottom of his hamster cage.

I guess I'm just getting old or maybe it's just that the nature of parenting has changed since my own days as a young'un. A teenage driver came in with her parents to contest the charge of failing to yield to traffic, after she pulled out from a side road and was immediately T-boned by a car proceeding along one of our major highways—hey, it's paved and has a breakdown lane! Simple enough, I thought; if you do that, you're guilty. You're not a criminal or a bad person, but you're guilty. Not true, apparently.

The girl—and her parents (who weren't in the car, but that didn't seem to matter)—claimed that a snow bank along the highway prevented her from seeing the oncoming car, so she shouldn't be held responsible for the violation. I thought about it while the mental picture was coming into focus and then decided that if snow banks—and other weather-related conditions—were to become absolute defenses to motor vehicle charges, I wouldn't be finding many people guilty up here between Thanksgiving and Memorial Day. "The snow on my windshield [or on the road or on the traffic signs] kept me from seeing the speed limit sign [or the stop sign or the double solid lines or much of anything else]." If that's the case—and it is sometimes—you have to be more careful [or observant or slow down or stay home] is how I see it.

My take on weather-related traffic violations was small consolation to the indignant parents, whose attempt to support their daughter was commendable on one level, but whose efforts seemed counter-productive to a valuable lesson they might have endorsed about being more careful and responsible in the future. If I'd been the driver back in the '60's or if one of my kids had been broad-sided like this in the '80's,

I'd [they'd] have been hauled into court by the ear and I'd [they'd] have pled guilty and then apologized for taking up the court's time, in case there was any chance I'd [they'd] missed the point.

Alright, I'll acknowledge that reasonable parents can differ about how best to handle a critical moment like this, but I'm not really at the nub of my discontent yet. The real beef I had with these particular parents was that they let their daughter show up in court wearing a largely see-through tube top, with no supporting undergarment—believe me, there was no room for a dissenting opinion on that issue—and her bare stomach hanging out. At least there was no navel jewelry or snarling dragon tattoo in view, so she had that going for her.

Actually, I spent more time wrestling with how to handle the wardrobe choice than in finding her guilty of the charge. Should I just keep my mouth shut and consider this either a form of free speech about the respect the court deserves, or, sadly but more likely, a clueless inability to distinguish a court appearance from a trip to the mall? Or, should I send the young lady home to take another crack at her wardrobe before hearing my decision? If I did the latter, I feared at least the parents would assume I was biased against their daughter because of her outfit or lack thereof, but if I just turned the other cheek to what clearly looked like a blatant affront to the court, there wouldn't be much left of the already blurry line in the sand about proper courtroom attire.

As with many pivotal decisions along my judicial road of life, I dodged it like a spineless worm and said nothing—not even a snippet about stopping at the Gap on her way home. What this experience reinforced—besides that I'm a spineless worm—was that the criticism I was getting from the parents about my decision was as off-base as their decision to let their daughter leave the house [un]dressed for court like it was the tennis court. Actually, I doubt there are many tennis facilities that would have let her get to 40-love in that outfit either.

It may have occurred to you by now that parenting deficiencies have been the thread running through many of our knottiest cases. If it hasn't yet, here's one that will smack you with a 2x4 right between the eyes. A kid we've had with us since he was a juvenile delinquent—and I use that term with all its pejorative connotations—was charged with boosting a CD player from a vehicle left unprotected within the kid's swath of crime. The prosecutor's witness was another kid who swore he saw the defendant get out of the car with the goods and run down the street toward home, black wires trailing behind him all the way. The defense was an alibi supplied by the mother of the young man, who claimed she'd called his girlfriend's mother in another town, coincidentally at just the moment of the crime, and then promptly driven the kid to the girlfriend's house to spend the night—all of which was corroborated by the father, who insisted he'd picked the kid up there the next morning. So their little angel couldn't possibly have committed this heinous larceny at the time alleged.

The fly in the ointment was the girlfriend's mother, who'd been sequestered so as not to benefit from the prior testimony. She insisted it was her daughter, not the kid's mother, who'd spoken to her about the kid coming over, and considerably later than the crime time, and then that it was the kid's brother, not the kid's father, who'd picked him up the next day. In other words, by the time the girlfriend's mother got finished, the alibi was smelling like the kid probably did once he ran all the way home lugging the CD player, which I found he'd done. I also predicted, this time on the record, that with parents willing to fabricate excuses when necessary to keep him out of trouble, this wouldn't be the last time we were concerned about the kid's nocturnal mischief.

Indeed, even before the Red Sox could blow a 10-game lead, the kid was back facing the claim that he'd made off with the contents of another vulnerable vehicle. This time the kid's parents took a pass, perhaps sensing that the jaundiced eye with which I'd greeted their last alibi might ripen into perjury charges if they tried to fudge their son out of trouble again. As for the kid, he's now got some quiet time either to think over how to resurrect his future—or to make sure no one's around to ID him the next time he sees someone else's CD player he can't live without.

A few pages back I was whining that my partner Jim had gotten tired of carrying around 170 pounds of my dead weight and had decided to throw in with a big Massachusetts firm that would take over all his administrative headaches, not the least of which, I'm sure, was how to cure my anemic billable hours. I took his suggestion about talking with the mega-firm myself, to see whether they might want something to do with a veteran of 35 years in the trenches but who was spending more and more time either on the bench or on vacations with his travel-happy wife and friends (a number of whom are less encumbered, shall we say, by inconvenient employment responsibilities).

None of that seemed to phase the firm's managing partner, that is, as long as I can round up enough revenue to cover my nut of office expenses, which I'm keeping my fingers crossed about despite the virally expanding demands of this job. (Sometimes I feel like Lucy trying to keep up with the dishes coming faster and faster down the conveyor belt—I haven't broken any of them yet, but I'm getting worried and my predicament isn't nearly as funny as it was on her show.)

OK, fast forward, and now I'm lawyer #75 or thereabouts in an aggressively expanding conglomerate of legal services that soon hopes to put roots down in all the New England centers of promising activity. I've only met two of the other lawyers so far—maybe my due diligence could have been better—but I'm assured by Jim that they're all just great guys and a few gals. What's going to be the greatest challenge is the bureaucratic red tape that comes with riding herd on so many other people, though I should have anticipated that factor if I'd remembered back to my first job out of law school.

Atlanta was the hot place to go then and I was lawyer #85 in the firm that occupied those three contiguous bank buildings I mentioned. Though that's pint-sized among today's monster firms, it was so populous in those days that it was someone's [sole?] job there to put out an intra-office newspaper every day and then to deliver it by hand throughout the buildings in those pre-technology days.

There were 14 of us fresh-faced, wet-behind-the-ears recruits who started as rat plebes in 1972, only one of whom stayed put long enough to become a full partner, the others either having been canned outright, having left for greener pastures at other firms in town, having taken jobs in-house with big corporate clients (like *Delta Airlines*, when there really were friendly skies), or, like me, having flown the coop entirely for parts largely unknown by my colleagues (did you say Vermont?). I also mentioned that after being gone for 30 years, the firm sent me a directory the size of our local phone book containing the present whereabouts of just the people who'd departed the premises since I was there—a nice gesture but hardly a testimonial to the firm's retention success.

Having tossed in a number of baseball references along the way, here's another. A week after leaving behind the glitz of that legal megalith and the 80-degree heat of April in Atlanta, I was sitting among moving boxes up here in Peterborough, with snow filling up the tulips outside, watching Henry Aaron, back down there in a Braves uniform, hit his 715th home run to break Babe Ruth's record. (If you don't know who Hammerin' Hank is, then most of the rest of this is probably a waste of time, too, so consult your favorite search if you have to.)

Anyhow, this week, 33 years later, as I started getting acclimated to my new legal environs, Barry Bonds was hitting his juiced-up 756th home run to surpass Aaron's final total. It boggles the mind to think of all the steroids ingested and injected in major league locker rooms between those two history-making events—not to mention all my own memorable at bats during those intervening decades.

Back toward the beginning of this self-absorbed wool-gathering expedition, I bemoaned the fact that once I'm out of here for a few months, no one will remember that I was ever here at all. Footprints in the sand is the image that just occurred to me—I know it's stolen, but I just can't remember the victim.

To buttress my case, I offer the local precedent in the person of one James Sweeney. He held the fort at the old Peterborough Municipal Court for 40 years, from 1915 until he dropped dead of a heart attack one day in 1955. And I bet there aren't still five people in town who even know his name, much less why they should. By the indications I've been able to excavate, however, he did just fine on the bench all that time and contributed all sorts of other commendable community service, too, like serving on the bank board and coaching youth baseball teams. Then he died, and poof. Bummer. Ironically, if he'd stolen all the fines or gotten caught in the wrong bed with his robe unzipped, we'd probably still be talking about him. That's an option for me, too, Right, Tiger, Eliot, Arnold?

I also cited the example of Justice Henry Billings Brown, who served on the Top Rung Court for 16 years and wrote the now infamous "separate but equal" decision in *Plessy v. Ferguson*—which I bet a majority of the current justices don't even know (the justice, not the case). Don't worry, I'm not going to bemoan that again, but I am going to mention a couple of tidbits I found in the second installment of his profile in my Supreme Court Historical Society newsletter. When he was a US District Court judge (before his final kick upstairs), he was quoted as saying that he found he could "easily dispose of the business [of the court] in nine months of the year, and that there was always an opportunity for a summer's outing.

Even when I was a young lawyer back in the '70's, the courts had spring and fall "terms", or sessions, when there were a flurry of trials and other judicial shenanigans, but summer was dead as a doornail at the courthouses. Most of the lights were off and if there was a judge on the premises at all, he—and I mean he in those days—had his feet up on the desk and was reading *The Wall Street Journal*, chatting with lawyers who might stop by for a signature on some inconsequential motion, but otherwise struggling to stay awake until he could leave for the golf course at 4:00.

Those days are gone. I'm certainly not a federal judge, but I bet none of them currently enjoy the old justice's laid-back schedule. Even around here the court runs at full throttle year-round—with dockets of 50 or more arraignments and trials on many days, and even without the boost in business provided by our local college students roaring around in cars full of beer. Right now, it's Friday of the week before Labor Day, probably the deadest week of the year next to the one between Christmas and New Year's, and I'm waiting for the prosecutor to queue up some of the dozen or so remaining trials we still have to wade through before we can enjoy our last "summer's outing" of the year.

So why is it like this? Is it just more people in general; more aggressive law enforcement; more laws for stuff that used to pass for boorish behavior but didn't get you hauled into court (see my confession about snowball throwing); more people scoffing the law; more people challenging the charges they get? Whatever it is, it's combining to make this a whole lot more like a full-time job than the after-school paper route it was when I started practicing, or when Judge Sweeney used to hold court in his kitchen up on Pine Street, which I hear he did. If I was inclined to eat lunch like most everyone else in the modern world and to close down our sessions from noon to 1:30, like they still do in the other courts I visit, and if I really scrutinized every defendant's understanding of all the constitutional rights being waived when he/she is pleading guilty—which I should probably do more of but figure most people don't really care about if they get the outcome they were promised by the prosecutor—we'd be running our dockets all the way to 4:00 p.m. every day of the week, then taking a potty break and cranking up a night session.

In fact, it happens that way for nearly all the visiting judges who fill in for me when I'm away (short of the night court part). When I get back from vacation, I'll ask how it went while I was gone, and the clerk says, "Judge so-and-so was here until almost 5:00 p.m. on juvenile day and had to continue several trials until another day because he wasn't going to reach them." If I did it all that way—and it's probably what our chief will "urge" me to do when/if he reads this (note to self: defer publication until after retirement party)—I'd have this and only this job, 'cause there'd be no time to practice law unless I did it in the middle of the night ("Oh, sorry to wake you, Mrs. Johnson, I didn't realize it was 11:15 p.m."). That would mean winning less bread than most lawyers in New Hampshire, which just isn't going to cut it after 35 years of working 60 hours a week and still trying to pay off a mortgage that ballooned when we used it to pay for the kids' college degrees. Not when some of my non-legal contemps couldn't spot a full day's work if it was on a flashing billboard and yet could buy and sell me.

Sorry to turn this into another episode of Whiny Boy, but after a week when a part-time job keeps you occupied for 4+ days and is still metastasizing like the Blob, and when you get back to the office, there are e-mails and phone messages asking when you're going to finish this will or that deed—the luster of having the judge for a lawyer having worn off years ago—and it's already 6:00 p.m. and you're trying to get out "early" for maybe nine quick holes of golf or some work in the yard before it gets dark, which is happening earlier and earlier now that summer is about gone and you haven't played more than 27 holes since this time last year, and you're facing the prospect of another hideously cold, dark winter of working until 8:00 p.m. every night, I hope you'll cut me some slack. Wow, that was downright Faulknerian.

On the bright side, I've still got my health and a great family and I don't have to worry how I'm going to keep the lights on, which is more than most of the people I'm dealing with everyday can say. Plus, there are undoubtedly dozens of other lawyers out there who'd gladly wear a black dress for the same money and be glad to have the chance—and I'm sure they're all convinced they could do it way better, too.

The fact that I'm not a full-time judge—and despite all my griping, I still prefer it that way—means there are times when I'm not in court but still carrying that mantle around while at large in my civvies.

I mean, it's definitely gratifying to run into a parent at the bookstore and have them report that their punk kid with the nose ring and Metallica T-shirt, who was on the road to state prison or worse, really got straightened out as a result of our get-together with him and that he's now managing a hedge fund on Wall Street, with a great wife and two kids and a tremendous 401k.

On the flip side, it's pretty embarrassing to be standing in the checkout line at the Piggly Wiggly, with my Red Sox hat on and my orange juice and blueberries on the counter, while some irate fellow customer, or even the cashier, berates me for finding her or her boyfriend or her stepson's girlfriend guilty of some charge several months ago that I have no recollection of whatsoever, all as my fellow shoppers are wondering how this unshaven guy in a dirty T-shirt could possibly hold such a position of authority, much less make a bonehead decision like the one being described. At those moments, I think about how I should have gone out of town to do my shopping or worn my dark glasses even in the dark—or maybe I didn't really need those groceries after all.

Even more difficult are the situations where a friend or client wants advice about something that may come before the court, even if I'm not going to be the one to deal with it. Maybe caller ID would help, so I can dodge those calls at 2:00 a.m. when there's no chance in hell that the subject is private legal business. If they don't get me, perhaps they'll find someone who'll actually tell them something helpful and won't waffle like a politician up for re-election.

In other words, as counter-intuitive as it seems, being a good friend to someone may mean doing nothing at all for them in their moment of greatest need—which I'm sure they won't have any trouble at all understanding—though it may also mean I'll need to start cultivating some new friends.

Enough with the hanky-wrenching; back to business. One of our regulars who ought to have his own toothbrush in the men's room was here for trial on a charge of telephone harassment of a former girlfriend who'd recorded his call on her home answering machine. The defense attorney wanted to hear the tape before the trial started—a commendable discovery request—but he was told we had no capability to play it for him, having converted our own equipment over to digital some time ago. The solution, in typical New Hampshire fashion, was for the prosecutor and defense attorney to repair to the prosecutor's ancient Honda (they don't pay those folks much) to play the tape on his dashboard cassette player.

As they left to do so, I wondered what arguments would be made if the vehicle ate the evidence, like an old Barry Manilow tape. In truth, the defense attorney was probably hoping for that kind of mishap, but the lawyers soon came back ready to proceed. The snag at that point wasn't the technology but the defendant's pungent breath, which our bailiff picked up on—I'm not talking about garlic here—and which, in turn, prompted the guy to cop the plea he'd been offered before you could say, *Make it a Bud Light.*

Apparently, this was one of the rare circumstances where alcohol can actually assist law enforcement. For my part, I don't mind admitting considerable relief, as I envisioned all of us squeezing into the Honda to hear the taped call for the record. I was hoping for shotgun at least.

The grandkids started back to school yesterday, and Labor Day weekend kicks off tomorrow. While I love hot weather myself and am always unsure in January and February why I live at this warmth-deprived latitude, I won't be sorry to see some temperature-related improvement in our customers' courtroom attire. I spoke on that not long ago and I've got my pants wadded up again. In doing so, I realize I may be showing how far out of the mainstream of modern life I've wandered, but I'll risk it.

I've decided most people don't dress for success here; they dress like they're hoping I'll think they're either too crazy or stupid to be criminally responsible. Shorts are only the tip of the iceberg (what's left of them these days), but I'm not even talking about shorts, despite that probably a third of our clientele show up with their knees exposed this time of year. I'm focusing here on the so-called "wife beater" T-shirts that have no sleeves and allow all of us to inspect some guy's tattoo art and crop of body hair. And then there are the tank tops the size of a tube sock that must be intended to feature a woman's pierced belly button, or, worse yet, a serious failure to work those abs. I used to send local people home to improve their appearance, but pretty soon there just got to be too many of them for me to keep up with, and I gave up.

Instead, when a really egregious outfit presents itself, and even biting my tongue can't stem the sarcasm, I say something like, "Did you forget you were coming to court when you got dressed this morning?"; or "Did you read the part about 'appropriate attire' on your hearing notice?" If someone's offended and complains to the Judicial Conduct Committee, I'll take my chances. We've certainly come a long way on many fronts since the Supremes ruled 35 years ago that my predecessor couldn't require men to wear ties to court, but we're still lost in the woods on this issue.

I wonder whether the smart guys in Concord would make the same call again if they knew then what a gaping hole in the floodgates of decorum they were blowing. On the other hand, all you have to do is go to church or a nice restaurant or take a commercial flight and you'll know that the wardrobe mirror is now as extinct as button hooks and detachable collars. Maybe a valuable post-judicial mission will be to wander the countryside handing out small mirrors, so people are better able to make themselves presentable when they appear in public—sort of like a modern-day Johnny Appleseed. Can you say "curmudgeon"?

Just as dress codes have undergone considerable mutation since the prehistoric days of my early practice, so, too, have other physical accoutrements. As I've mentioned already, when a charge of DWI is brought, the killer evidence is often the breath alcohol reading produced by blowing into the Intoxilyzer. I love that name, because it always makes me envision a Rube Goldberg sort of contraption with tubes and beakers.

If the result that emerges is over the legal limit of .08%, a defendant sometimes claims that the cops didn't wait long enough for alcohol in his mouth to dissipate before making him blow. Another defensive ploy might be that alcohol was trapped in the nooks and crannies of the driver's false teeth and caused the result to be so high—that one's getting rarer, though, as our clientele tend to do without teeth entirely if they're dentally challenged. Now the culprits tend to be tongue studs and lip rings, often paired with extreme wardrobe choices to round out the statement being made.

The pierced-up kid we had this time claimed he was using Listerine to prevent infection from the recent hole poked in his tongue and that it, rather than lots of alcoholic beverages, must have caused the Intox reading to sky-rocket. While I admired his imaginative thinking, there was no science offered to back up this theory and the officer failed to detect any whiff of disinfectant amidst the overwhelming odor of other alcohol-based substances. So, I filed his defense in the "nice try" folder and sent him to see the clerk about his fine and license surrender.

By the way, back in the days of the three martini lunch and getting totally wasted at the office party, the threshold presumption for alcohol impairment was .15% blood or breath alcohol. Now, that kind of reading gets you nearly to an aggravated DWI charge, which would necessitate an enhanced fine, 5 days in the county lock-up, 2 years without a license, and then a year's use of an ignition lock you'd have to blow into before you could start up your vehicle. That array of penalties would hurt a lot more than a tongue stud and be way more expensive.

Cathie and I have finally accepted the long-standing invitations of several good friends and we're now near Vail in Colorado, after visiting other pals in Salt Lake City and Jackson, Wyoming. In Salt Lake we toured the Mormon complex with a couple of lovely young South American women who were fulfilling their "mission" by telling us—many times, in case we didn't get it—how much difference their religion is making in their lives (and how the new conference center holds 21,000 souls).

Then, while in and around Jackson we did some breath-taking high-altitude hikes in the Tetons and Yellowstone. As crowded as all the main sites were, we found that all it took to achieve maximum solitude was to head about a hundred yards down one of the trails, the common mind-set among most visitors apparently being that if you can't see your car or the snack bar, you must be lost.

We're also hiking here in the Vail area with some friends we've known for more than 30 years, having first met them in Bermuda when we took our maiden vacation sans children. These folks are our age but have been extremely comfortably retired now for about three years, dividing their time between the water's edge in Rye (New York, not New Hampshire) and a truly unbelievable home here (15 telephones and so many bedrooms that no one's ever slept in a couple of them) with spectacular views way out over their golf course and . . . . are those really the Canadian Rockies? The only concerns today in this household are whether to play golf, go fly-fishing, or do some bird photography, and then whether to do sushi or Tex Mex for dinner tonight.

Meanwhile, I'm checking my office e-mail every couple of hours, trying to keep from having 500 messages to sort through when I get back in the saddle Monday morning and also wondering where along the line I veered off the track that might have had us weighing the same kinds of challenging options as our hosts. I'm sure it was the decision to move from the big Atlanta firm to the tiny one in Peterborough, where my starting salary was about what it now costs to get your house painted and where it's still way less than these folks spend on bathroom fixtures. I don't regret the road taken, however, except occasionally— like now—when the rewards for taking the other road get heaped up in front of us so dramatically. As soon as we get home and back into the swing of things there, I'll calm down and be happy just to have clean underwear and to be doing this, even if it takes at least another 10 years of doing it before having the luxury of taking up bird photography. In the meantime, though, I need to have the house painted.

PS—Just a few months after getting home from Vailhala, we got a call from the Mrs. out there, to the effect that she'd thrown her hubby out with his fly rod and telephoto lens, on the ground of 17 years of philandering with enough other women to fill all his bedrooms. You could have knocked us over with a hummingbird feather. Cathie and I were dumbfounded and so were all their friends and family members, none of whom had any idea there was trouble in paradise. I guess we're a lot better off than we thought we were, which is usually the case when you think about it. After all, 15 telephones won't do you much good if there's no one who wants to hear from you when you call.

Just as we were heading west, the news broke of one of my Superior Court colleagues being suspended from most of her judicial duties for doing some shady lawyering to help her husband avoid a large financial obligation. While I'm sure that kind of hanky panky, if proven, would be grounds for sanctions during any period in our history, the story got me thinking about how standards of acceptable judicial behavior have morphed over the years—like spanking your kids.

Not long ago I read the biography of New York Judge Learned

Hand—not only one of the most colorful legal monikers ever, but also the judge often cited as the most qualified never to make it to the top rung. Hand clenched a slightly lower federal rung for much of the first half of the 20th century and was known as much for his unblemished moral rectitude as for his intellectitude. Yet in the chapter on Hand's life called "The Peak of Political Enthusiasm", the author describes how Hand also regularly made financial contributions to political campaigns and even wrote much of Theodore Roosevelt's 1912 Bull Moose Party platform while juggling his paying work with the other hand.

Hand may not have lost any sleep over that extra-judicial behavior, but in this so-much-more-civilized time of extreme political correctness, his conduct would be scandalous and would get him run off the bench in a nanosecond, no matter how distinguished and unsullied his prior record and reputation might have been.

Just look at the uproar caused by Justice Scalia's bird hunting trip with Vice President Cheney, whose case was likely to be coming up for the justice's vote but who apparently never said more than "duck!" during the whole boondoggle. It took a 50+ page memo from Scalia to dig himself out of that hole, yet chances are if it takes that many words to set the record straight, it's more likely to look crooked and you probably should have gone fishing instead, by yourself.

Speaking from personal experience now, I recall getting reamed out once by a local reporter for hearing a small claim involving a guy who was a fellow member of our savings bank's largely ceremonial advisory board. And it didn't seem to matter that I'd never met the guy, had never been to a meeting with him, and had no idea he was even on the board.

Not long afterward, when I'd apparently failed to learn my lesson, someone reported me to the Judicial Conduct Committee because I was announcing the auction items at our summer theater's annual benefit. I wasn't actually hawking the stuff or badgering people to up their bids for, say, a year's worth of home-baked pies, but I guess they thought I was still a cog in the wheel of soliciting funds for the organization. You see, asking people for money, even for admirable and non-controversial causes, is taboo even for part-time judges these days, because it might suggest we're trading on our official positions to coerce their contributions. (As an aside, if this is reminiscent of judges in other states asking—perfectly legally there—for contributions to their re-election campaigns, it's not the same thing at all; no, it's not nearly as blatantly unethical.) Luckily, by immediately confessing my outrageous transgression and by promising never, never, ever again to act so irresponsibly, I narrowly escaped with my judicial career intact.

To be honest, because I'm a part-time judge who's a private citizen most of the time and because I never connected the ethical dots the way my more perceptive critics were able, I got completely blind-sided by that one. So, while I still go to the auction (I'm assuming I don't have to give up all my civil rights), I don't go anywhere near the podium and I spend most of my time scarfing up all the chocolate-filled or -covered things I can find at the hors d'oeuvre table. My wife even does the bidding—so no one feels intimidated by competing with me for an item. I wonder what Judge Hand would do?

Turning from the niceties of judicial ethics to the truly bizarre, today I considered the stalking petition of a woman in her 20's whose claim was that a former co-worker had been making unwanted sexual advances toward her. Specifically, she said he'd slipped into her bed on several occasions and was discovered to be in the throes of having sex with her when she woke up. During another moment of intimate stalking, he allegedly ate a chocolate bar from one of her private orifices, which I'll leave to your imagination to explore further. Then she said he proclaimed her his "sweet tasting love slave." Seriously.

Given this young woman's perhaps limited prospects for future relationships—this is just an subjective estimate on my part—as well as her entirely pleasurable accounts of the incidents she was alleging, I must admit to wondering why she was asking for restraining orders. I also spent much of our time together trying to picture the alleged assailant, but all I could envision was a skinny little Jack Sprat sort of character.

When the guy finally came in for his day in court, he turned out to be an average-sized guy (though still considerably smaller than his alleged love munchkin), but a bit slow and in need of a ride to court from his sister because he didn't have a car. As it turned out, the sister was critical to sorting through the sordidness, because in response to the woman's elaborate diary entries about all the months of lewd behavior the hapless guy had forced upon her, the sister said it was all simply impossible because her brother didn't even know where the woman lived, and in any event couldn't have gotten there from his home 35 miles away unless she'd driven him, which she hadn't.

Not put off in the least by that defense, the woman claimed the guy had been fired from his job at the supermarket where they both worked due to his ongoing harassment of her. Aha! That seemed like an objectively verifiable fact that might lead me out of the weeds, so I eagerly suggested she get me some proof of that smoking gun before I ruled.

Perhaps I shouldn't be surprised, but it's been more than a week now and nothing has materialized. Maybe the store is reluctant to provide confidential information about another employee, or, to be completely callous and sexist, maybe the woman has already gotten what she wanted from the process. Those are just wild guesses, however, because we haven't heard anything more at all from the woman herself.

PS—It's been another week now and still nothing. I'm vacating the temporary orders and dismissing the petition today, but I have no idea what really happened here and why (or why not). Maybe I've completely failed this woman based on my male-oriented skepticism about the plausibility of her claims. On the flip side, maybe the proceedings were some kind of erotic vehicle by which the woman could recount her fantasies about the guy while he was forced to sit there and listen to them. Maybe the guy even liked what he heard and the two have now embarked on a kinky but voluntary liaison—while the sister sits outside with the motor running.

Wherever the truth may lurk in this scenario, I'm certain that in the immortal lyrics of Jim Morrison, "people are strange." And that as one of the strangest characters in rock history, the Lizard King would know.

I don't know how many criminal and motor vehicle complaints I've looked at over the last 25 years, but I'd guess it's close to 75,000. I'd also guess I glance at the date of birth listed on nearly all of them, particularly those of people who appear about my age or older.

Today is the first time, however, that I've had someone standing there who was born on exactly the same day as I was. The guy actually looked pretty good for his advanced state of decrepitude and he seemed like a decent enough fellow, even though he didn't seem to know he couldn't have an open container of beer in the car with him. I was skeptical. Whether it's the law or not, anyone our age ought to know that to be drinking in a place where it would be inconvenient to find a bathroom is hazardous to your personal hygiene.

When we got finished with his plea, I started to say something about our birthday convergence but decided against it at the last moment. There was a courtroom full of people and it just didn't seem like the time to get into a chummy conversation about where he was born, how he made his way from wherever that was to this area, and what he'd done with himself all these years. If it ever happens again, though, I'm resolving now to take a recess and have a heart-to-heart in chambers with whoever it happens to be—where was he/she when Kennedy was shot; did he (if a he) manage to avoid getting shot at in Vietnam; did he/she ever think the time would go by as fast as it has?

That is, we'll have our chat unless the offense that gets the next customer in here is too scurrilous for cordiality. I'm not going to huddle with someone charged with molesting his stepdaughter or abusing his/her partner, though by the time this happens again, the transgression will probably be something like negligent use of a bedpan or theft of a walker.

PS—I'm now within a month of having to turn in my robe for a bathrobe and slippers, and it's never happened again.

Before reading further, please consult my lament about people believing all's fair in court, as well as in love and war—in other words, saying whatever they need to in order to get off, even under oath, whether it's true or not. I've heard it referred to as "testilying", which actually makes it sound like a marginally legitimate alternative to the truth when the latter could be inconvenient. It reminds me of the Watergate hearings when a witness might declare his prior perjury "inoperative", or when our new president's assistant declares his departure from the truth to be a case of "alternative facts".

This time we had a guy about 25 who was charged with DWI after wrecking his car. When the cops arrived, he told them his friend Chris had been driving, because he—the kid—was too "cocked" to get behind the wheel. Of course, by that time there was no sign of Chris anywhere and our guy was too drunk even to cook up a plausible description of his alleged chauffeur. Understandably, that led the police to cast a jaundiced eye and make the arrest rather than put out an all-points for Chris.

The case would have been a tad out of the ordinary if that's where it ended, but at trial the fellow took the stand, swore soberly to tell the truth, admitted he had fibbed about Chris after all, and then went on to say that he was actually perfectly sober when the accident occurred. What really happened, he assured me, was that he was so distraught about the accident, and about his grandfather's recent death, that once he cracked up the car, he did what anyone would do and immediately started drinking heavily. By the time the cops arrived he had already pounded 4 or 5 beers, thus producing the .16% blood alcohol result he blew (double the minimum legal threshold for being cocked while driving).

This time it was my turn to do the eyebrow raising, and upon finding him guilty I also volunteered that this total fabrication of events went way beyond the modest exaggeration I might tolerate. In fact, I suggested that his performance fit the definition of perjury, in my humble opinion, and that he would be lucky if the police didn't slap him with that, too. I should have slapped him myself, but I didn't want to sacrifice my judicial career (lowest rung that it is) for this kid. Instead, I said I took personally his utter disregard of the oath I'd administered and that I wasn't quite as stupid as I must look.

After finishing with all that, the fellow decided to appeal the conviction. Perhaps he thought that given this rehearsal, he could improve his performance enough to blow the tale past a jury of his peers. I doubt they're likely to be that stupid either, but maybe this rehearsal will make him more convincing. More likely, he was just buying some time before serving the maximum sentence he'd done more than enough to earn. If he's unsuccessful next time, too, he'll at least have the consolation of creating Pulitzer Prize-winning fiction, and he may have career prospects with the Disney folks in Fantasyland.

Conflicts of interest are the bane of the part-time judge, because they blind-side you in ways you least expect. The worst are the ones that crop up after you've already heard most of a long case, and then suddenly a witness is called who's a friend or client. The whole thing starts to implode at that point. You announce the conflict, which the parties are usually anxious to waive because they want to avoid the expense, delay and inconvenience of having to start all over again, but that doesn't really solve the problem for me. I still feel extremely awkward at the prospect of discounting, even disregarding entirely, the testimony of someone I feel my own obligation toward—not to mention maybe losing a good client or friend in the process.

I usually handle the situation by announcing that although the parties may not have a problem, I'm going to believe everything this witness says and that if that approach is OK with everyone, we can proceed. It's generally fine with the party who called the witness, but rarely with the opponent, so we either stop and rewind right there or the witness is excused and we proceed without him. Either way, one of the parties suffers because of me, a result no judge wants.

This is all a lead-in to the conflict that cropped up today. A nervous fellow in his late 20's or so came in for a small claim hearing, but said I probably shouldn't hear the case because of a conflict of interest. I didn't recognize the guy's name or face, so I asked him to explain the problem. He said I might be biased against him because he'd stolen my law partner's snow blower. I acknowledged that this might be a troublesome complication and that he might have second thoughts about my objectivity if he lost, which probably would have been the outcome 'cause how could I give an awful lot of cred to an admitted thief?

Needless to say, the other party was outraged, not only because he'd have to come back to get the judgment he was sure he deserved, but no doubt also because he'd been dumb enough to do business with a confessed pilferer. Now I'm going back to the office to find out whether my partner knows who stole his snow blower. If not, I think I can give him a pretty good lead.

It may seem hard to believe, but even after all these years of honing in on the nuances of body language and voice patterns, I really have no idea what my rep is with the local cops and defense attorneys. I mean, I can certainly tell when lawyers are pissed about my rulings and think I blinked on the crucial fact or argument they thought had won it for them, but that's not a reputation.

I hope the predominant opinion is toward the fair and impartial end of the spectrum, but I'm sure there are some who think I've swung way past fair, beyond impartial, maybe all the way over to soft as a grape on crime. Just as surely, there's probably a camp of aggressive defenders who think I run rough-shod over their clients' constitutional rights and wouldn't throw out an illegal confession or search even if it smelled like three day-old fish in the hot sun.

Another litmus test of my true colors was administered this past week and I'll let you make your own assessment of the hue that emerged.

My first impression of the kid from Keene was that this wasn't his first trip through the metal detector. That is, he didn't seem at all wide-eyed or jumpy at the prospect of unknown and potentially serious consequences, as most newcomers do. In fact, he seemed downright indignant at being hauled in here for allegedly trying to return some high-priced sneakers (at least that's what I called my Keds or PF Flyers) to the local branch of the sporting goods chain from whose sister store in Keene the shoes had been stolen not long before. On top of that, the kid actually had the brass nuggets to wear the contraband to his trial, where they were positively ID'd by the Keene store manager.

The trouble was that the manager said this wasn't the actual thief who made off with the goods, and the kid couldn't really recall (really?) exactly where he'd happened upon them. Unfortunately for the cops, they hadn't been able to track down the first culprit in the chain of crime, so that guy wasn't here to complete the link to the defendant.

I guess I could have put two and two together circumstantially, as the cops urged me to do—I mean, really, what were the chances that this obviously street-wise kid actually ended up with a brand-new, premium pair of sneakers like this without knowing pretty clearly what had happened? The problem was that the public defender also had a decent point when he argued that no matter how fishy the situation looked (or smelled), there could have been any number of other, non-criminal ways his client might have come into possession of the shoes without knowing they were stolen.

In other words, when there was this degree of plausible (if not probable) uncertainty about what the kid knew and when he knew it, the hurdle of reasonable doubt hadn't been cleared. I saw it that way myself, even as the cops gnashed their teeth and the kid symbolically re-tied his shoes and smirked at me on his strut out of the courtroom. At that moment I'm sure there was no doubt among any of them, including the kid, that I'd have let OJ walk, too.

With just a couple of weeks until Halloween, Cathie and I took out a second mortgage on the house and loaded up the shopping cart with enough candy to service the 350+ kids who descend on us every October 31. We live on a street near the elementary school, with a good sidewalk, and it's evolved into the place to be if you want to run into all your friends and make sure your kids get all they'll need for a near-fatal sugar buzz.

That reminds me of the college freshman who came to court this time last year charged with underage possession of alcohol due to the six-pack found among his Halloween goodies. The incident was memorable because the kid was wearing a full gorilla suit at the time he was pinched (captured?). The officer said he stopped the kid because he (the gorilla) looked under 21, so I guess either the suit was a juvenile model or his (the gorilla's) behavior fit that description, though no one inquired about the cop's credentials to make that kind of anthropological assessment.

To my great dismay, the kid just pled guilty, so we never got to explore what tipped off the cop that there was a sweaty teenager under all the fur. If there's a lesson to be learned here, it's either that underage possession of alcohol is not a risk worth taking under any circumstances, or that if you're going to take the risk, you could improve your odds by dressing up like Father Time or at least a clearly adult creature of some variety.

In a related story, there's a reason why kids don't get their licenses until 16, even though they may be tall enough to reach the pedals and see over the steering wheel before then. Turns out it has more to do with attaining a critical mass of maturity and judgment, although if that was the real test, I'd kick the age up significantly, even if it meant the hormonal young folks had to convince mom or dad to get them to the drive-in and then disappear for a couple of hours while they steamed up the back seat. (We still have one of those nearby, so it's not entirely hypothetical). See, it's one thing for an 18 year-old to screw up the country by voting recklessly, or even to point a loaded weapon toward enemy lines, but I don't want a teenager still shedding baby fat drifting over the center line toward me in a couple of thousand pounds of reinforced steel.

As authority for my concern, I offer the case of today's 16 year-old, who was motoring along at 104 in a 40 zone while texting on his smart phone, the phone being considerably smarter than he was. (Permit me to digress long enough to observe that you can't text while driving in the Granite State, but you don't have to wear a seatbelt even if you're going 104. Go figure.) Maybe the kid was texting his mother about which emergency room to visit him in, but I suspect that instead he was, like, making plans to hook up with his buds somewhere and, like, chill. Following his court appearance he'll need to re-text his pals to arrange where they can, like, pick him up, because he'll be hoofing it now for as long as I can make that happen.

This is a PS to the account above about our fleeting moment of national notoriety for those creatively-prosecuted illegal immigration cases. The "reporters and editors at New Hampshire newspapers and radio and television stations" ranked our cases as the 5th biggest story of the year, proving once again that it doesn't take much to be a pretty big fish in our New Hampshire kiddie pool.

I mentioned that one of the ultra-conservative radio guys who was all over me about the decision was an occasional diner at the same place we have breakfast when we spend a weekend up north in the Lakes Region. This past weekend we were there again and who sat down at the counter next to me but the loudmouth himself. Except for spreading his considerable girth into my personal space, he gave no indication of acknowledging me and woofed down his eggs, bacon and hash browns without any concern that one of the great threats to America's borders was just 16 inches away. I kept eating my pancakes without a peep—even though there was no digital recording device in the vicinity—not wanting his over-worked circulatory system and dangerously-clogged arteries to suffer a life-threatening surge in blood pressure. I mean, I don't want him to die, just to shut his big fat mouth.

Yesterday while walking a letter to the Post Office before it closed, a beat-up Jeep passed me in the opposite direction, from which a young male voice blurted out, "F**k you, Judge Runyon," in a distinctly hostile tone. Instead of taking offense, I was encouraged to think that at least some former customer didn't find me a total pushover—in spite of being so obviously soft on illegal immigration.

I've heard enough horrifying domestic violence and stalking cases not to take any of them lightly, but they're not all matters of life and death. This time a high school girl charged her ex with stalking her, claiming he wouldn't leave her alone and take no for an answer. His defense was that if she was so freaked out by his advances, she should stay out of the produce department where he worked after school. The girl said she wasn't leading him on, just shopping for broccoli, which was, like, positively her most favorite veggie ever. His parry to that claim was that there was a huge produce department at the mega-grocer about a mile down the road and that it had an even more abundant and varied selection of broccoli than his. He may have been risking his employment with that negative assessment, but he may want to consider the legal department somewhere in his future, and he could chalk this up as his first courtroom victory. Petition dismissed this time.

Sex crimes and the life-long obligation of sex offenders to register their whereabouts is serious business here in New Hampshire. Not surprisingly, many offenders slip into a new town—often a small one where they think no one is paying attention—and then don't register with the local authorities. They either hope to continue doing their despicable thing under the radar or, at best, hope to find a job without freaking out every employer in the neighborhood. Either way, it's hard to develop much sympathy for these guys—and they're nearly always guys, except those female high school teachers who, bewilderingly, seem drawn like moths to pimply 14 year-olds.

The case at hand seemed to warrant that knee-jerk response of contempt, as it involved a 20-something guy who was charged with failing to register in one of our towns after being convicted of rape in Massachusetts. It got more complicated, though, when I learned the offense happened more than 10 years ago, when the guy was a teenager and his "victim" was his 14 year-old girlfriend. On top of that, the kid denied ever actually having sex with the young lady, despite pleading guilty because he said his public defender worked out such a favorable deal that it seemed the easiest way out for all of them, including the lawyer.

When the guy eventually found that having the conviction on his record would continue to haunt him forever, even keeping him out of the rough-and-tumble military, he said he'd had the conviction successfully expunged, or so he thought, and that he didn't need to register anymore. In fact, he said he'd never have been eligible for induction—much less one tour in Iraq so far and another one about to start—if he was still on the books as a convicted rapist.

So, what to do? Even if I believed very little of what he said, the guy didn't look like our typical offender. He and his girlfriend may have gotten an illegal start on their sex life, but there was no indication that force was involved or that he was more responsible for what happened than she was. Clearly, the guy had also done some pretty responsible things with himself since then.

When the dust settled, I decided to give him a few weeks to prove he'd annulled the Massachusetts conviction; however, even if he can't come up with anything, I'm not going to prevent the guy from heading overseas again. I mean, let's face it, another session of dodge ball with all those IEDs is likely to be considerably more punitive than whatever I could do with him.

The case highlights a common shortcoming in the legislative process, however, one that, as judges, we repeatedly have to contend with. On the one hand is the public outrage about a particular societal abuse—i.e., convicted sex offenders re-abusing because no one is aware they're living next to our children. That's coupled with the chronic fear that our duly-elected or appointed-and-vetted judges won't serve us well (remember the $54 million pants case?). All of which leads to an inflexible statutory fix on the other hand that inevitably drags in many more fish than we really want to catch. Ergo, our teenager who [may have] had consensual sex with an underage girlfriend and now has to register as a sex offender for the rest of his life.

If we have no choice but to apply the letter of the law without any flexibility or discretion whatsoever—which many would have us do rather than, heaven forbid, "legislating from the bench"—we may ruin a young life because there's no provision in the law for what to do with a round peg and a square hole. Actually, despite my less than hard-ass bent in most cases, I'm opposed to the dreaded "judicial activism" we all get charged with, and I often reach results I hate in the interest of leaving the lawmaking to the people elected to do it. On the other hand, if there's any latitude at all provided to allow for discretion, I'll take an honest crack at tailoring the outcome to the circumstances I'm faced with, not all of which even the most carefully constructed laws can envision.

In this case anyhow, I dodged the ball temporarily, and I'll see where we stand once I've got all the facts—always the preferred course, I think, even to the most blood-thirsty fighter of crime.

The differences in life between the haves and the have nots usually manifest themselves in the kinds of cars people drive—new Lexus versus '79 Chrysler Cordoba with cracked windshield and tail light out—or in where they live—1790 Colonial on 10 wooded acres versus third floor walk-up with rats and inadequate heat. There are more subtle differences, though, and we had a peak at one of them today.

A woman from one of our economically-challenged towns was charged with "kindling a fire without a permit" because she was cooking her weenies on a fire she'd built in her yard in a concrete drainage culvert she'd cut off and stood on end. If instead she'd had the fire in a fancy Weber grill or in one of those trendy iron fire pits people spend a lot of money on these days, the cops would have driven right by and not taken a second sniff. I know that because I asked them, even though they couldn't tell me what the functional difference was between the woman's crude setup and the more upscale cookout equipment.

Nevertheless, despite the equal protection arguments the woman might have raised, she just pled no contest—and she did it with such hopeless resignation that it must have seemed just one more of her life's unwinnable sparring matches with the cops. The prosecutor wanted a fine of $100, so it wasn't a huge penalty, at least not for a Weber owner, but for someone cooking on a drainage pipe it was probably a life-threatening setback that could lead to having the power turned off and the oil tank running dry.

I went along with the plea, but suspended the fine as long as she doesn't do any more illegal culvert cooking for a year. Maybe she'll take my suggestion to scout the yard sales and recycling center for a rusted-out hunk of metal that looks more like a real grill. Or maybe she just ought to get some help rolling her concrete cylinder behind her behind her building where the cops can't see it.

I'm writing this while listening to the Senate Judiciary Committee's hearing on Samuel Alito's nomination to the U.S. Supreme Court. The questions relate to his views on "federalism" (the role of the federal government in relation to the states), and to whether landmark cases like Roe v. Wade are untouchable precedents or are subject to reconsideration as new judges express their cents' worth.

Meanwhile, I'm trying to decide whether a single-mother tenant trailing a bunch of kids who needs her security deposit back to put down on a new apartment should be charged $50 for extra cleaning the landlord said he had to do. Although the debate in Washington may be more critical to the nation's future, I'm sure the $50 I'm dealing with will be considerably more significant to the woman who's waiting downstairs to hear whether she'll be able to fill up her car with gas or will need to be living in the car for a while.

Last night my son and I went to the Red Sox playoff game against the Angels at Fenway and agonized through inning after inning of runners left on base, until Manny Ramirez launched a monstrous shot into the ozone in the bottom of the 9th and everyone in Boston went home abuzz with glee. The challenge for me was that it was 1:00 a.m. and I was supposed to drive 2½ hours up to the lake house for our last weekend of the season and the annual buttoning up for winter that's depressing as hell but has to be endured this time of year.

I had the new Springsteen CD to keep me awake and I guess I was charged up enough by the combination of the music and the game to be going about 10 above the exit ramp speed limit as I came off the interstate in Concord. I know that because a state trooper pointed out my speed as he walked cautiously up to the window about 2:30 and asked for my license and registration. Ordinarily, no cop would bother with someone doing much less than 15 over, but at that hour of the morning the trooper was fishing for possible DWIs and was using any pretext— uh, reasonable suspicion—for checking to see who'd been drinking a beer an inning. That is, speeding to any extent, not going as fast as the speed limit, having a plate/tail/head light out, not using a turn signal even when there's no one else on the road, executing the ubiquitous California stop, even flicking a cigarette out the window these days (now called "improper disposal of lighted materials"), would provide a chance to sniff the inside of a car—and maybe bag a really big one. I doubt even Driver Ed himself could make it past one of these guys if he really wanted to come up with something to justify the stop.

On the other hand, over 40% of all traffic fatalities last year involved drinking before or during driving, so the odds of nabbing someone with alcohol under his belt, particularly at 2:30 in the morning, have to be a lot better than hitting the Powerball—or hitting one out of the park in the 9th.

Anyhow, once the trooper confirmed that my breath was bad but not alcoholic, that my license wasn't suspended, and that there wasn't a warrant for my arrest out there somewhere—and I mean anywhere throughout the land, now that they have the internet at their immediate disposal—he asked me how the Sox game came out, which seemed to win me just enough leniency points, and he sent me on my way.

People often smirk that it must be cool to know you can go as fast as you want and never get a ticket 'cause you're a judge. They appear confused when I explain that I'd never tell a cop I was a judge and that I'd be much better off paying the ticket than trying to get special treatment—only to have the cop tell a buddy about the nerve of that judge, and then have the buddy tell a reporter who runs an expose on this shocking abuse of authority. Of course, that ends up getting me hauled before the Judicial Conduct Committee to explain the whole sordid affair.

Then, after that whole kerfuffle, one of the same whistleblowers who started the whole thing would call two weeks later to ask if I could talk to the prosecutor about his kid getting pinched for underage alcohol possession even though the 30-pack was all the way in the back seat.

Using alcohol as the segue, I'll note that we recently had a 21-page docket of 80 cases, of which 40 involved either alcohol or drugs, and of which most were in the internal or external possession of college students during a huge party weekend. The total take at the clerk's window that day was over $6,000, not even counting the additional amount many of the kids will have to scare up from somewhere ("Uh, Dad, the prof says we need a new $360 book for chemistry class").

Drugs weren't an issue when I was in their shoes, but I can relate on the subject of alcohol-soaked partying long before the law would have allowed us to partake. Why is it so prevalent? Easy. You're living on your own all of a sudden, having to deal with adult stuff like running a checkbook (I won't say balancing), collecting from your mates to pay the cable bill, and debating the meaning of life at 3:00 in the morning. Consequently, you feel entitled to the adult perks that come with those activities, like drinking yourself into a puking stupor after a tough week of Comparative Social Mores.

The trouble is, unlike the days when my friends and I were drinking a grain alcohol concoction called "hairy buffalo" out of plastic trash cans and the security officers were just pouring it on the ground and helping us stagger back to the dorm, today's U-cops get right on the phone to the local police department. Then, before you can clean the barf off your shirt, you're cuffed and stuffed and maybe spending a night in jail, too, if you're too drunk to tell which of the twelve blurry cops is the real one. If you're so drunk that they have to take you to the ER for physician-assisted barfing, you end up paying for all those services and fees, as well as the considerable fine.

Actually, most of the change in response is driven by safety, which morphs into liability and the fact that most schools have been burned by expensive lawsuits from the families of drunken freshman who choked on their own vomit or went into alcohol shock after being released by security. Just another case of lawyers ruining a good time, I guess.

Let's go for three alcohol-infused cases in a row. A 17 year-old whose parents gave up on him long ago was standing in front of me for a DWI arraignment, his first adult charge after years of one juvenile scrape after another. I remembered that he lives with his older sister, but she wasn't there to help him decide what to do this time. He was all set to plead guilty because he couldn't afford a lawyer, even though he didn't think the charge was fair and we couldn't appoint a PD for him on this kind of charge, albeit a serious one.

When the prosecutor started telling me what happened, which I always ask them to do before accepting a plea, it turned out that the kid was found passed out in his car, which was parked with the keys in the ignition but wasn't running. Gee, that seemed like a pretty close one to me, so I stopped the prosecutor in his tracks and asked the kid whether perhaps he wanted some more time to see whether he could get a little free advice from a lawyer before deciding what to do. One of the public defenders here on something else heard the cop's account and offered to go over the police report with the kid. Once we circled back to the kid later on, he said he guessed he would change his plea to not guilty and ask for a trial date.

The unfortunate part is that this kid is going nowhere no matter how this case comes out. He's surrounded by a family full of poor male role models, a number of whom I represented when they were juveniles themselves 30 years ago and who pretty much see the alcohol, drug and driving laws as the game pieces in their age-old battle of cat and mouse with the cops. If the cops win one time, it only hardens these guys' genetic resolve to continue the good fight as soon as they get out of jail, which is where they now go on nearly any charge because their records read like Russian novels and nothing less makes even a dent in their commitment to continue waging war against the tyranny of law enforcement.

I have no idea how the kid's DWI will come out, but I would be willing to stake my entire judicial retirement account—all four figures of it—on the fact that he'll still be visiting our facility long after I've returned to earth from this mighty rung. If there's a way to break this inbred crusade of criminality, I don't know what it is, unless someone throws the kid in the trunk of a car and drives him so far away he can't afford to come home. Then, he'd have to be reprogrammed to accept that most people don't spend all their take-home pay on beer, marijuana and fines, and don't try to outrun the cops every time the blue lights go on. I'm not sure it's possible to drive that far without hitting an ocean or an international border.

I've been fortunate so far to do my job and make my decisions without spurring too much public outrage. This week, though, I drew the following comment in a letter to our local editor:

"Judge Runyon has again let a person off that has broken the law! What the judge said is that it is OK to speed if you are not posing a threat to anyone or anything. Isn't this a bad message to send to all of us, especially teens? What is the use of having speed limit signs?"

I bet you're asking yourselves, "Why would a speeding case attract any comment at all, much less outrage about how it came out?" The reason is that the alleged speedster was none other than a local cop who peeled off from a chat with a fellow officer at over 100 mph. That was pretty well established because the other officer said so, based on, what else, his radar gun. Then he reported his [not such a] buddy's burn-out to their chief. Apparently, the lead-footed cop was already persona non grata around the station, prompting his chief to bring a charge not of speeding but of reckless driving, even though it was the middle of the night and there were no other vehicles in the area at the time.

So the philosophical crux of the case, not unlike the tree in the forest, was: If you're going really, really fast on an empty road but there's no one there to be endangered by it except yourself, is it really reckless driving? I was all set to dig out my Kant and Nietzsche but thought I'd try the New Hampshire Supreme Court first. As it turns out, they'd recently gathered the wool on this very issue, pronouncing that if there's no potential harm to anyone but the foolhardy driver, there's no reckless driving.

So, since my job description doesn't include yelling a second-guess up to the top rung, I found the cop guilty of speeding and fined the hell out of him; I just didn't take the reckless driving bait. I may not be totally impartial, but this doesn't sound much like what Mr. Letter-to-the-Editor was complaining about, does it? Am I way off-base here? If so, just keep it to yourself.

And that wasn't all the guy said. His next paragraph went this way:

"This same judge let several illegal aliens off who clearly violated U.S. laws. When are our justices and courts going to back our law enforcement officials in upholding the laws made by our representatives? It is time for citizens to push these liberals out!"

I've already yammered on about our immigration cases as much as I plan to, and I'll accept that I'm more liberal about my decisions that some of my colleagues. After all, we've got a few former Marines among us and I couldn't get to the right of them without a shoe horn and an AK-47. Once again, though, the rap here bears little resemblance to what actually happened, in my humble opinion. Whatever. I just let it roll off as best I could, although it was interesting to get a first-hand view of what candidates for office face every day and how difficult and frustrating it must be for them to keep their records and positions accurately reported.

Just for instance, this morning on the way to court I heard that in the presidential campaign debate last night, Rudy Giuliani claimed that Mitt Romney raised taxes 11% while governor of Massachusetts. Not surprisingly, Romney denied the charge, saying he'd actually reduced taxes during his administration. I'm pretty sure only one of them could be correct, but which one, and how are the rest of us to know?

And how are our local letter readers to know whether I ought to be kicked out for gross disregard of the law due to my blatantly anti-law enforcement agenda? Luckily, no one's filed an impeachment petition yet, even the irate letter writer, although it may be in the mail.

By the way, despite all the venom and vituperation, I know the letter guy personally and thought we'd always been on cordial terms. With friends like that, I guess. . . .

There's a debate getting louder and louder in our State—others, too—about whether judges should continue to be subject to mandatory retirement ages. It's 70 here, by virtue of our 1792 Constitution. Those in favor of the limit seem to be "throw the bums out" conservatives who see nearly all judges as promoting their own liberal, activist agendas, without any degree of accountability, and who want to get rid of as many of the trouble-makers as soon as possible.

Ideally, they'd like to see all judges serving short terms and never getting comfortable enough to make decisions without considering the career consequences on the next election day. Then, if the chosen ones didn't make the "right" decisions, it wouldn't take long to boot them out and try to get someone else in there who'd "follow the law"—in the way they view it, that is.

On the other side of the issue are those who argue that 70 is the new 60—maybe even 55—and that with many people now living robustly into their 80's at least (that is, a lot more people than 200 years ago), there's no reason to lose out on all that pre-70 wealth of judicial experience and judgment just because some outdated, biological milestone has been reached.

In case you haven't parsed it yet, I'm of the latter view, and not just because I'll be bumping up against the gray ceiling pretty soon myself. No, it's because I do feel like it takes a number of years to get the right perspective on this work, and that to toss it all into the dumpster out back at 70, without any consideration for whether the individual judge might still have a few years of effective deciding left, is counter-productive to maintaining a competent cadre of judges.

I'd even go for a three-score-and-ten reconfirmation process, to let all the nay-sayers vent about the cantankerous old fool, and then put the issue to an "up or down vote" in the Executive Council, where a new judge would have to be approved anyhow. Do it all again in another 5 years, too, so you won't have to worry that some nursing home patient in a drool-stained black bathrobe will wander onto the bench and ramble incoherently. I'd probably be out of work already if that was the test.

The bottom line for me is that if we let U.S. Supreme Court justices make decisions affecting the course of our very lives until they themselves decide whether they've staggered over the hill, might we not take the chance that I'll screw up some $50 small claim because my hearing aid was off and I didn't catch some nugget of critical information from the plaintiff? Eh?

One of the likely raps against post-70 judges might be their tendency to nap on the bench, because, as we all know, that's de rigueur for people of such advanced age. In fact, I can hardly wait. I recall with pleasure the naps I often snatched—at 22—before the late nights of law school prep, and I hope to put a similar bookend on the other top end of my legal career when the time comes.

Actually, a Superior Court colleague who's younger than I am was recently brought up on charges of dozing off during a trial, although she was eventually cleared after a very high profile and extremely embarrassing hearing. I don't think anyone claimed she was multi-tasking on purpose, just that she didn't—or couldn't—stay awake and hadn't taken a recess to splash on some water and snap out of it. She never admitted losing consciousness, but she must have been pretty drowsy or no one would have noticed. It could have been plain old insomnia the night before, or maybe some cold medicine that warned against operating heavy machinery (like the wheels of justice), or perhaps she just stayed up 'til the bitter end of an extra-inning Red Sox game. (I hope at least they won.)

Whatever the reason, I guess I don't understand why this accidental lapse, even if true, was deemed a capital offense and warranted all the attention usually accorded wanton abuse of judicial responsibilities. Maybe now she gets ordered to take her vacation sooner than she'd planned or has to be tested for narcolepsy, or maybe she has to head for bed after the 7th inning. But really, getting de-robed and hounded from the bench like someone who took a bribe, which is the way the media made it sound?

If she's a lousy judge, then hit that issue squarely, but let's not make a federal case over something that was surely unintentional in the first place. I mean, who would really pick a conspicuous setting like that to nod off, with several dozen people staring you in the face and with important rulings to make every few minutes? Was this actually as outrageous and news-worthy as all those other things public officials are doing wrong, consciously, on a daily basis? No, but it's fodder for the cannons that are rolled up to the gunnels whenever there's a chance to claim judges are under-worked, over-paid and unaccountable to anyone for rulings that advance their own secret wish lists without regard for the rule of law.

For my part, I don't think I've ever committed that unspeakable indiscretion—snoozing on the job, that is—although some of the lawyers I've listened to make it an awful challenge not to go completely slack-jawed and slide right out of my chair. Maybe someone should review the tapes of my beleaguered colleague's case and see whether the lawyers should be charged with contributory, sleep-inducing monotony. If so, they should be banned from courtrooms and sentenced to spend the rest of their careers representing the estates of retired judges who've already nodded off for good.

Some people don't need anyone causing trouble for them because they do a much better job of it themselves. Today a fellow from just over the border in Massachusetts was standing in front of me with a blank look on his face and a charge of DWI to deal with. Despite an uneasy feeling that he wasn't completely absorbing my unusually thorough explanation of his rights and the long-term consequences of a conviction, he insisted on pleading guilty, in order, he said, to get it all behind him as quickly as possible. He didn't qualify for a court-appointed lawyer on the charge or I would have insisted on it; that's how clueless he seemed. So after doing the best I could to lay it all out for him, we finalized the sentence and, as I always do, I asked him whether he could get home without driving—since I'd just relieved him of his right to do so up here. I emphasize that because many people come to court without realizing they'll be license-less when they leave the premises and won't even be able to drive back to where they came from. He said he planned to call for a ride and then left to see the clerk about paying his fine.

That was that. We moved on down the docket and I didn't give it another thought—until the fellow was standing there again about an hour later, this time in handcuffs, charged with driving away from the courthouse at the wheel of his car. Now we were talking about an even more serious offense that requires a mandatory jail sentence. This time he acknowledged that he'd better have a lawyer, which this offense provides for, mumbling as he was led away that he was just driving across the street to McDonald's to get a coffee and wait for his parents to come pick him up.

I won't say anymore at this point, because the guy will have the right to remain silent if we try this case, and the State will have the burden of showing he was on his way to the drive-through window. Let's say they do that successfully, though. My question is why anyone who's been warned not to drive would risk it when you can see the golden arches from the prosecutor's office—and from the bench, for that matter—and when you can walk to McDonald's in less time than it takes to buckle up? Sometimes people don't need guns to shoot themselves in the foot.

Let me comment briefly on what may be going through your mind at this point—other than how many more pages you've got ahead of you here. Correct me if I'm wrong, but you're probably wondering how I can hear that last guy's case when I've already heard him blurt out what he did at his arraignment. Right?

The short answer is that we hear so many cases, one after the other (remember the Lucy analogy), that by the time this guy comes back for trial in a month or two, I'll have absolutely no recollection of him (he wasn't wearing a gas mask or a white sheet), much less the comment he made, and the slate will be as clean as a whistle. Another reason the slate will be so uncontaminated is that my advanced age prevents new information from taking any firm hold unless reinforced many times in rapid succession, and then it's only a 50-50 proposition. Cathie would be happy to confirm that for you.

The main reason, though, for pressing on despite the information leak is that it happens all the time and we just don't have any choice in a court like this. If this was Manchester or Nashua or any other court a few rungs up the ladder where there are multiple judges all the time, we'd simply flip this guy over to another courtroom and there'd be no fear that the well might have a skunk in it. Here, though—and in most other courts with part-time judges—there's only one judge available day in and day out and you'd have to transfer the case to an entirely different court at least 20 miles away; then everyone would have to troop over there for trial. I'm pretty sure that wouldn't make any of the participants too tickled, and in all but the most serious cases the prosecutors might well drop the whole business to avoid the trip and the overtime their departments would have to pay to get the arresting officers there. So, everyone lets these blips fade away and assumes we judges can erect something like a Chinese wall between what we hear one time and what we can legitimately base a decision on.

This is also totally different from the way the process works where there are jury trials, which we don't have at this court level (despite a pilot project a few years ago). When I mentioned back there that the press was sitting in the jury box during our immigration cases, it's because our courthouse was built when it looked like we might be doing the "12 Angry Men" [and Women] thing here, too. That project was aborted, though, either because the Superior Court judges didn't want their jury trial turf encroached, or because someone concluded that our largely part-time judges weren't sharp enough to give the right jury instructions and would bugger the whole thing up.

Anyhow, where there are jurors, they are carefully protected by the judge from hearing any shred of testimony or evidence they're not supposed to. If something big pops out that shouldn't—like the fact that an insurance company may be paying the damages for an accident, which is a common faux pas—there's a great gnashing of judgely teeth, the case comes to screeching halt, the infected jury is sent home, and the whole trial has to reboot with a spanking new 12 that haven't been contaminated with the taboo information.

On the other hand, our cases often go like this: The cop testifies that he yanked the surly kid out of the car because he was worried about his (the cop's) safety and wanted to frisk him (the kid) for weapons. While patting the kid down, he didn't feel anything hard or dangerous like a gun or knife, but he felt something soft and crinkly that he was sure was a baggie of marijuana, though he didn't have any other reason to think so— no odor of dope in the car, no roach in the ashtray, etc. Instead of letting it pass (because it clearly wasn't a weapon), he told the kid to empty his pockets, and lo and behold, there was the incriminating weed.

So now I know the kid had a stash of marijuana, which makes finding him guilty of possession pretty much a slam dunk, you say. The trouble is, the kid's lawyer doesn't take all this lying down and claims the contraband was snatched illegally because the pat down was lawful for weapons only, and producing none, had to stop there. Beyond that point, it became just a fishing expedition, which is never a wise trip for a cop to take when we're talking search and seizure rights. I agree, and reject the baggie as evidence, but still know that the kid was really guilty except for the tiny technicality of the Constitution.

At that point, everyone's counting on me to develop a quick case of Alzheimer's about that baggie, and so I do—as would my colleagues—telling the kid he gets to hang onto his fine money this time, but he'd better spend it on a Slim Jim and some Red Bull from now on, or even his constitutional rights may not save his bacon if the cops go by the book next time.

What makes the process work is the little birdie whispering in my ear: "Look, if you're not going to play by the rules, or if you're just going to bend and distort them to make the cases come out the way you want, you may, ironically, become the darling of the gun-toting, law-and-order fruitcakes, but there'll be a whole lot more wrong with your judging than taking a cat nap on the bench."

Last Friday I attended one of our increasingly rare judges' conferences. We used to have several of these every year, and they were usually two or three day sessions at an old hotel somewhere up north that we could pretty much take over. This one was in and out in about six hours and it was held at a drafty banquet room in a poorly-maintained Manchester restaurant.

It was nice to see my long lost compadres, but it had been so long since our last gathering that I had to peek at a lot of name tags to come up with greetings for people I used to know well. There were also quite a number of new judges I hadn't met at all and will never remember unless we get reacquainted more than once every presidential election year.

This particular session was on the growing tendency for people to self-represent themselves (it's also called being pro se, but you Latin scholars knew that). We needed professional guidance about this trouble-fraught phenomenon because people say and do the darnedest things when they don't have lawyers who know (or should know) the rules.

Not surprisingly, my colleagues were all over the lot in this minefield. Some thought the self-represented should be held to strict compliance with even the most arcane court rules, just like everyone who shows up with—and pays—a professional mouthpiece with knowledge of those ins and outs, while others felt the court has an obligation to loosen up the rules considerably and to provide guidance to people who need/want to represent themselves, all in the interest of achieving "substantial justice".

That raises an interesting conundrum. When we think about the self-represented segment of our constituents, we tend to assume that everyone would hire a lawyer if they could afford one. There's a growing knot of people, though, who distrust or dislike lawyers and make a voluntary choice to go it alone. And should those folks be treated just the same as the indigents who just can't afford a lawyer? If it makes any difference in your thinking, I will add that many who purposely go solo seem to have a large smelly cow chip on their shoulders and radiate antagonism toward the system as a whole, the judge being at the root of the problem in their view.

Consequently, the goal of many of these folks is not just to prevail, but to co-opt the process for their own purposes, even to the detriment of everyone else's rights. Instead of presenting their claims and defenses as expeditiously as possible, their approach is often to monopolize the court's time, as though they'll win by filibustering the issues and by wearing out everyone's patience, including the judge's. They file repetitious and rambling, almost stream-of-consciousness, pleadings, and if their positions don't carry the day, they continue filing objections and motions until they convince themselves the judge is out to get them—and then they file an indignant complaint with the Judicial Conduct Committee. If you've guessed that I see this self-represented constituency as different than those who are going it alone by necessity, or who are making a good faith attempt to understand and comply with the rules, you've nailed me.

As for the latter who are doing the best they can, I have no problem pointing them in the direction of the right forms and instructions they need—the recipe, if you will—and then leaving it to them to bake the cake for themselves. If they get most of the ingredients in there, even if the thing looks pretty messy when it comes out of the oven, they'll get credit for substantial compliance and I'll interpret their efforts liberally, figuring anyone's going to be able to tell it's supposed to be a chocolate cake even if it looks like mud pie.

To shift the metaphor, what I won't do is to put my thumb on their side of the scale to such an extent that there's no potential for a lawyer to add any value for someone making the financial sacrifice to hire one. You see, I don't share a popular view that lawyers are a cancer on the system and that we'd all be better off if the courts could be weaned away from them—like trying to get rid of cigarette smoking by making it more expensive and inconvenient for people to light up.

Actually, my experience is just the opposite. When I survey the docket prior to a session, I'm always relieved to see at least one lawyer involved in a case. Contrary to the conventional wisdom, and despite all the stereotypical jokes at lawyers' expense, even the greenest lawyers greatly facilitate the processing of cases, usually by helping to resolve them, rather than by forcing all of them into long, convoluted hearings—which is nearly always the result when both parties are self-represented and have no idea how to engage in productive settlement negotiations.

Back to the judges' conferences. The longer ones were often a waste of time when it came to the official content—how to reduce the stress of the bench is one I recall, where we were all given small Nerf balls to throw at each other when we thought they were full of grits. Even the lamest sessions, though, afforded time to meet informally and talk over the challenging experiences we all bump up against (see everything I've already written so far). Those sessions probably reduced stress more than anything, because we came away with a sense that we weren't entirely alone out there, and that we were all struggling with the same challenges. In fact, I often felt pretty good on the drive home, thinking at least I didn't screw up as bad as that judge did— or at least I didn't have to worry about that cluster of muck in our court (yet at least).

I was often amazed, too, at the different approaches my colleagues took with virtually the same situation. One would try to reason with and calm down a customer who's lost it in the courtroom—that's my approach—while another would just toss the person in the holding cell and wait for an apology for some rude affront. One would ream out or fine an attorney for being late, while another would let the random indiscretion roll off his back—which I do many times a week, particularly for the public defenders who always seem like holiday postal workers in ties and skirts. You know, with that glazed look in their eyes like they're about to crack under the never-ending onslaught of new cases.

Still, despite the variety of approaches, there's nothing like having others in the same lifeboat to make you feel like maybe you'll survive after all.

I sense there's at least one other big difference about the way judges do their business in our tidal backwaters. Some of my colleagues prefer to haul the lawyers and prosecutors into their chambers at the drop of a hat and sort out all the preliminary issues there—stuff like, should the drug evidence be squelched because of how the cops came up with it, or will the judge buy the plea deal the parties have worked out.

My colorful predecessor used to cram all of us into the glorified closet that was his chambers and demand a thumbnail summary of the evidence before starting a trial he was hoping to avoid—'cause he was a part-timer himself—whereupon he'd tell us how he was planning to rule. That way, he said, you could take your appeal without having to waste your time on what was certain to be a fruitless run-through.

It was great if he saw things your way—your work was largely done without having to swear in a witness—but if the unpredictable pendulum of justice swung the other way, your fate was pretty well sealed and no Oscar-winning amount of histrionics for your client's benefit was likely to stem the predetermined march toward guilt. I'm still wearing the scars of defeat from many such futile efforts.

It's taken me so long to get this down on paper that I've now been to another judges' conference, this one about how to deal as best as possible with mentally-ill defendants.

I don't know whether mental illness is a more prevalent societal problem in the 21st century or whether we're just diagnosing it more often and more broadly than ever before. What I do know is that as a young lawyer 30 years ago, I never remember anyone suffering— or claiming to suffer—from anxiety or panic disorders (other than from having to come to court in the first place), post-traumatic stress disorder, or major depression, just to name a few of the ones I can think of. We occasionally heard about one of these ailments, but the person was treated like they had one leg shorter than the other, and no one considered it a defense to the offense charged.

Now we if someone even mentions one of these names, the whole process often grinds to a stop right there. In fact, the consequence of any of these conditions is usually that the person is not competent to stand trial, or at least not without considerable treatment, including years of therapy and high-powered (literally mind-altering) medication in many cases. And mental illness in all its permutations has gotten so prevalent that some of our courts have set up special "mental health" sessions to deal with nothing but this geometrically-expanding segment of our constituents.

I'll start by saying I'm not dismissing or discounting the seriousness of these illnesses. After all, it would be hard otherwise to explain why people increasingly walk into schools, public meetings and shopping malls and start shooting everyone in sight. I'll overlook for now that despite the voices in their heads, they're typically armed with military assault weapons that they're constitutionally able to acquire even easier than a pint of cheap wine (I'll get started on that subject again later).

Even here in New Hampshire not long ago, a deranged, disgruntled and heavily-armed coot—not a healthy mix—killed one of my colleagues by shooting her in the back, then gunned down a couple of others, none of whom had done anything memorable to incur his wrath. He would have kept on blasting away had he not died in a shootout with the local authorities, and so never got to describe the delusional basis for his deadly rampage—as if that would have provided reasonable justification.

In other cases, based on the notes they leave or the statements they make before they finally turn the guns on themselves—or before the cops do it for them—it's pretty clear these guys (and why is it always guys?) are seriously deluded about any number of weird impulses that tell them to resort to this kind of mass and random violence.

Maybe it's just that we have real names for what's going on in people's heads now, whereas we used to shrug our shoulders and just call these guys "wackos". I remember thinking that way in the '60's about the guy who started shooting people from the tower at the University of Texas, and then certainly about Charles Manson, and in the '80's about that Hinckley "nut" who shot Ronald Reagan because of something having to do with Jodie Foster. Just last week, too, there was the previously-model-student-who's-now-off-his-meds who suddenly shot up the campus at Northern Illinois University for no apparent reason.

The blossoming of labeled mental maladies has also led to increased requests by defense lawyers for evaluations to determine whether their clients are competent to stand trial. To be somewhat callous about these "tactics", if the lawyers can get a professional person to put one of the magic names on a client's mental state, they stand a good chance of sucking the wind out of the prosecution's sails and having their clients walk, perhaps with a largely hollow admonition to take their prescribed medications.

This was confirmed at the conference I just mentioned, where the State's psychiatrist noted that he now performs several times the number of competency evaluations he did when he first started keeping track. (A tragic postscript is that the psychiatrist himself recently died very suddenly—not because of the dramatic increase in workload, I hope.)

I'm somewhat at a loss to know what to make of all this. On one hand, there's no question that increased violence in our society is at least partially the fault of untreated mental illnesses, coupled (in my view) with the NRA's cowboy fixation on having unlimited access to all the guns and ammo we want, and on the inclination now to shoot first when settling our differences.

On the other hand—again in my view—there are too many people using marginal mental illness claims as a defense strategy, which not only keep eccentric bad guys from being held criminally responsible, but also leads to many seriously-ill people getting sprung free to offend again, perhaps really violently the next time. Without having done the research, I think we'd find that many of the tragedy-causers we've seen in recent years have passed through the criminal justice system, but have skated right out again without any accountability and without any sufficient assurance that they received the help they needed to prevent another round of explosive eruptions.

Oh, and in the meantime, it would help if we'd ensure they don't get their hands on things that shoot projectiles or blow stuff up. Just not gonna happen, though, that's all there is to it.

There was a front-page article in *The Keene Sentinel* on Saturday about how a vehicular homicide case had been plea-bargained by the prosecutor to get a conviction, much to the horror and dismay of the victim's outraged family who hadn't been consulted about the deal and who felt the loss of their loved one had been disrespected by letting the driver off so leniently. Interestingly, the large photo that appeared with the story wasn't of the prosecutor, the defendant, or even the victim, but the judge who validated this terrible miscarriage of justice by giving the agreed-upon sentence his official blessing.

I've known the judge in question since the first few weeks of my arrival in New Hampshire 34 years ago, and he's not only a good one but not nearly as mushy on crime as I'm probably thought to be. So my take on the story is this: The reporter's ear was bent severely by the family's vocal opposition to the deal; the factors pro and con giving rise to the proposed sentence were not adequately reviewed with the family, much less exposed to public view; and plea bargaining as a general practice has such negative connotations (like being a liberal) that this case presented an easy opportunity to take another pot shot at it.

As usual, the judge won't be able to say anything to defend his decision, and for that I feel his pain. Since it's not my case, though, I don't have to keep my big mouth shut. I'll just say that when you've got a high-profile and emotionally-charged case like this (we actually touched the case briefly for the probable cause hearing because the accident happened in one of our towns), courts need to be very careful before allowing a plea to go forward without ensuring that the prosecutor has given the family a thorough analysis of the case (and his or her decision-making), in order to get them on board with the plea, if at all possible.

I don't mean the judge should be hamstrung by what the victim's family wants in deciding whether to accept the plea—they probably wanted the kid executed in this case—but the family needs to be well educated about why the deal behind door #2 makes sense. Maybe there's a real problem with proving the charge that might enable a really despicable deed to go completely unpunished—a missing witness, a critical piece of evidence that the rules wouldn't allow to be used, or a confession the defendant made without first having his rights explained, to name a few common snags.

If the family fully understands those potential problems, they might prefer to take the retribution in the hand, rather than go for two life sentences in the bush—and risk having the defendant skate out the back door entirely. If the family wants to roll the dice no matter what, the prosecutor still has to make the call, but maybe the family's reaction will at least be tempered by having been in on the huddle and understanding what prompted the deal. Who knows what happened here; all I know is what I read in the paper.

One more tidbit about plea bargaining: It's absolutely necessary, no matter what its slimy reputation. Without it there would be so many trials that we'd be running three shifts, 365 days a year, and part-time judges would be a distant speck in the rear view mirror. Just in this court we often have 20 cases (sometimes many more) scheduled for trial on a given day. Let's say they all took 20 minutes, which is way less than even the simplest ones usually eat up. That's almost 7 hours, even if no one comes in for emergency DV restraining orders, and we never need to break for the potty or a quick banana. Our day is only 7 ½ hours long, and if we need more time, we either pay overtime to our staff—a distinct budgetary no-no—or I turn out the lights and lock up whenever I'm finally done. If we really don't get finished with all the trials, then we just compound our problems on another day.

And this doesn't build in any time for arraignments—people's first appearance when they tell us whether they want a trial—of which we usually have 25 or 30, each eating up another five or ten minutes. That's another couple of hours, and it would definitely keep me from getting home in time to play along with *Jeopardy*, much less to see who's getting voted off on *The Voice*.

So, the line has to be drawn somewhere, and plea bargains—reasonable ones, that is—are the only solution we can afford. What's actually reasonable, though, is always the rub. I'm not talking about giving the ranch away on charges that could easily be substantiated if the case went to trial. I'm talking about calculated compromises based on careful assessments of the risks of trial. When those deals are proposed, it's the judge's job to decide whether what's on the table is within the range of predictable outcomes.

That's what my buddy judge did in the case that got me started down this street, and I have no doubt he got the math right. It's just that someone needed to clue in the victim's family about how the pluses and minuses were being totaled. It's sort of like when you were doing math in school. If you showed your work but got the wrong answer, you'd still get partial credit. Just the wrong answer wouldn't get you anything; in fact, the teacher would probably think you copied it off the girl in front of you, and send you to see the principal.

Nothing's more polarizing than when politicians start blasting judicial activism and preaching judicial restraint. You can read a lot of confusing stuff about the fine line between those philosophical extremes, but I've got a simpler rule of thumb: Judicial activism is when the judge knows the result he wants and then comes up with a legal theory, usually thinly-veiled and implausibly lame, to get there. Judicial restraint works the other way: The judge determines what the law really is, and the result—whatever that result might turn out to be—flows smoothly and logically from it. If you look carefully, you can nearly always tell which way it went.

Don't get me wrong, I'd love just to make up the law as I go along; it would make the job a whole lot easier, and I'm sure I'd like the results better, too. The trouble is, if you start fudging things that way, pretty soon you're taking campaign contributions from lawyers with an agenda, and before long that agenda starts showing up in your decisions. OK, maybe not in New Hampshire (no elections, remember), but if I can make the cases come out however I want, pretty soon I might start taking pens home for personal use—that's more like the scale of things here—and who wants his case heard by a pen thief?

Last week the temptation to test the waters of judicial activism became more than theoretical for me. A twitchy young guy with a degree from the Marines and a chip on his shoulder about "the Man" appealed the local police chief's suspension of his concealed pistol permit. The chief said the kid had a suspended fine for theft of something stupid I can't remember, and he said that showed "questionable judgment and character." The permit statute allows for an appeal to court, so the righteously indignant kid promptly marched himself over here from the PD and dumped the whole thing in my lap.

Now if you've been paying attention at all so far—a dangerous assumption, I realize—you'll know I'd like nothing better than to yank that gun out of the kid's hand, whether concealed or otherwise, smack him upside the head with it, and tell him to get himself a big dog if he needs personal protection. Unfortunately, the statute says nothing about smacking or dogs, but it does require "clear and convincing proof" of "just cause" in order to deny a guy his beloved hidden gun. Maybe I'm just lacking in imagination, but I couldn't see how a suspended fine for a non-violent theft made the grade—so I reversed the chief's call and reinstated the kid's permit.

Now I'm in that weird no man's land where the kid probably won't shoot me with his gun, but where I may get blasted to smithereens by the entire police department. I'm envisioning getting stopped for a headlight out and ending up looking like Swiss cheese when I reach into my jacket for my license. The cops' story will go, "We swear it looked like he was going for a gun, so we shot him 43 times in self-defense."

Important disclaimer: None of the police departments in our area are weapon-happy. In fact, most of them have saved the lives of more than one defendant by showing restraint in the face of circumstances where they might have legitimately started blasting away.

Before wrapping up this low-rung, occupational memoir, I want to say a word about how I got into this line of work in the first place. A lot of it has to do with Abraham Lincoln, which would leave him scratching his head if he could still do that after what Booth put him through.

You see, my mother's mother was from southern Illinois, the "Land of Lincoln", and she talked about the tall man in black all the time (and I don't mean Johnny Cash). She even claimed he'd sat in one of her rickety old wooden chairs and that the dark stain on one arm was where he'd bled after cutting himself whittling. (I wish I knew where that chair was now and could run some DNA tests on it—I might be able to retire a little early.) My grandmother was born less than 30 years after Lincoln died, and she said her parents remembered seeing him riding the circuit as a practicing trial lawyer, long before he gained even statewide prominence, much less headed off for Washington. Then, too, my grandmother's brother, my great uncle, was also a lawyer and a pretty Lincolnesque-looking character himself (think Jimmy Stewart), so the profession was held in pretty high esteem when the family gathered around the dining room table. The seed was planted there but remained dormant awhile.

Fast forward to the war in Vietnam and the critical importance of a student deferment to keep you from ending up face down in a rice paddy in a place you couldn't pronounce. As my remaining college days dwindled dangerously in the late '60's, troop levels were multiplying like ebola cases, and my own deferment appeared seriously in jeopardy. Just before I got the dreaded "Good Morning Vietnam!" letter from my draft board, I looked in the mirror, asked myself what Lincoln would do, and quickly decided it was time to water that old law school seed.

I don't think that plan had to do with being chicken, but maybe I've mentally blocked out that unpatriotic character flaw. I recall more the sense of utter futility and tragic human sacrifice [of perhaps myself, as well] from that misguided boondoggle, which was also dawning on lots of others about the same time. It was ill-conceived to begin with and got worse from there—remind you of anything?—yet way more young men were being sacrificed there than even in the more recent post-9/11 debacles.

Eventually, I, too, got poked, prodded and branded I-A, even after showing the docs much more than they cared to know about my purported back and knee problems. The experience was "Alice's Restaurant Redux", though Arlo Guthrie and I never ended up naked together.

Then, just as I was swallowing hard and fearing that my first year of the Paper Chase would be my last, a lifeline suddenly materialized, courtesy of that sweetheart, President Nixon, and the lottery system he cooked up to re-structure the draft. Cathie and I sat on the sofa in our tiny married student digs, unable to blink or breathe as we watched the Selective Service guy pulling birth dates out of a bin, like lottery numbers. And then for the one and only time in my brushes with games of chance, I hit the jackpot. Of the 365 places that April 20th could have popped up, it held out gamely until 356, and just like that I was through the rapids and on to clear sailing toward my JD (Just Deferred).

If I'd been number 56 instead, I'm sure I'd have manned up and gone—and I don't mean to Canada—but just as surely I'd have used my fledgling powers of persuasion to try to land a desk job somewhere in Indiana. The rest, as they say, is history—spineless and boring history, no doubt—but history nevertheless.

Do I regret not being one of the almost 60,000 who didn't come back from that tragic conflict—or who came back without a limb and dragging a lifelong case of PTSD? Not a bit. Do I regret not having done more for my country in some other non-life-threatening way? I do, and I'm still working on a plan, even now, to make up for it. I swear I'm telling the truth, so help me.

Sticking with Lincoln for a moment, which is never a bad idea, I note that we're coming up on his 200th birthday. When he was born in that dirt-poor, one-room cabin in backwater Kentucky, his chances of rising to the presidency were akin to hitting the Powerball—once I learned the real odds of that, I quit buying the tickets. He didn't have as much formal education as my 7 year-old granddaughter, yet somehow made himself into the most inspiring wordsmith of all our presidents—also managing in the process to save the Union and free the slaves. Any one of those accomplishments would have launched him onto the presidential all-star team, but he hit the trifecta.

When he left home in Springfield, he told his well-wishers that the challenges he faced were greater than those that confronted Washington. It wasn't an exaggeration. By the time he took the oath on March 4, 1861, seven states had already packed up and left home, and four more were halfway out the door. At that moment there were no completely united states and there was a distinct chance the country of the same name would end up just another failed historical experiment—sort of like the Weimar Republic. And who remembers that?

So how did he pull it off? The historians keep taking their shots, but they rarely seem to get their arms all the way around it. One key is that Lincoln read a lot. It may have been for fun at first, but it helped him develop a keen ear for what makes language effective. He learned how to turn a phrase that would vividly and memorably make his point, and he didn't bury it in a swamp of verbosity that would make it hard to find. Remember, in those days when you said something out loud, that was basically it. If you wanted people to remember it, you had to make it succinct and pithy enough for them to repeat to others.

On that score (four score?), the parallels with Obama are profound. Lincoln wasn't a serious presidential candidate until his speech at Cooper Union in New York in February, 1860, rocketed him into the top echelon of contenders. Obama was a little-known Illinois state senator until his riveting speech at the 2004 Democratic convention put him in the national spotlight. You know, "There is no red America and no blue America; there's only the United States of America. That's right up there with "of the people, by the people, for the people", in my humble estimation.

The other mega-factors for me are that Lincoln was infused from head to toe with common sense, and he was a pragmatist who didn't have a doctrinaire bone in his body. He preached for three years that the key to winning the war was attacking the Confederate armies until they couldn't respond, not trying to capture the flag flying over Richmond. When he finally found U.S. Grant, the only general who shared that view and was willing to walk the talk, the war was over in 11 months.

Likewise, just a couple of months before the big proclamation, when he was accused of being soft on abolition, he said his goal was to save the Union, not to destroy slavery. In fact, he promised that if he could save it by freeing none of the slaves or by freeing all of the slaves or by freeing some and "leaving others alone," he'd do whatever it took And he did.

On the flip side, Johnson and Nixon were so stubborn about winning in Vietnam—we'd never lost a war and they weren't about to start, dammit—that almost 60,000 Americans were sacrificed needlessly. (I just got back from a vacation in Vietnam and the former Vietcong were nice as pie. What were we thinking?) Then there's our last CIC, who not only started a wholly unnecessary war that's blown up our rep around the world, but then wouldn't let go of the bone before sending more than 4,000 of our best and bravest to their deaths so far. Forty-three was no 16, and now we'll see how 44 shapes up, though he professes that 16 was his kind of guy, so at least he's got that much going for him.

Our central court office in Concord just sent me an ink stamp that says "order vacated". I don't know how to take this. Is it a not-too-subtle suggestion that I get so many things wrong I may need an expedited way to get back on the right track? If so, maybe they could also tell me which decisions to use it on, so I don't screw up the ones I've managed to get right the first time. I'd also like to know whether I'm the only one who received this dubious gift or whether these quick-correct devices were also dispersed among my colleagues. If the latter, I don't feel quite as severe a blow to my self-esteem, although there must have been a pretty major eruption of particularly stupid and outrageous orders to warrant spending the judicial branch's scarce resources on all these expensive labor-saving devices. I mean, I can write "order vacated" just about as fast as I could find the stamp and get it all inked up.

The news deliverers have been completely preoccupied this week by the revelation that New York Governor Elliot Spitzer has stumbled off the moral high ground and into the arms of a high-priced prostitute. No matter how you spin it, it's a tragedy of epic proportions for the

Spitzer family, particularly the governor's wife who stood stoically behind her husband while everyone in the world (of the male variety at least) wondered what was wrong with her that had caused him to spend not-even-a-small fortune on the company of other women. Seriously, though, a high altitude fall from grace like this is a real shot to the solar plexus, in that it shakes the very foundation of my [our?] perpetually precarious faith in the innate honesty and goodness of human nature.

It's also further glaring proof that there's just no way to know what's really going on inside anyone or whether what they say squares with what they know to be the truth—do I hear an echo? Spitzer's always seemed—and that's the critical word—like such a Mr. Clean about ferreting out corporate corruption and other crimes of moral turpitude, yet now we see that he's been a total hypocrite about it the whole time. He professes contrition at this point, but it's clear he'd still be shacking up like the cad he is if he hadn't been snagged in the sting that, ironically, was made possible by the electronic financial monitoring system he himself put in place. The guy must be arrogant beyond even his statemate, the Donald (and that's a high bar to clear), because he can't possibly be as stupid as he'd otherwise have to be.

This is a particularly troubling revelation for a guy in my shoes, because it adds significant ballast to my earlier discourse about people's propensity to lie their asses off if it serves their personal interests, and if they think they can get away with it. It also makes it awfully hard not to go completely cynical about any of the testimony I hear, unless it's backed up by objective corroboration. I may be able to come back from this blow eventually, but it's going to take a lot of positive reinforcement, and even one more serious setback could prove fatal. I feel like the poor trusting spouse who wants to believe her repeatedly philandering partner won't ever stray again, until he does.

The ink wasn't even dry on that last lament when less than 24 hours later I was totally down for the count. I'm still groggy, but I think this is the way it happened. The kid charged with aggravated DWI (that is, driving while being really drunk) after an accident on his way home from his friend's house, admitted to the trooper that he'd had a 6-pack before heading out and re-confirmed that story in a written statement at the station after being fully Mirandized ("you have the right to remain silent . . ."). Then he blew a number on the Intoxilizer that was more than twice the legal limit. No problem so far, and I was even admiring how cooperative and stand-up the kid had been about his monumental lapse in judgment. That's when the trouble started.

The State rested, and the defense lawyer proceeded to call three of the kid's party pals, all of whom testified, even after the most convincing oath I could muster, that the kid hadn't been anywhere near a 6-pack—in fact, hadn't drunk more than Coke—before driving off and flipping his Neon about 100 yards down the road. So he was stone-cold sober at the time of the accident, they all said, using just about the same words, and didn't start drinking until he walked back to the house and proceeded to drown his sorrows in many large glasses of undiluted vodka. That seemed like an odd story to offer up, not only because the defense lawyer knew what the kid himself had said about the 6-pack, but because it seemed implausible that a person just involved in a serious accident—one where the police were sure to show up and start asking hard questions—would voluntarily turn himself from merely a lousy driver into a totally blotto DWI suspect. Also, when you think about it, why would the kid admit to downing a 6-pack before the accident, which might well cook his goose, but say nothing about the vodka afterwards, which might get him completely off the hook? Unfortunately, the kid himself never took the stand to resolve these perplexing discrepancies, which prompted me to ask, when the dust settled, which of the utterly inconsistent versions of the facts the defense lawyer wanted me to put all my faith in. This is where I took the knockout blow.

The lawyer said he wasn't going to help me with the truth part, and that since there was no way for me to tell which version of the facts was the truthful one, I had to have reasonable doubt about which one to believe—and thus had to find his kid not guilty.

Now, if you've made it this far, you know I'm often presented with the dilemma where each side of a case offers a totally different take on the same situation (see the loan/no loan girls above), but this was the first time a defendant had come up with both versions himself and tried to bewilder me into saying not guilty. In the interest of trying to do the right thing—and to avoid the public gnashing of teeth—I took the case under advisement. Yet even after the last three days of almost constant reflection, I still don't know what to do.

One side of me just wants to believe the cooperative and stand-up kid—who couldn't possibly have had the guile to make up such a complicated plan of deception so soon after a discombobulating accident. That path would lead to a finding of guilty and the typical consequences. Next case. The other side, though, wants to find the kid guilty for the same reason, but also to refer the hotshot lawyer for ethics enhancement therapy and to report the three musketeers to the cops for a perjury investigation.

One thing is clear, however: I feel like a contestant on the '60's show "To Tell the Truth", where it's a given that someone's lying and I have to figure out who it is—only this isn't a game show and that oath I deliver isn't just for entertainment value. Another clear result: It's going to be a long time before I swallow anyone's testimony without a dose of salt as big as our highway department dumps out for winter road work. I think I said that just a couple of days ago, but I really, really mean it this time.

Remember the judge I thought got a bum rap for falling asleep at the wheel in her courtroom? Well, yesterday she finally succumbed to intense public pressure and resigned. Harsh result, you say, for something she never intended in any event. Ah, but that incident wasn't what did her in. Just as she seemed to have put that public nap thing behind her, she shot herself in the foot while wide awake.

It seems the judge's lawyer-husband was having problems of his own, not the least of which was getting disbarred and running up a lot of debts in the process. All that certainly would have been embarrassing to the judge, but not career-threatening. Where she jumped the shark was in using her non-judicial legal skills to set up a trust, and then help her husband slide his threatened assets into it just days before he was supposed to start paying off his debts. She said it was for "estate planning" purposes, which I guess it was if you mean hiding your assets from your creditors so you still have an estate. On the other hand, the judge had once been a member of the Judicial Conduct Committee, which left little doubt that she appreciated the rank aroma of this particular planning strategy.

I mention this sad tale of self-destruction not to rub it in on one of my colleagues, who's causing enough trouble for herself without my help, but because it slaps all of us upside the head. The public has a chronic suspicion that judges cruise along above the laws they nail everyone else with, and incidents like this one just underscore that feeling. Sure, they say, she got caught but there must be dozens who escape the ethical speed trap. It's what makes people wink and snicker when I tell them I'd get cuffed and stuffed the same as they would if I drove home after too many brewskies at the judges' conference. They assume the cops would either chauffer me home like a rock star or head in the other direction while I careened along toward my driveway. Not so, of course, but now even harder to convince them of because of my troubled benchmate's conspicuous flame-out.

I think a lot about time; always have. I think about it a lot more these days, as I motor past the two-thirds milestone of my judicial odyssey. Almost 18 years down, and just about 9 to go if I'm lucky enough to avoid the biological, oncological, and other -ogical obstacles rearing up before a nearly 61-year old, not to mention simply running out of gas or blowing a fuse along the road.

Not that it's a revolutionary observation, but the most intriguing characteristic of time is how it accelerates to warp speed as we ourselves are drastically slowing down. When we were kids, time seemed eternal. Trips in the car took forever, school classes seemed like they would never end, and waiting for your father to get home from work to dispense the discipline necessary to get you back on the right track was agonizing. All that time eventually passed, however, and another 50 years for me since then.

Today the years fly by like days, and it's hard to believe that what happened last year was more than a couple of weeks ago. You (Cathie, that is) carefully plan a once-in-a-lifetime trip to Africa for two years from now and suddenly it's a year and a half ago and you've already taken another vacation since then.

One of my favorite lines is from Jackson Browne's song "The Pretender", where he observes that "in the end they say it's the wink of an eye." Emily Gibbs makes a similar observation when she comes back from the cemetery to watch her family on a typical morning in the final act of *Our Town*, and countless other poets and writers, now long dead, have expressed the sentiment in their own memorable or forgettable words. ("Gather ye rosebuds while ye may. . . ." is another chestnut that comes to mind, and the proof of the pudding is that the guy who turned that phrase has been feeding insects for more than 300 years.) I keep trying to slow down my own steady march toward oblivion but I'm pessimistic; it's never worked for anyone else, and I'm pretty confident that everyone alive when Lee surrendered to Grant has also surrendered by now.

The only shred of a chance I've got is to try slowing down the perception of time racing away, by focusing on the moment in front of me and by pretending like I'll never do this or that thing again. Maybe I should posit a terminal illness and give myself six months to live—hypothetically, I hope. That would mean no longer being driven by my Blackberry (yep, got one) to the next stop on my schedule, but trying instead to savor what I'm doing right now—like the "slow food" or "mindfulness" people would have us do, savoring each bite and moment to the fullest extent.

That last tactic is particularly difficult here in court. The dockets are longer than ever and everyone wants to get it over with as soon as possible. The defendants who have jobs are losing money the whole time they're sitting around, so they want to get back on the clock, and the lawyers are always champing to get on to their next case somewhere else, where they're already an hour late. Indeed, if I could get through it all in an hour less time, I could get back to my office and return the calls and e-mails building up there. There may even be clients sitting in the conference room, drumming their fingers on the table, coming to a slow boil because I'm keeping them waiting, too.

So, despite my best intentions about taking a deep breath and breathing through my eyelids like the lava lizards of the Galapagos (see the dugout conversation in *Bull Durham*), that's a goal, not reality. And as I heft the new docket before each session, it's nigh impossible not to get caught back up in the swirl of it all and lose track of that elusive whiff of perspective.

Oops, really got to go—the clerk says the prosecutors have lots of pleas lined up for me. Apparently, no one has the time to come back another day and deal with the hassle of all that pesky evidence, so I need to help them cut and run and get back out there on the road. By the way, Jackson Browne's *Runnin' on Empty* is my all-time favorite. Freudian, right?

Lately, too, I've been having dreams about imaginary cases I've never actually seen in court. They're quite vivid and detailed and they involve the full cast of characters for whatever species of case it might be. Criminal cases seem to predominate, though there've been a smattering of juveniles to deal with, as well. Only one case presents itself at each session, so I know I'm just dreaming, but the frustrating part is that no matter how hard I work at them, I never get any of them fully resolved before the radio comes on in the morning. Maybe my subconscious is telling me I've been at this job too long.

No more dreams this week, although today's paper may produce a few nightmares. A woman we've never had any contact with in court wrote a letter to the editor that started out, "Why operate a district court if Mickey Mouse and Goofy are letting everybody off?" I'm not sure whether I'm the rodent or the mutt, but since there's no other critter on the premises but me, I must be some ghastly mutant hybrid of the two. Her beef appears to be that I let all the druggies and drunks off, while hammering all the hapless speeders and unlicensed drivers. I'm not sure how she'd know about that nefarious plan without ever having set foot in the courtroom, but she seems pretty sure of herself. Maybe it's just that my intentions are so blatant that she can put two and two together right from the weekly court report in the paper. Gee, and I thought I was being so careful to cover my tracks. Here I've been trying all these years to get the poor drunk drivers and drug users back out on the street (where we hope they'll bring us more business, of course) without anyone being the wiser, and now I've been caught red-nosed and exposed for the Goofy I am. Cathie told me not to worry about it; she said that's what people think anyhow, so this letter shouldn't come as much of a surprise. Maybe I have been at this job too long.

My father died two weeks ago. We were at the lake with the whole family for Memorial Day weekend. It was a gorgeous Sunday morning and I was sitting on the dock wandering through the *New York Times* when I heard the phone ring in the house. Despite lots of ups and downs over the past few months, my mother had feared that Pop might not make it through this weekend, so I held my breath while I waited to hear whether this was the call. It was, Mom saying he'd just taken one deep breath about 2:00 a.m. and that was it. We'd all been down there to say goodbye about a month before, and since then it had been like pins and needles every day. I'd find myself thinking about him during a hearing and then have to race to catch up with the evidence in order not to appear more out to lunch than usual. I think I managed successfully most times, as no one seemed [more than usually] horrified by the decisions I was making, but the wait for what was inevitable was starting to preoccupy me.

The rest of that beautiful day was a blur of booking flights and making sure things were lined up for the graveside service—my parents were always as religion-averse as I am, so the lack of a lot of singing and praying in a strange church wasn't going to be a disappointment. I reached our clerk at home and asked her to do her best to cover the week's sessions, but just to cancel them if she couldn't find a pinch hitter on such short notice—she couldn't. With all the cutbacks in judicial time, last minute needs like this are nearly impossible to fill, so a lot of kids dodged another boring lecture from the dorky judge and a lot more people got a welcome reprieve in coming up with their fine money.

We successfully battled the holiday weekend surge at the airports and got to the house in the midst of a constant stream of friends and neighbors who, in the best of Southern traditions, all came bearing their special dishes—blueberry dump cake, pimento cheese sandwiches, and enough fried chicken to decimate the local coops.

I struggled all night with whether to say something at the service, but in the end, due to 90+ degree heat and a lot of Pop's contemporaries teetering precariously in the sun, I kept my mouth shut and let others take charge for a change. The casket was draped with an American flag, and a detachment of Marines, I think, did a nice job of folding and presenting it to Mom, followed by a very moving rendition of Taps. Afterwards, as I watched these guys pack up their van, I couldn't help thinking how many other times they'd performed this detail recently, as the World War II soldiers who look so young and invincible in the old newsreels are now falling away at an alarming rate. Mom had mentioned that she wanted to conclude with *The Battle Hymn of the Republic*, but she didn't see how that would be possible out there at the cemetery. Cathie wasn't deterred, however, and when it seemed like we were all said and done, she just started singing. Everyone else joined in, and I did my best, as well, despite getting even more choked up than I usually do when I hear that fiercely patriotic song. The best part was that Mom got her wish, unexpectedly, and Cathie earned as much gratitude as if Julia Ward Howe herself had shown up.

I was surprised by how little emotion I felt during the trip. I think it was because Pop had died gradually for me over the past year or so and there was almost nothing left of his old self at the end. Also, it's hard not to be thankful for the 91 years of life he had. By all accounts, his childhood was happy and not lacking in anything he needed or wanted. He served his country with honor when it called on him and he came home in one piece. He was married to the Florida State homecoming queen for 62 years; he had a long and stable career, working for the same company the whole time; and he got to enjoy 30 years of retirement among his closest friends. What more could any of us hope for? In fact, most of us would settle for a lot less and be very grateful for it.

Back at the court the following week, a young public defender aggressively reamed us all out for delaying her juvenile's hearing while I was away. I let her vent her full tank of righteous indignation, all the while biting my badly scarred tongue. When she finished, I thought about asking her whether my father's death and the need to be with my 85 year-old mother for a few days were good enough cause for extending the hearing for a week, but then I passed on getting that personal and just explained that a family emergency had taken me out of town unexpectedly. She backed off reluctantly at that point and her client promptly pled to the charge. I'm giving her the benefit of the doubt because she didn't know the real story and I'm hoping she'll feel the need to drop everything, too, when her father's time comes.

Every time I sneak off on a vacation (Croatia this time—the Adriatic was gorgeous) and we manage to coax a colleague from another court to cover for me, all I hear when I get back is how tough they were on people paying their fines. "No one was allowed to leave the building until they came up with the money and it was amazing how many of them did it by the end of the day." So, instead of having two weeks to pay up, which is the slack I usually cut, and getting to go back to work to earn it, all those financially-challenged souls, which is nearly everyone these days, spend an agonizing day on the phone trying to scare up the funds, wondering what's going to happen if they can't pull it off and missing out on the money they might have made in the meantime. I guess it makes us look like titans of law and order to be so hard-nosed, but it ends up working an even greater hardship on people who are behind the eight ball already and wondering where next month's rent is coming from.

There is a line to be drawn, however, and on the other side of it are our cadre of notorious scofflaws who sorely need their feet held to the fire or we won't see them again until they run amuck next time. Most of those folks don't have jobs anyhow—I have no idea where they get what money they have, but they seem to spend it on tattoos and smokes, if you'll pardon the condescending lapse in PC-ness—so another two weeks isn't going to help much. They need to expect that if they can't come up with the dough, they're going to be working the fine off at $50 a day at the house of correction. (I've always loved that term, like the house of carpet.) Some of them, in fact, end up doing just that without batting an eye, but more likely, a disgusted parent or a girl/boyfriend will miraculously come to their rescue about the time we're dialing the phone to have the sheriff come get them. Either way, the theory is that they'll think twice before driving yet again with a suspended license or writing another bad check at the convenience store—but probably not, because history repeats itself on a small scale, too. And it's a good thing, because we'd never have enough customers to keep our bottom line in the black without our regulars, much like the airlines counting on their frequent flyers.

I've often lamented the state of parenting in the early years of the new millennium, but today it sunk to an even lower low. A barely teen came in charged with lovingly raising three 5-foot marijuana plants—hell, trees—probably enough to make joints for every kid in the school district. Yet instead of twisting the kid's ear off and encouraging some effective drug treatment before adult convictions start taking root, the mom assured me her son didn't have a drug problem at all; he "just wanted to see whether the plants would grow." Admittedly, she's got plenty on her plate as she and the kid's father slug it out over their divorce, but sticking her head in the sand like this is the quickest way to ensure that the state will have custody of the kid by the time they decide who gets the flat screen TV.

When it rains it pours. A little later in the day, we were faced with a 16-year old whose parents are already divorced and whose current POSSLQs don't like having the kid around. So, both parents—and I'm using the term very generously—were pushing me to let the kid move in with his 16 year-old girlfriend's family. Oh, and there's no harm done, because the kid's already impregnated her, so how much worse could it get? After finally recovering the ability to speak, I explained that while they might want to abandon their parental responsibilities and teach their son a lesson he'll always regret, the court wasn't going to be an enabler.

Instead, I closed the case, which had already accomplished as much as it could, given the raw parental material we were working with, and everyone left the courtroom happy as a clam. The kid probably thought he'd died and gone to heaven. I wonder whether he'll feel the same way in about nine months.

In case you've been in a cave the last six months, we're now wallowing in the worst economic quagmire in a long time. Some are comparing it to the Great Depression of the '30's, but I don't see it as quite that dire yet. Still, because New Hampshire is on a starvation diet when it comes to revenue sources even in the best of times, our court system is eating nothing but bread and water these days, so maybe the governor can button his fiscal pants.

What this means here in Jaffrey is that instead of getting our usual 155 or so session days to service the annual caseload—which is what they've always told us it takes to do the job—we now have only 135 days to handle the same number of cases. You do the math, but I'm thinking that's going to mean either a lot less time to spend on any one case or a considerable amount of unpaid overtime.

Please don't get me wrong, I'm not so big for my big black dress that I can't do my part alongside other state employees now working four-day weeks. On the other hand, we're not making widgets here and it's not like you can just ratchet up the assembly line to get the job done quicker. The cases do require a certain amount of judgment to handle properly—or at least not to screw up too royally if you're assuming the worst.

The problem is, if you keep doing your darndest at the usual pace, you keep falling farther and farther behind, and when the delays stretch to a certain critical length, the system begins to break down entirely. Witnesses disappear or get so foggy they're worthless, and the people who couldn't make bail end up spending more time in jail waiting for trial than if they'd pled guilty at arraignment. Then, after about six months you start getting motions to dismiss for failing to provide speedy trials—you know, that constitutional stuff.

And on top of all that, unlike the effect of recession on big screen TV sales, it turns out that the number of cases is inversely proportional to the current economic climate. Why? Well, because economic adversity breeds new business like a 30-pack in the hands of a teenager. When people can't pay their bills, they get sued for writing bad checks and for defaulting on their car loans, credit cards and medical expenses. That makes some of them desperate enough to turn to shoplifting or maybe cultivating a little marijuana to raise some extra cash. It also leads to the drowning of sorrows at the VFW on the way home from the unemployment office and then to pushing and shoving about it with one's domestic partner. We'll get through it, but it won't be pretty, and there'll be some bloody noses.

No, it won't be pretty, but I'm actually a lot more concerned these days about a colleague at a neighboring court who's almost exactly a year younger than I am. Shortly before Christmas he and his wife were out shopping for a tree, when he fell down in the lot a couple of times without apparent cause—and it wasn't sticker shock over the price of the trees. It turns out he'd been having headaches for a few months, so this episode prompted his wife to get him right to the emergency room where they didn't see anything obvious but they X-rayed him up and down. A strange mass appeared in the photo of his head, so they rushed him to the big hospital up at Dartmouth and opened him up for a better look. The thing was about the size of a large lemon, and they worked for six hours to get out as much of it as possible. Then they all waited for the biopsy results.

By now you've probably guessed that it wasn't good news; in fact, it was a dangerously malignant brain tumor. The judge is back at home now and as chin-up about it as he can be under the circumstances. We talked yesterday about what happens going forward, the first step being a trip to Boston today for another opinion about the best plan of attack. I'm hoping they come up with an aggressive counter-offensive of radiation and chemo that will clean up the rest of what's there, but wishful thinking is what we all resort to at times like this. So many cancers go into hiding for a while once they're zapped, only to crop up again in a couple years in another place, just when there might be reason to think they're dead as a doornail.

I have more than a passing interest in all this. Not only is my robe mate a valued friend of 30 years, but I myself am about six years beyond having a malignant melanoma carved off my chest. The dermatologist said he got it all and that there weren't any rogue cells in the area around the area, but something must have gone wrong in the first place to incubate those mutant invaders, and who says there couldn't be another batch hatching somewhere else in there. I'm keeping my fingers crossed, observing even more numerous superstitions than I usually do, getting my annual skin checks, and watching like a hawk for any weird changes in skin color. As for my judge buddy, I'm sending all the good vibes I can in his direction and hoping for miracles.

Cathie and I have been avid supporters of our really fine professional summer theater since the '70s, and we haven't missed a production there since Jimmy Carter was president. In honor of the theater's 75th anniversary this summer, they're doing *Our Town*, which Thornton Wilder wrote about this area in the 1930's while holed up at the MacDowell Colony, a famed writers' and artists' colony here.

If you're not familiar with the play, one of the themes is that we all take our lives too much for granted and fail to savor those many, many (most, really) days when nothing at all of any lasting importance happens. In the final act—which I've yet to watch without tearing up, even though I can lip sync all the lines at this point—Emily, the young protagonist who's died wants just one more day on earth (remember, I dropped her name a few pages ago). She gets special dispensation from the Stage Manager to come back on a morning like so many others and can't believe her family members aren't swirling the precious moment around their taste buds like a fine Merlot the way she is.

Play or no play, I think about this mindless human shortcoming all the time and yet am just as deficient as the next guy no matter how hard I fight it. Dull and boring days aside, I can't even remember most birthdays and Christmases, which you'd think would imprint themselves on the hard drive more indelibly than the typical Tuesday. In fact, if I hadn't written all this stuff down within moments of its occurrence, you'd have been finished with the ordeal of reading it in about two and a half double-spaced pages, and you could have spent a lot more time trying to keep track of your own lives. It would have been a tragedy, though, to miss that one about the Gas Mask Lady—am I right?

I'm not sure why the spirit moved me, but I've written a poem for this holiday season. I can't remember ever doing that before, unless it was some sappy doggerel about Cathie's birthday or my juvenile attempt to compose a limerick as memorable as the one about Nantucket guy. Maybe it has something to do with wanting to branch out from my comfort zone and figuring a decent poem is easier to accomplish than playing the piano, which I'm still hoping to do but probably won't get to until I have a couple of hours a day to work on my scales.

Anyhow, it's not Eliot or Auden, or even Seuss, but at least it's mine:

> The bailiff taps quietly at my door and
> I shrug on the dark trappings of authority
> While this week before the silent night
> Many anguished souls wait wondering
> Whether they will spend meager earnings
> Here or, worse, what might have been
> Precious hours with familiar faces
> Instead with joyless, nameless strangers
> Which I am charged to determine, hoping
> Always I may deliver a lawful dose of coal
> Without dousing all tiny embers of hope
> For the new year.

It's a week now since Barack Obama was sworn in (the second time, after the CJ's botched attempt to recite the oath from memory) as our 44th president, and the feeling of hopefulness in the land—at least the land I roam—is palpable. The only thing this has to do with the court or the law is everything.

On a personal level, I feel like the victim of chronic abuse whose PTSD is so severe that he doesn't even flinch anymore and whose tormenter has finally been hauled off to a long prison sentence. The sense of relief is almost overwhelming, and while my expectations for improvement are high, it won't take much to create pretty stark contrast with his predecessor.

On the judicial landscape (as seen from the top rung of the ladder), I don't believe it's too optimistic to proclaim that the Supreme Court has been saved from at least a generation of regressive decisions that attempt to undo rights that so many fought so hard to secure over the past 50 years. Justices Stevens, Ginsburg, and even our own Souter, are sounding anxious to retire, and they might now be replaced with qualified centrist jurists who have no dogmatic agendas.

To put it bluntly, we can look forward to justices who are willing to respect well-established precedents, rather than distorting them beyond recognition or completely overruling them based on personal convictions thinly veiled as "originalist" readings of the "plain language" of the Constitution. Refer back to my disgust with the latest gun rights case if you're wondering what I'm getting at.

Likewise, the new president raises hopes that he will insist on the rule of law—ah, what a fresh breeze—and will not continue to undermine our system of checks and balances, that is, by holding suspects without warrants or judicial review and by violating the rights of citizens without establishing probable cause in the well-established fashion.

While I agree that the global war against terrorist activities presents unique challenges, I can personally attest that even on my minimal rung, judges are frequently awakened in the middle of the night to rule on traditional warrant applications. I see no reason why that 24/7 process wouldn't be perfectly adequate to preserve our national security interests, as well. All in all, I look forward to spending a few righteous years in Obamanation. He won't make all the right calls—I can relate—

but I take some comfort from the fact that he'll be trying his best.

Speaking of warrants, I got a call for one from a PD in the middle of the night, and instead of telling them I would meet them at my office to review the application in person, I tried having them fax the application to my home machine. The technology worked well enough, despite that I didn't have enough paper for the printer and had to use scraps of anything I could find, but I found I was still so sleepy that I'm not sure my review of the application was much better than it would have been if I'd had a six-pack first.

From now on I'd better just get dressed and head down to the office. The cold night air would at least fully wake me up before I issued a warrant likely to be bounced for some pretty obvious lack of important information.

Having read this over again, I admit that a small claimant could get nervous that I wouldn't give her claim its lawful due, even if she had a slam dunk for me, or on the flip side that I'd pound a claimee's face into a pulp just for showing up to offer some lame excuse.

So, I want to add the reassuring caveat that I promise to raise a disbelieving eyebrow at both parties equally—and without prejudice of any kind—and thus to decide their cases completely impartially, though without even a shred of joy in my heart.

On a recent trip down to see how Mom is doing on her own, I made a trip with her out to see how Pop's grave was being tended. While standing there looking at his newly-chiseled name on the gray granite and wondering where the plastic flowers had come from, I happened to glance across the street to the concrete block quarters of the New Birth Sounds of Thunder Christian Center. I doubt I'd have much in common with the world (and hereafter) view of its congregation—though I'm sure we could agree that we all love the local Short Sugars barbecue.

And if the NBSTCC'ers were the ones responsible for the flowers, whether fake or not, I'm ready to tip my Red Sox cap.

I've hear it said, "A Democrat is someone who cares more about people than property." Based on my experiences here on the lowliest rung, I'd say that's an accurate aphorism, though the Republicans all seem to be way on up the ladder, so it's kind of hard to tell about them.

Cathie was out of town last weekend, so on Saturday morning I was on my way to our local breakfast establishment for some coffee to take to the office. On the way in I passed a fellow who looked vaguely familiar but not enough to call up a name. We made eye contact, nodded briefly and kept on going, and I was about to pull open the door when I heard him call "Judge Runyon". That's not usually a good sign, because it often means someone is about to bring up a subject I really can't talk about when we're not staring at each other in the courtroom and speaking on the record.

He said I wouldn't remember him, but that about 13 years ago I heard a number of cases he brought on himself through severe alcohol abuse. He said he wanted to thank me for the way I dealt with him and that it helped him finally get things under control. He said he's now been sober for a long time and that he appreciated what I'd done for him. Then he turned and kept on going, and I floated into the coffee place.

It was a cold, gray day in early March and I hadn't been looking forward to spending my whole Saturday working. Suddenly, though, it was warm and bright, and I didn't even need the coffee to perk me up. The guy didn't realize it, but he'd done a lot for me, too.

Turns out even Holmes had fears that his long lilting name would be forgotten before long. We know that because in a speech to a Bay State bar association he attempted to self-rationalize by saying his work as a judge would live on and continue to affect future generations even after his name had drifted into the ozone. After all, he argued, do we really remember who invented the wheel?

Ironically, many Americans of the 21st century might say they've heard that impressive name somewhere—Holmes, not wheel—but have no idea whether he was a judge or a British private investigator with a deerstalker and a fancy pipe.

Justice John Paul Stevens announced this week that at 90 this will be his last term on the penultimate rung of justice. I e-mailed my cell phone number to the White House just in case, but haven't yet been pinged with a reply. I'm pretty optimistic, though, 'cause I'd have no trouble couching my personal views in wobbly judicial terms like I've seen the right-wingers frequently do ever since they got away with it in *Bush v. Gore*. I mean Justice Scalia doesn't even attempt to explain that one; he just tells anyone who asks, "get over it." I could do that.

The big debate at the New Hampshire Statehouse these days, apart from how much more to slash out of the judicial budget, is whether to allow loaded and concealed handguns on the legislative premises. If your eyes have completely glazed over by now on the subject of firearms, you won't need more from me here.

The part I'm having trouble with, though, is how any of the reps could really claim to be seriously at risk on those premises; that is, after they've already walked through the metal sniffer and are surrounded by a small regiment of beefy security people. As far as I know, there's never been an assault there, so aren't we just making it more likely for that to happen if everyone's armed to the teeth?

Talk among yourselves, but leave the guns at home, just in case the discussion gets really heated. I mean, would you want to disagree too vehemently with someone you thought might be packing?

The judge of the old Peterborough District Court died last week. He was 92 and had been retired for 22 years, per that constitutional mandate

I wailed on awhile back. He's also the one I mentioned who could remember his immediate predecessor but no one farther back than that. Now it will be interesting to see how long it takes until there's no longer anyone who remembers him. I may not live to see that door completely close, but it's always surprising, shocking really, how much faster that happens than we anticipate—sort of like how quickly an abandoned field starts to grow saplings and then to disappear completely.

If he retired in 1988, anyone born prior to 1970 probably wouldn't have much reason to remember his bench time, and those saplings are now 40 years old already and probably past their own primes. Like me, most of the lawyers who actually plied their trade in front of him are nearing their dotage, so the colorful tales of his judicial career are already fading to charcoal gray.

Still, I recall that nearly every time I lost a case I felt I should have won—which seemed to happen a lot—I'd barge into the judge's chambers after the session and moan about the outrageous injustice of the outcome. That sounds pretty brazen on my part, but his chambers were about three feet from the clerk's desk and his door was always open, so if I was just grousing to the clerk, he didn't even have to stand up to join the conversation. He would let me blow off my steam with great patience and equanimity, and then tell me he thought I had an excellent case for appeal. That always made me gnaw my briefcase even more, however, 'cause if the appeal was so airtight, why couldn't we just straighten out the whole mess right here? That appeal line may have helped some when I explained the options to my client, who was seriously pissed that the fee he'd paid me (or would never pay me now) hadn't gotten him off, but I don't remember ever pursuing such an appeal. The client never seemed willing to send good money after bad, at least not with me on the case any longer.

Eventually, the judge and I worked out a system in the courtroom that let me know where I stood before I wasted more breath than was healthy. If he started looking out the window while I was talking, that was my signal to wrap it up in a hurry because he had made his call and was no longer interested in being persuaded otherwise. Of course, I always tried to comply, hoping that a willingness to cooperate would work to my client's benefit. I never recorded any statistics, but I'm now firmly convinced that zipping my lip helped more than hurt, and it definitely got us both back to our offices a lot quicker.

By the way, there was no security in the courtroom in those days either. Once when I went out in the hall to discuss a plea deal with the arresting cop, my client, who had been at the county B&B (bars and boyfriends) but was now sitting in the courtroom alone, jumped out a window and started hoofing it through the center of town before someone noticed the handcuffs and thought maybe the authorities ought to know which way the guy was headed. I think the deal the cops were offering was off the table at that point.

The economy has been sucking jobs and people's retirement plans into its black hole for about two years now, and even the court system is feeling the tug of oblivion. Judge and clerk vacancies aren't being filled, and we've instituted "furlough days" to cut our budget enough to keep us from having to sell judicial favors. ("Say, I could probably keep that smoking gun out of evidence for, say, a grand in small bills in a paper bag left in my car.")

The furloughs mean the courthouse has the "gone fishing" sign on the front door, but that we can't really go fishing because we have to hustle back here if something super-serious happens that can't wait even another day—like a guy who was told not to contact his old girlfriend who then decides to text her that he's sorry for throwing that TV remote at her.

The State's got to whack something like $250,000,000 out of its expenses, and the court system has to do its part. The trouble is, we get such a pittance of the `budget in the first place (I think I said 3% somewhere back there, but it's even less) that every few thousand dollars means we have to start straightening out our paper clips and checking the courtroom for loose change.

It also means that when I have a conflict with a party in a case, the people involved have to wait a long time until we can find another court to send them to because we don't have anyone else here who can step in. We had another judge for years, which didn't cost us much because he didn't get paid unless we used him, but when he left to make more at the convenience store down the street, the position went poof.

On top of that, this morning I read a piece in the paper by a legislator who's long been one of the court system's loudest critics, who basically called us a bunch of spoiled whiners. He said we could live just fine on what he and his buds give us if we decided to spend our money on streamlining our administrative work instead of protecting everyone's jobs. He suggested we could save lots of money by consolidating stuff like data entry and scheduling and getting rid of the people who duplicate those functions in each court.

The rep is probably right that we could use technology more efficiently, but that's not likely to help us over the upcoming fiscal year. System-wide changes like he's proposing take forever to work out and implement and usually require a huge slug of start-up money to roll them out—that he's not likely to give us. Plus, he's clearly never been around a clerk's office when, say, a woman with a baby walks in because she can't drive until she pays her fines. Or maybe her car was repo-ed and she needs help understanding a notice we sent her or finding out where she can do her community service within walking distance. This kind of scenario presents itself several times a day.

The fact is, so much of what we do isn't standardized to the point where a keyboardist in Concord can do the same job on it that a person standing face-to-face can accomplish. I mean, we all hate calling some large bank or government agency—or customer service of any kind— and getting stuck with electronic menu options that don't sound like what we want, only then to have to listen to someone tell us over and over while we're waiting that our call is so very important to them that we'd better not hang up or we'll have to schlep to the back of the line.

I don't think that's the way people want their courts run, too, any more than they'd want to have their health care dispensed that way: Press 1 if it feels like you're having a heart issue; press 2 if you're constipated; press 3 if stress is ruining your life; press 68 if you're mad as hell and you're not going to take it anymore.

A 77 year-old guy has been charged with standing naked on the roof of an industrial building I can see from my office. I don't know yet what prompted this public display of his shriveled shortcomings—I missed the show myself—but I'm sure there's a story behind it. Maybe he was trying to make a statement about the company stripping him of his dignity by promoting some inexperienced whipper-snapper past him; maybe his wife left him and he hasn't figured out how to use the washer and dryer; or maybe he's just starting to lose it and thought he was someplace else entirely—like in the shower. I'll add a postscript after the arraignment.

Here's the PS—The gent came in fully dressed in khaki safari clothes and looking like the twin of Marlin Perkins of "Wild Kingdom" (ask your parents). His hair was slicked backed in that 1950's "Mad Men" way, and he had the same pencil-thin mustache as Marlin. I had all sorts of questions I wanted to ask (see above), but I opted to spare the guy the gory details and to count on a mental health evaluation to figure out what the full story was.

As you've probably gathered by now, we often deal with repeated substance abuse or violent outbursts by having the abusers get their heads examined by someone with real professional credentials. If we didn't do it that way, I'd just be shooting from the hip about what to do and there'd be little chance I'd hit the broad side of a barn.

Nearly every day there are unscheduled cases that muscle their way into line because someone's done something so stupid that he needs an immediate dope slap. This time it was a young guy in cuffs who'd failed to follow through with the anger management evaluation we'd given him the chance to do instead of spending the best part of a year at the county HOC—oh, and being angry with me about that. The ironic part was that when he shuffled in, he was wearing a T-shirt that boldly proclaimed, "I don't have an anger management problem, I have an idiot problem."

Truer words were never reproduced on textile, which made me wonder whether there's a lucrative retirement niche for me in the ubiquitous shirt-message market. Courts could require their customers to don the appropriate garb for the circumstances, so the general public would be warned of the potential danger in their midst. I missed out on "I'm with Stupid", but I could make a fortune on "I'm the Stupid She's with", due to the geometrically expanding market for that one, and how about "I beat my wife [or girlfriend or dog—the variations are as plentiful as kudzu in Carolina], so take a free poke at me", or maybe "DWI means Death Wish Incarnate".

I almost asked the guy whether he'd looked in the mirror after getting dressed, but I thought the question might be too abstract for someone suffering with the idiot syndrome. When I did ask him why he hadn't followed through with the anger management option in order to stay out of jail, he had nothing for me but a clueless shrug, which was further verification for the appropriateness of his attire. Perhaps he'll use the quiet time now afforded him to sort out once and for all how this mysterious result befell him.

Despite the furlough days we've taken and the paper clips we've re-used, the budget crisis up and down our ladder of justice has become even more dire. The first manifestation of that was when I had my court days in Jaffrey cut by 30 this year—about one-fifth of the total—and then was assigned to commute all the way to Derry—a 93 mile round trip, but who's counting—to help out there for 20 of those days. Except for all the driving, that sounds like a net gain of 10 days, but let's scratch the surface a bit.

The 30-day cutback at our home park means I still have to hear those cases; I just have 30 fewer days to do it. I thought each day's docket was already reading like Tolstoy's masterpiece, but I guess we'll have to add an epilogue, a bibliography and an index now. Plus, the legislature sadistically decided last year that judges who travel less than 100 miles to their assigned benches—even for away sessions—get no reimbursement for mileage.

Based on a little quick math, that means my personal contribution to solving the budget dilemma will be about $400 for gas alone. Oh, and my lavish salary is also getting cut for those 10 days they now say I have off. Still, I do have a job—unlike many of our hard-working staff who are being told their positions really weren't all that critical after all. So while I'm grousing at you here, I'm keeping my mouth shut otherwise.

Chapter 3: Within weeks of all that mumbling in the mirror, the bottom has fallen out again. Now the news is that even with all the loose change we've pulled out of the furniture, the State says it's still not enough. I'm beginning to think of the governor like that brother-in-law you avoid at family gatherings because you know no matter how much you've slipped him in the past, he's got a million reasons why he still needs a little more.

So now the plan is to completely reconfigure how we do business from the ground up. Instead of having separate district and probate courts and a family division, they're going to lump them all together into "circuit courts" and try to do business with about 18 clerks instead of the 50+ we now have for those three separate courts. And instead of having your friendly local court staff to call about your case, you'll contact another ubiquitous call center where someone somewhere unknown will try to access your records in the computer system and tell you what you need to know. That philosophy has improved the customer service of our cable and credit card companies so much (dramatic pause) that we can hardly wait to give our own customers the chance to reap the benefits.

Understandably, all the clerks are nearly apoplectic about having to polish up their resumes and apply for one of the new jobs, knowing there aren't nearly enough to go around and that within 30 days they could be standing in an unemployment line or supersizing fries across the street at McDonald's. I wrote a hurried letter of recommendation for our clerk, but she's going to be up against a popular clerk from a larger court that's also going to be in our circuit, and even though he doesn't have nearly as much seniority "in the system", he's a lawyer. I tried to emphasize the factors that aren't dependent on legal training—happy disposition, good organization, proficient personnel skills, excellent baking talent for staff birthdays and holiday brunches—but that J.D. is undoubtedly going to be the clincher.

That's especially true when you consider that lots of unfamiliar breeds of cases will be lumped together and that our clerk's eyes would glaze over if you started asking about the ins and outs of probate administration or marital parenting plans. She could certainly pick it all up, but I doubt they want to wait for her to navigate the learning curve when there's someone who can hit the ground running.

My assessment was prophetic. The lawyer got the job; our clerk is being reassigned to a deputy position at a court location nearer where she lives; and we're getting a new deputy who lives so far away that I've only been there once in my 37 years of wandering the Granite State. I hope she's got snow tires and good shocks, because the winter snow and spring frost heaves will make it a harrowing ride during many months of the year. The saying is that New Hampshire has 9 months of winter and 3 months of bad ice fishing.

I'm not a native, but I've lived here 37 years now and that's long enough to opine that New Hampshire has its collective head up .... somewhere dark and aromatic. I've already mentioned that there hasn't been an execution here since the late '30's, yet that detail didn't keep our capital punishment statute from being amended to include murders that occur during home invasions.

That legislative move was prompted by public outrage at the case of a couple of high school kids who broke into a house and killed the young wife. It was a terrible, brutal, senseless crime, but I doubt the stupid kids who acted on the spur of the moment would have stopped to debate whether to go through with it if they'd known they might be facing executions. Plus, what about all the other forms of grisly murders you can think of—those killings aren't bad enough to warrant the same consequence? Just run-of-the-mill murders, I guess, but try explaining that to the families of those victims. Maybe their local representative should get that assignment.

Soon after that round of judgment-proof law-making, the same block[heads?] voted to reduce the tax on tobacco products—to get people to buy more of them. In a day and age when we know for sure that tobacco causes all manner of health catastrophes—no to mention lots of uninsured medical expenses we all pay for—wouldn't it make more sense to increase the tax to [maybe] keep kids from being able to afford those coffin nails in the first place? And [maybe] to encourage their financially-challenged parents to opt for bread and milk for their families instead? Apparently not.

Meanwhile, those same people have all but gotten rid of the juvenile cases we call CHINS, which stands for "child in need of services". Those cases often involved kids not minding their parents—like about coming home at night—or going to school the next day. Since those are actual problems—unlike the nano-chance of getting shot in the Statehouse—those cases may now have to be brought as parental neglect cases—on the theory that the kids would have come home or gone to school if the parents had been doing their jobs.

Apart from that shaky logic, neglect cases are much more complicated affairs involving lots more human resources and usually requiring many more hearings. By the way, despite all the complexity, our reps initially decided, too, that parents no longer get lawyers to help them navigate these treacherous waters; they'd just have to fend for themselves to try to keep their children from being taken away. Witnesses tried to point out that last insanity at the hearings on the bills, but the deciders must have been too busy cleaning their .44 magnums to pay attention. (PS— Much of this foolishness has more recently been undone, but the fact that it passed in the first place is the frightening story.)

And last but not least are the real killers—and I mean exactly that. This is the only state in the nation that doesn't require drivers to wear seatbelts and it's one of a handful that doesn't require motorcyclists to wear helmets. These are bloody proof of our *Live Free or Die* mentality, and they make it possible for us to legally splatter our guts and gray matter all over the roadways in the interests of personal freedom.

Last fall I was out for a bike ride—wearing my helmet like a pussy—and was the first on the scene of a Jeep Wrangler rollover where the guy whacked his head on the roll bar (intended to save his life) on his way out of the vehicle, then soon died from the wound, all because he wasn't wearing his seatbelt.

Unfortunately, our motto had become *Live Free and Die* for this poor guy. If it was simply a matter of personal choice to take that risk, you might say OK, he rolled the freedom dice and lost. But the rest of us are also involved, because trying to save the fellow consumed a lot of expensive health care resources that we're all subsidizing. And what about the guy's family that may have lost its ability to stay afloat? No one asked them whether they wanted to assert their personal freedom.

Like I said, it's pretty dark and smelly these days in Concord.

Back to the death penalty—like a dog with a bone.

I don't have time for more than a skim of the print media during the week—we used to call them newspapers—but Cathie and I spend the first half of Sunday mornings with *The New York Times*. Cathie checks out the travel section in the hope of getting tips about new and outrageously costly vacation destinations and how to get to them as cheaply as possible, and I surf the rest of it, particularly the book reviews for promising additions to the precariously perched piles in my office that are growing much faster than I can read[-uce] it. (If I spent my time reading instead of writing this nonsense, I might have the pile under control by now.)

Last Sunday as I was finishing my blueberry bagel, I came across an op-ed about the recent execution of an African-American man who had been on death row for 22 years and who even the Pope and a former FBI director thought should be spared due to insufficient evidence of his guilt. The author of the piece talked about the risks of executing innocent people and how we should only be killing the ones we're really, really sure about.

That approach to the subject got my robe bunched up, so I started composing a dissenting opinion. By Tuesday I had my indignation honed down to the tweet-like length the *The New York Times* will consider running, so I fired it off electronically to wherever those things get read. Almost immediately I got a reply from a real editor that maybe, possibly, I was sufficiently onto something to warrant letting their readers decide for themselves.

This Sunday, not having received anything else that knocked me off my soapbox, the paper actually printed my mini-tirade (yep, I was as surprised as you must be). Here's what they let me say—and you could look it up:

> "Mr. [op-ed guy] speeds right past the central issue. The problem with the death penalty is not that we may be executing innocent people. Notwithstanding widespread concern about the [recent] case, we're doing much better at avoiding questionable executions with the help of DNA testing and multi-level review of the evidence and trial process. Beyond Mr. [op-ed guy's] reservations, the problem with the death penalty is not that it fails to provide effective deterrence to serious crimes, or that botched executions are cruel and unusual punishment. And it's not that opposing the death penalty is being soft on crime or coddling our worst criminals at the expense of their victims. I'm a part-time judge and I believe in law and order. The problem with the death penalty is that it's just plain wrong for a civilized society to kill people. That's why all our friends in the community of nations have abolished the death penalty or no longer use it, and why China, Iran, North Korea, Yemen and Syria continue to use it. Using it diminishes us as a country. People who commit our most heinous crimes should be removed from society for the rest of their lives, but they shouldn't be killed."

It occurred to me just after I'd hit "send" that maybe I should have used a pseudonym or shouldn't have mentioned I was a judge, 'cause I'm probably not supposed to sound off publicly on topics like this. That angst lasted about 10 minutes, until I decided that if Justice Scalia could go hunting with someone whose case he was about to ponder, I could say killing people (as opposed to ducks) was wrong.

Plus, the higher-ups don't trust me to send people off to death row anyhow, no matter how many DWIs they ring up down here on my rung. Plus, plus, it's been about a week now and no one in the court system has balled me out, so whatever my judicial indiscretion was, it must have flown under the media radar here in the Granite State. That's either because no one cares what I think about any issue, legal or otherwise, or, more likely, if it ain't in Manchester's *Union Leader*, it didn't happen or it ain't worth knowin'.

I spoke a little too soon about remaining under the radar. The State's Chief Justice paid us a routine visit a few days after that last entry, and while she said she agreed with my sentiments—it's always nice to know a higher court concurs—she raised an eyebrow at my public declaration in the "kill 'em, don't kill 'em" debate.

Still, it's comforting to know our chief reads something other than the *Onion Loader*, as we call the local grill starter. She suggested, just to be safe, that I report myself to the Judicial Conduct Committee, which I dutifully did and which I'm now actually looking forward to hearing from. I mean, really, if I can't express myself on such a life or death factor in the administration of justice, which the Code of Judicial Conduct specifically allows judges to do, then I'm moving to North Korea where they have a more liberal and tolerant policy toward public expression.

PS—Just got a letter from the JCC, saying they had no problem with my letter and not even warning me to keep my mouth shut on such topics of legal interest in the future. I guess I'll cancel the mover after all.

The new circuit court structure I described is wreaking havoc on my alter ego as a lawyer. Totally unrelated to the moves made to tighten our belts and reduce administrative expenses, the court legislation slipped in a prohibition against anyone in the firm of a part-time judge appearing in any other circuit court in the State. It's sort of like Congress passing a health care bill and tucking in some funding for a dam project in Nevada.

Whatever the motivation, that little tidbit buried in our new law bars anyone in our whole mega-firm from showing up on behalf of a client in any of the 10 shiny new circuit courts, not just the one where they might run into me. The fallout is that the firm is majorly miffed, to the point of totally dumping us and looking for another Granite State affiliate that's not so hamstrung. I've offered to excise the cancer that is myself in order not to contaminate everyone, but as they say, the damage is already done, the die is cast, the horse is out of the barn, and the water is both under the bridge and over the dam.

I'm officially even a pariah now to my original partner Jim, who's got good clients he doesn't want to lose by being banned from representing them himself in any circuit court anywhere. And who could blame him, with two kids in college at today's horrifying tuition levels (one year routinely costs more than my house did).

Still, that's going to leave me going it alone for the first time since I was a fresh-faced JD in June, 1972, a prospect that has me as anxious about my future as if I'd embarked on a solo career at that seminal moment in my distant and hazy past. It was the same month as the Watergate break-in, for Pete's sake, if anyone can remember what that was all about.

It's finally here: The first business day of the New Year and the first time in 40 years that I'm a sole practitioner, at least when not still clinging to this brittle, sagging rung. Actually, it feels more like walking a flimsy tightrope without the benefit of a safety net to keep me from splattering my guts all over the pavement. On the bright side, it's the first time I've been able to make decisions without consulting at least one partner or having to run the idea through a whole executive committee.

Back on the precarious side, though, I have no idea yet whether my old clients will really stick with me or will figure they need more frontline troops and backup reserves to wrestle successfully with their pressing legal matters. Even so, I wouldn't worry so much if I was there at my desk full-time, but I'm not while I'm still flailing around over here. If I was stressed before, when there were others back at the office helping to pay the rent and the malpractice premiums, it can't help but ramp up when there's little or nothing happening over there until I can get back to start the time clock. It's a good thing my blood pressure has never been an issue, but maybe I should get one of those home monitoring gadgets, just in case.

Several weeks ago I heard the case of a social worker at a sheltered workshop who was charged with assaulting a troubled 12 year-old in his care. Outrageous, you say, but the kid was a whirling dervish of non-cooperative and oppositional behavior who was also prone to head for the woods whenever there was a chink in supervision. This time the boy was acting out his usual MO to the nth degree and the defendant was getting really frustrated. Finally, it appeared to the defendant's colleagues who witnessed the incident that the defendant "just lost it", picking the kid up and throwing him to the ground from waist height.

The defense was that this was required under the circumstances, but none of the defendant's co-workers backed him up on that, and neither did the worker trainers who described what was supposed to be done under these often difficult circumstances. Apparently, the protocol is just to hold on for dear life and call out for reinforcements.

I wrestled with this one for longer than most. I think we can all see how a boy like this could really get our goat and cause a momentary blip in good judgment. On the other hand, we all have kids who occasionally push us to the brink of mayhem. Whether we slip or plunge over the edge is all that separates most distraught parents from those who end up here for criminal assault or juvenile abuse—or in this case, whether we lose our jobs and jeopardize our own families' welfare.

In the end, I found the worker guilty—really no choice there—and he did lose his job, though the workshop had canned him long before my pronouncement. I thought that seemed like just about enough without piling on, so the fine was suspended, due to no ability to pay, and he had to comply with the results of an anger management evaluation.

Yesterday was a rare mid-week day off from court, but it didn't take long to get a call to drop everything and present myself anyhow. The cops had picked up a 17 year-old we've known since he was about 11, and they wanted a lot of cash bail set. We'd closed the kid's juvenile case at 17, as we have to do, even though he'd been in one or another placement facility for nearly all that time because he couldn't function without someone following him around all day making sure he wasn't leaving trouble in his wake. He was sort of like Pigpen, except with more serious debris than a dust cloud. And when we finally cut him loose to walk out into the world, I don't think anyone in the room felt like we'd seen the last of him.

Whether he's found guilty of this offense, he'll be back here again and again, probably for the rest of his life. He has no independent living skills whatsoever, despite my harping the last couple of years that it would be grossly unfair to dump him out of the juvenile safety net and into the adult world totally unprepared.

Apparently, even this otherwise clueless young man is perceptive enough to know all that, because he was heard to say that he only did what he's charged with so he could "go back in" where someone else will tell him what to do. The tragedy is that he functions just highly enough not to qualify for a sheltered workshop of some sort, yet he's not as likely to make his way alone as my 9 year-old granddaughter. She might not be tall enough to reach the pedals of a car, but she could balance a checkbook, live on a budget, and even get up to go to work every day— particularly if the break room had a supply of M&Ms.

This fellow can't do that stuff now, and he's not likely to be doing any better at 40 than I'll then be doing in my drooling, demented dotage. So, as he's figured out, his only alternative is to keep himself jailed up on minor offenses, but to avoid doing something so unwittingly dangerous that he gets himself killed along the way.

Abraham Lincoln knew all of this. So did an almost completely unknown Scottish poet named William Knox who wrote "Mortality", Lincoln's all-time favorite poem. That's saying something, too, because the president was an avid poetry buff and recited many poems from memory. This was no brief bit of doggerel either; there are 14, 4-line stanzas containing way more words than his own 272-word address at Gettysburg.

Lincoln probably knew the poem so well because he recited it so often that people came to think he wrote it himself, prompting him, when asked, to say that he'd "give all [he was] worth, and go in debt, to be able to write so fine a piece . . . ." That's pretty high praise from one whose own prose is considered so worthy that it's chiseled in granite and marble all over the world. What do you think?:

Oh, why should the spirit of mortal be proud?
Like a swift-fleeting meteor, a fast-flying cloud,
A flash of the lightning, a break of the wave,
He passes from life to his rest in the grave.

The leaves of the oak and the willow shall fade,
Be scattered around, and together be laid;
And the young and the old, the low and the high,
Shall molder to dust, and together shall lie.

The infant a mother attended and loved;
The mother that infant's affection who proved;
The husband, that mother and infant who blessed;
Each, all, are away to their dwelling of rest.

The maid on whose cheek, on whose brow, in whose eye,
Shone beauty and pleasure—her triumphs are by;
And the memory of those who loved her and praised,
Are alike from the minds of the living erased.

The hand of the king that the sceptre hath borne,
The brow of the priest that the mitre hath worn,
The eye of the sage, and the heart of the brave,
Are hidden and lost in the depths of the grave.

The peasant, whose lot was to sow and to reap,
The herdsman, who climbed with his goats up the steep,
The beggar, who wandered in search of his bread,
Have faded away like the grass that we tread.

The saint, who enjoyed the communion of Heaven,
The sinner, who dared to remain unforgiven,
The wise and the foolish, the guilty and just,
Have quietly mingled their bones in the dust.

So the multitude goes—like the flower or the weed
That withers away to let others succeed;
So the multitude comes—even those we behold,
To repeat every tale that has often been told.

For we are the same that our fathers have been;
We see the same sights that our fathers have seen;
We drink the same stream, we feel the same sun,
And run the same course that our fathers have run.

The thoughts we are thinking, our fathers would think;
From the death we are shrinking, our fathers would shrink;
To the life we are clinging, they also would cling -
But it speeds from us all like a bird on the wing.

They loved—but the story we cannot unfold;
They scorned—but the heart of the haughty is cold;
They grieved—but no wail from their slumber will come;
They joyed—but the tongue of their gladness is dumb.

They died—aye, they died—we things that are now,
That walk on the turf that lies over their brow,
And make in their dwellings a transient abode,
Meet the things that they met on their pilgrimage road.

Yea, hope and despondency, pleasure and pain,
Are mingled together in sunshine and rain;
And the smile and the tear, the song and the dirge,
Still follow each other, like surge upon surge.

'Tis the wink of an eye—'tis the draught of a breath -
From the blossom of health to the paleness of death,
From the gilded saloon to the bier and the shroud
Oh, why should the spirit of mortal be proud?

When I was finishing up the morning session in the Keene court a couple of weeks ago, the last woman who came up said, "I've been watching all morning and I think you're a kind judge." I thanked her for her vote of confidence, but joked that I was sure the judge who heard her case at trial would also be just as kind. Then she asked if she could request that I be her judge. I said she had quite a number of rights in court, but none of them involved being able to choose her judge. We gave her a trial date, and that was it.

As I walked out at lunchtime for some fresh air, though, one of the bulky bailiffs who I'd never seen before, said, "You got paid quite a compliment today." I felt the same way, although I didn't recall doing anything particularly kind for anyone that morning, certainly nothing that I could consciously repeat. The woman and I hadn't launched into a penetrating colloquy about the basis for her comment, so I didn't know whether she meant I went easier on people than I could have, or just avoided the level of arrogance and intimidation she was expecting from a judge.

Whatever prompted the comment, I'll take it and keep plugging away just the same. I figure that after all this time, either I've got that kindness thing down, or just managed to hit a lucky one out of the park—sort of like a light-hitting second baseman does every so often.

There was another terrible shooting last week, this time in Aurora, Colorado. An unassuming young guy dressed in riot gear and carrying assault weapons walked into a theatre that was showing the latest Batman movie and opened fire. He killed 12 and injured about 60 more, then just surrendered to police like nothing had happened. When they checked out his weapons, they found he acquired all of them perfectly legally.

Some commentators predict that the incident will reopen the national gun control debate, but most figure it won't cause even a blip on that screen. That's largely because no one in public office can suggest tightening up the gun laws, even reinstating the ban on private ownership of military-style assault cannons, if he expects to keep his job. The argument is that if you crack the door even that much, it won't be long before you can't have an air rifle to shoot beer cans in the backyard. It goes on to claim that if guns are restricted, then only criminals will have them, and we'll all be huddled defenselessly in our basements.

The problem is that the statistics from unarmed countries we call our first cousins show something entirely different. While we have gun-related violence rates that rival unstable places like South Africa and

Mexico, we're many orders of magnitude beyond places like England, Canada, France and Germany where there are tight gun regulations.

Ah, but they don't have the Second Amendment, you say, that our Founders insisted on to protect us from ourselves. The trouble is, unless you contort the language of that simple sentence beyond reason, as even the Supreme Court has seen fit to do, there's no guaranty of an individual right to have handguns for self-defense. It's only a right for local or state militias to arm themselves against oppression by a too-powerful federal government—the kind we fought that whole Revolution thing to get free of. Saying any more about it is a total waste of pixels, so I'll save them for something likely to achieve an actual improvement in the human condition.

PS—That talk I gave to the Rotarians was more than 10 years ago. After they gave me a letter opener with the Rotary seal on it, no one came up wanting to sign on as a mentor to one of our troubled kids. Then, last week, completely out of the blue, I came back from court to a voice mail message from a woman who said she was a guest at that Rotary lunch. She said she had a son who was in the throes of juvenile turmoil at that very moment and that she took to heart my entreaty to do whatever it took to keep the child safe while he struggled with his challenges. She said she managed to get him through that rough water without permanent scars and that he was now cruising, without any more potential for disaster than we all face on a day-to-day basis. She thanked me for offering those words of encouragement and just wanted me to know how things had worked out for her family.

Wow! I'm sure Chief Justice Roberts got lots of kudos for his courageous vote to save the health care law (we'll overlook the death threats for the moment), but I doubt he ever gets this kind of direct feedback from a real person.

I guess my choice of OWH, Jr. as one whose name is chiseled forever in granite wasn't as safe as I thought it was. I mentioned his name to some family friends in their late 20's, and they looked at me like I'd said it in Mandarin. And it wasn't that they'd heard the name but couldn't place the context; there was just no flicker of recognition at all. These guys hadn't dropped out of school to work at McDonald's either; they were all college grads with grade points their parents were proud of.

So think about this. Holmes died in 1935 as the best known jurist of his day, probably also as one of the top 10 best known Americans. Because he had no children and his wife had already died, he left the bulk of his estate to the United States of America. My friends were born in about 1985, just 50 years later. Yet even his name, not only his life's work of more than 90 years, had faded to black in our collective memory.

Sure, most lawyers and judges remember at least the Holmes name, though I doubt even most of them could cite one of the cases he decided during almost 30 years on the Supreme Court. I always think of *Abrams v. United States* from 1919 for his "clear and present danger" test about public dissent. Ring any bells at all? Buehler, Buehler? I'm getting more discouraged by the minute.

Our own Justice David Souter has come back to earth from the top rung, and he's moved into a more substantial house where all his books won't fall through the floor of his ancestral but dilapidated homestead in Weare. Where? He's also kept his mouth largely shut since then, but he made a rare appearance last week and opined on some of the recent shenanigans of his former breth- and sistren. Of most significance here is his comment on Justice Scalia's Second Amendment decision. You know, the one that cut an individual right to an AK47 out of whole cloth. Now I've got some heavy artillery to fight back with. Souter said,

> "It was so obvious that the Second Amendment is written with the first clause that refers to a well-regulated militia, therefore the right to bear arms shall not be infringed upon. I don't know how you can read that language and not say they would have put the militia clause (in) if they were trying to provide a right that had no relation to the militia and the carrying of arms for that reason."

Alright, maybe not the most artful sentences he's ever put together, but it wasn't scripted like Scalia's carefully-crafted decision of more than 35 pages that miraculously blew away the militia clause—sort of like an AK47. Those Supremes just have more fire power, after all.

While we're on the subject of Scalia, I'll also mention his recent dust-up with Judge Richard Posner over Posner's outrageous charge that Scalia actually uses legislative history to determine what the final version of a law means. Imagine that, consulting what the people who passed the law had in mind when they did that!

My comment really isn't about any of that. It's about sitting judges, particularly ones way up top, keeping their big traps shut and doing their paying jobs. If they have something to say, then put it in the actual decision and move on. If their meaning wasn't clear, then they should have hit the delete key and tried again to make it better.

One of the facts of life about judging is that you take your lumps about unpopular decisions, bite your tongue until it bleeds (maybe whimper to your spouse or clerk about being misunderstood), then spit the blood in the bucket and come out for the next round.

Frankly, Justice Scalia, with all due respect, no one cares or remembers why you made the decision. It's just the bottom line that counts, so work on getting that right.

I'm sitting in the airport in Tokyo, waiting for the long flight back to Boston after a week of hiking in Bhutan, the lesser-known neighbor and cousin of Nepal. They're close enough to claim portions of the same impressive Himalayan peaks, and they're cousins because they share the Buddha as an ancestor.

The hiking led from one spectacular vista to another—my camera's memory cards are full—but the highlight of the experience was the concentrated exposure to Buddhism. Not being a religious person myself, I don't mean the chanting while fingering a string of rosary-like beads or the turning of prayer wheels. I mean the gentleness and inner calm the people bring to daily life and the focus they have on living in the moment, without dwelling on past disappointments or worrying about what the future may bring.

I mean "staying within themselves", to cop another athletic metaphor, by avoiding the trivial distractions and stresses that constantly try to blur their appreciation of the beautiful tapestry of life right before their eyes. See, I'm talking like a Buddhist already and I haven't spent years in a monastery with a shaved head and an orange bathrobe.

The key will be whether I can maintain this inner calm when I'm hit tomorrow with dozens of voice mail messages proclaiming urgent deadlines and a bloated docket of unresolved cases that have been waiting for more than two weeks. I've expressed this concern in non-Buddhist terms before, but now I've seen it revealed as a sanctioned way of life. That doesn't make it any easier to pull off, but it is comforting to know there are others—many, many others—who see the pursuit of this brand of happiness as an effort worth devoting their entire lives to.

Alright, there's finally good Wi-Fi here now, so I need to start tackling my e-mail.

Over the past 10 years New Hampshire has attracted a group of virulent libertarians known as "Free Staters". I've never seen any indication that they're a dangerous tribe like Skinheads, but when they run afoul of the legal system and get dragged into court, they don't take it lying down. In fact, they take pains to draw as much attention to themselves as possible, by refusing to stand when speaking, by refusing to remove their hats in the courtroom, and by refusing to pay their fines.

They also show up in great numbers for even the most minor charge against one of their flock, and they usually bring a video camera to record the proceedings. That may be to send a not-too-subtle message to the judge that they're watching for telltale signs of constitutional abusiveness, or because they prefer home movies of themselves during judicial proceedings to commercial television. I think I'm with them there. These folks thrive on confrontation, however, and when a judge takes the bait and attempts to challenge them, they ramp up the righteous indignation, in the hope of showing how governmental authority is trampling their natural rights.

Today we had a regiment of the righteous show up in support of a young kid charged with driving without a license and failing to register his truck. He acknowledged both infractions of the Man's Law, but said he could drive perfectly well without a license and that registering a vehicle was just an excuse to take money from the people to support corrupt government.

Thus, looked at through the lens of morality, the kid saw himself commanding the high ground, and he proclaimed it an immoral act to find him guilty—which I did. When I said I wasn't really charged with assessing what was moral or not, just whether he'd violated the laws on the books, I heard a distinct gasp of righteousness issue from the guy manning the video camera. I pretended not to hear.

Then, when I fined him, he said he couldn't pay but would do community service in lieu. The reason he said he had no money was because he couldn't work without a Social Security number, a societal brand he wasn't willing to suffer. I didn't ask how he expected to support himself once he left the nest, but maybe if he does community service for all his financial obligations, he'll never need any money. It was at that point that I recognized the kid's mother as one of our prior soldiers of principle, whom I'd sent to jail to satisfy her fines when she refused to pay—or even to yield to community service. The apple apparently hadn't fallen far from the tree.

Yesterday was election day 2012. Being what we call the "moderator" in New Hampshire town government, I spent it standing next to our ballot box from 7:00 a.m. until considerably after 7:00 p.m., while thousands of my friends' and neighbors' ballots were run through the voting machine. Apart from trying to keep my feet from going numb, I passed the time by playing the "guess how they're voting" game. That is, I gave everyone the hairy eyeball as they approached the ballot box, and in a matter of seconds I factored in their facial expressions, their manner of dress (suit, work shirt, T-shirt logo), their gender and age, their hair (facial, length, ponytail) and personal artwork (tattoos, piercings, etc.). Then, because I had to make sure they correctly fed their ballots into the voting machine, I really couldn't avoid seeing how many of them voted. Some people even showed their ballots to me—like I was supposed to grade their papers—and I could see they voted a straight Republican or Democratic ticket. After thousands of glances, I couldn't help deciphering their choices even when they put the ballots in face-down. Those black marks are pretty dark after all.

My take was this. Most young people seemed to vote for Democrats, as did most people 55 and up who I knew were college-educated or were concerned about their Medicare and Social Security benefits. The people who voted Republican were primarily in the 35-55 age group and were either "social" conservatives, blue-collar workers still in uniform, or hard-nosed small business people, college-educated or not, who I guessed didn't like the prospect that their taxes or employee health insurance costs might further expand. I loved the fact that the latter thought I was a kindred spirit and gave me a big knowing grin as they fed their ballots into the maw.

Some people, though, just baffled me with their choices—the young woman with pieced nose and eyebrow, and the guy my age I thought was pretty crunchy—and voted against what I thought were their clear personal interests. Whatever their decisions, I thanked them for coming in to vote—which I didn't get to say to more than a quarter of our registered voters.

A substance abuse counselor in Maine, not New Hampshire (just want to be clear about that), sent us a letter saying our defendant (who now lives up there) has been dismissed from the program due to "lack of precipitation". Those programs must have a terrible time in Arizona and New Mexico.

More mass gun tragedies have occurred in the past few months, at a shopping center, a movie theater, and just last Friday at an elementary school where 20 six and seven year-olds were shot multiple times and killed, and 6 teachers and administrators were also gunned down trying to protect the kids.

Up until this last episode, the dead were mourned, but the NRA got away with claiming that we'd all be safer if we had even more guns, and anyone wanting more regulation was shouted down by the Second Amendment wavers. This time, though, it looks like the gun control scale may have tipped. I guess it took an event of total tsunami-like horror to drown out the fanatics and get the gun control dialogue back on the radar screen.

Here are a couple of things I've heard said or written in the last few days that increase the size of the wave:

> "One failed attempt at a shoe bomb and millions and millions of travelers now take off their shoes at airports all over the world. Thirty-one school shootings since Columbine and no change in our regulation of guns."

> "OSHA has five pages of regulations about ladders, while federal authorities shrug at serious curbs on firearms. Ladders kill around 300 Americans a year, and guns 30,000."

> "More Americans die in gun homicides and suicides in six months than have died in the last 25 years in every terrorist attack and the wars in Afghanistan and Iraq combined."

I don't know what will come of it all, but I do know that the only way to salvage something hopeful from the deaths of those little children and their protectors—and to bootstrap something positive from the other tragedies that got us up to this precipice—is for there to be a real paradigm shift in the way we're willing to deal with what and how certain guns are sold. If we're just paying lip service to the issue to make ourselves feel better in the face of this most outrageous tragedy yet, and if the NRA is just lying low until the wave recedes and it can counterattack, then all those who died this time will again have died in vain.

It didn't take but a week for the NRA to parry the new assault on guns, by announcing that the best way to avoid future Newtowns is to make sure there are armed security officers in all our schools. So rather than dampening the flames of our gun culture, the solution is to pour gasoline on it and to put even more guns out there. We don't need to prevent people from having assault weapons or multi-round magazines of ammunition, and we don't need to subject private sales of guns to background checks. Those things would just lead to greater government control and make law-abiding citizens less safe.

I don't know where we'll end up in this gun standoff, but I've got a better solution and it's pretty darn elegant if I say so myself. Because there hasn't been [but one now] attack by a deranged woman in any of these mass shootings, I suggest we simply take the guns away from men—that is, unless the militia gets called up—and let women keep all the guns. Then, since there won't be any gun-toting men around to attack women and their children, women won't need most of their guns, so they probably won't mind if we take most of them away—certainly not the bulky ones with huge magazines of ammunition that they probably can't lift anyhow and probably clash with their outfits.

This line of thinking is non-PC perhaps, but on the money. My assistant always says, "If we can send a man to the moon, why can't we send all of them?" Well, here's a nice alternative to an otherwise expensive space program, and it would keep men around for what they do best—like ensuring that the beer, jerky and recliner industries remain healthy.

PS—Since this last tirade, there've been a couple more male-perpetrated mass slayings, which further underscores the wisdom of my proposal. Seriously, though, even the president has thrown in the towel, saying at the Navy Yard memorial service (12 more dead there) that he can't save any future victims without congressional action, that they're too spineless or frothing-at-the-mouth idiotic (OK, my assessment) to act, and that it's going to take the American people speaking with their votes to foster any meaningful change.

Speaking of voting, I liken this issue to the history of the 19th Amendment. The first significant women's suffrage initiative took place in 1848, and then it took 72 years to achieve its goal—a goal even the most strident gun-toters probably support today, though that's making a risky leap of faith, I know.

It's the week before my 23rd Christmas shivering on this lowly rung. The ground is frozen but there's just a dusting of snow on it so far, probably due to climatic changes since the days when my rung was already under 6 inches of the white stuff before Thanksgiving. Don't get me wrong, apart from the concern that we may all soon be incinerated by the lack of an ozone layer, I'm just fine with not having to shovel the driveway more times than I can count on the numb fingers of one hand.

Still, another reason to be numb is that the scheduling plans for next year's court sessions just arrived, and it looks like we've been naughty again. After a 20% cutback for all the judges last year, they've apparently decided they can get away with that again. And it's a clever way they do it. Instead of walking right up and slapping us in the face with a 20% pay reduction, they reduce the number of court session days by that amount, theoretically lavishing all the judges with more time to shed their robes and relax in the sun. Of course, they don't send out a memo to all the police departments advising them to charge 20% fewer people with driving while stupid, or make sure 20% fewer parents are neglecting their children, or ensure that 20% fewer domestic partners are smacking each other around. No, they just expect you to do the same amount of work in those fewer court sessions—in our case, 23 fewer.

The clincher is that no one else in the court system is receiving this coal in their stocking. I guess the budgeteers figure the judges are already being pampered more than they deserve—they don't have to walk through the metal detectors and they get to take a break whenever they want to call their financial advisors. Plus, they don't have a union and can't open their mouths about anything they don't like, so what the hell.

As I've said before, though, at least I have a job. Some—actually quite a lot—of the people we deal with don't have one at all, are about to be kicked out of where they live by yours truly, and may find themselves in jail for New Year's if they can't come up with the fines they owe in the next couple of weeks.

Consequently, much to the chagrin of Cathie, who thinks we're all pussys for not standing up for ourselves, I'm opting for the Bob Cratchit approach: just being thankful for what we do have and trying to enjoy this moment in time as much as possible. One day, it will be thousands of years from now. My ashes will be in the spleen of a future creature of some description—if spleens haven't evolved out of existence—and no one will know or care what I was getting paid to do something called "judging" in the late Dark Ages of 2012.

I was in our local bagel store this morning, getting a supply of carbs to bolster us for the day's onslaught of juvenile cases, and as I was walking out the door, *The Sounds of Silence* started playing on the shop's sound system. I won't insult anyone's intelligence by identifying the artists— they're as iconic as anyone in American musical history. Sure, the song first hit the airwaves in about November of 1965, almost 50 years ago and easily 30 years before any of the kids slinging bagels were piercing their parents' silence. Still, I guaranty the kids all recognized it.

I myself have heard that song thousands of times by now. Somehow, though, it affected me differently at that moment. Instantly, I was a college freshman again, riding home for my first Thanksgiving break in a Chevy Nova convertible driven by one of the upperclassmen at the Sigma Chi house where I'd pledged. The song was playing repeatedly on the then AM-only stations we'd pick up and lose as we headed north. We'd never heard anything quite like it before, but we figured this was just another one-hit wonder by the duo with the funny name. We had no idea they'd go on to create a literal soundtrack for that time in our lives—but then we didn't know a lot of things at that point.

I who had barely had a date in my first 18 years didn't know that in just over a year I'd meet the woman I'd spend the next 45 years with. I had no idea I'd go to law school and would soon move my young family to a small town in New Hampshire where I'd spend 40 years-and-counting— or that someday I'd have been a judge there for more than 20 years.

Now I can point to just about every twist and turn that eventually brought me to that bagel store yesterday, but it all would have seemed like a crazy fantasy during that chilly ride up the New Jersey Turnpike. Then again, Martin Luther King, Jr. and Robert Kennedy were still very much alive; the World Trade Center hadn't gone up yet or come down; and Barry Obama was a toddler in Hawaii.

I've grumbled several times about the prevailing mindset that a judicially-administered oath to tell the truth means little or nothing if it's a matter of saving your bacon. Two recent cases once again made my point.

In the first, the defendant, who was the new boyfriend of a woman formerly married to the victim, testified that when he went to confront the ex-husband about allegedly putting nails in the defendant's driveway, the ex, who was half the defendant's size, pulled the defendant into the house and began beating him. When I found this totally implausible, and that the beating occurred the other way around given the size disparity and the telltale lumps all over the victim, the defendant just shrugged and took his fine without complaint, as though he'd given it his most imaginative shot, and though entirely fabricated, there was no skin off his nose.

In the second case only yesterday, this defendant was charged with reckless driving for going like the proverbial bat and passing other bats in prohibited areas. He claimed that his electric blue vehicle, tricked out with spoiler and fog lamps, wasn't the vehicle in question, though it fit the description of the alleged rocket car to a T. The defendant even went so far as to add that he'd been passed himself by the real offender in an identical car, who he said had shrewdly turned off the road before the cops intercepted the defendant.

Now I may still suffer from the remnants of youthful naivety when it comes to assessing the truthfulness of witness testimony, but cases like this have helped me overcome it. When I finally pronounced the guy's story complete hogwash, he quickly admitted he would have pled no contest except that losing his license for 60 days would have jeopardized his job—as a lawyer.

What he didn't say—but should have—was that he was terribly sorry for lying through his teeth to the court and that he hoped I wouldn't report him to the [Massachusetts] Professional Conduct Committee. I haven't done that yet, though I'm definitely straddling the fence. The part of this that's got me really bummed is that if even a lawyer—an officer of the court—feels that making it up as he goes is par for the course, then I've got more of a problem on my hands than I thought.

Adult softball is a popular after-work pastime during the summer months here. It's a chance to blow off the steam of the day, to show that your youthful athletic prowess hasn't totally eroded, and maybe to quaff a beer or two between innings. All in all, a relaxing way to unwind.

Not always, however. Particularly when both of the women you've been two-timing happen to show up at the same game to cheer you on and then suddenly realize that there's someone else in attendance for the same purpose—and she's clearly not your mother.

Fireworks quickly erupted in the stands, as each woman the guy had assured was the one-and-only began trading R-rated remarks about the other's virtueosity. Each, of course, assumed the other must have known about her nearly-nuptial relationship with the guy, and thus accused the other of being nothing but a cheap one-night-stander.

I entered the fray because one of the ladies (probably too generous a descriptor) was sufficiently incensed to file a stalking petition against the other. Once the evidence emerged, it became clear that the only one really at fault was the guy in center field, who would have been smart to stay out there even when his team came to bat. He did manage to get safely into the dugout without being beaned from the stands, but he'd be wise to keep his batting helmet on for at least a few weeks and perhaps only to show up for away games.

Oh, and I threw out the stalking petition. The two fans soon made up and were last seen checking the schedule, so they'd know when a grand slam might be in order. Baseball provides so many apt terms for whatever the conflict may be.

As I write this, the Congress and nearly all its constituents are debating whether to launch punitive strikes of some kind against Syria for President Assad's alleged use of chemical weapons on his own people. The debate has focused on what kind of response is appropriate to make sure he never, never does this again.

My problem with how this is playing out is that we've gotten to the sentencing stage a little prematurely if we compare this to a criminal prosecution. Usually, before a sentence is imposed, the defendant is entitled to have the charge proved beyond a reasonable doubt. The Administration has assured us that we can fire away because it's really pretty clear that Assad was responsible for all these Syrian deaths, many of them children graphically photographed in burial shrouds—I mean, who else would have had that capability, right?

Still, Assad vehemently denies the charge, and we haven't gotten any more conclusive proof of this than George W. had of WMD in Iraq 10 years ago. So, if we assume, with reasonable certainty, that at least some innocent person will die if aerial strikes are made on Syrian sites, what we're basically saying is that it's OK to impose that death penalty without even knowing for sure whether the real defendant is guilty as charged. I'm not soft on crime of any kind, but having been conned so recently in our political history with unreliable evidence, I'm not willing to impose this sentence without being shown the smoking gun.

I've got about 3 1/2 more years trying to stay vertical on this rung, and after 23 plus at this point, I think it's fair to say the bloom is off the rose for Cathie. Aspects of the job that used to roll off her back are really starting to rankle. Like when the phone rings at 2:00 AM and it's a cop from a town halfway across the state who calls me for a warrant because he can't find his own judge. I tell her I'm sure that happens to other judges when we're off gallivanting, but that old line isn't cutting it very well anymore. Like when one of the officers calls just as we're heading out the door to go somewhere and then we're 45 minutes late by the time I review the warrant application, maybe call for more details, and then fax the stuff wherever it's going.

And tonight when I told her we have to drive home from our

daughter's in Virginia on the Sunday after Thanksgiving, with everyone else on the east coast—instead of waiting until Monday—because I have court that day. Which means the normal trip of 10 hours probably balloons to 12 at least, once we battle our way through all the metro areas between there and home. Actually, it means she'll be doing the extra battling because I don't get to drive on these long trips anymore, due to my penchant for adhering to the posted speed limits. Cathie views the "limit" concept as more of a suggested minimum. I tell her that doctors have the same issues, but she's not buying that either, as doctors, she says, are only on call like that one weekend a month or so. Not 24-7-365.

Maybe as I get closer to where I can actually see the finish line, she'll wax nostalgic about the whole experience and realize she'll miss all the valuable perks of being a judge's wife. Like what I don't know, but I'm not going to push that button, for fear of, "You mean like the perk of having them cut your pay 20% every year when they cut the number of court sessions and then they expect you to hear all those same cases on 20% fewer days?"

Unfortunately, I don't have a good retort for that one, so I'll just keep my mouth shut and hope the cops don't call tonight from some town she's never even heard of. At least I've got the ringer turned off on her side of the bed now. I've got about 3 1/2 years to go at this gig now, and after 23 plus at this point, I think it's fair to say the bloom is off the rose for Cathie.

This is a milestone year for two of the greatest American speeches. In August we marked 50 years since Martin Luther King, Jr. stood on the steps of the Lincoln Memorial and told us about his dream for America, and it's been 150 years today since the man who was sitting silently over Dr. King's shoulder delivered his own address on the Gettysburg battlefield. Each was remarkable in its own way.

Based on what we now know, the most moving portion of Dr. King's long speech was completely off his written text and was prompted by Marian Anderson's whispered encouragement to "tell them about your dream." What came next was the miracle of words that catapulted the civil rights movement to the forefront of public attention and contributed significantly to passage of the Civil Rights Act of 1964 and then the Voting Rights Act of 1965.

One hundred years earlier, President Lincoln's address at the dedication of the Gettysburg National Cemetery was remarkable, too, but as nearly the antithesis of Dr. King's. By all accounts, Lincoln was an effective speaker, though not one who would have gotten a Southern Baptist congregation on its feet like Dr. King. And unlike King's booming baritone, Lincoln's twangy, rather high-pitched voice must have seemed odd coming from a figure almost a foot taller than most Americans of the day. Also unlike King, who was comfortable delivering unscripted sermons, Lincoln rarely spoke more than a few public words extemporaneously, nearly always deferring those requests until he'd precisely written down what he wanted to say.

That brings us to Gettysburg. President Lincoln was invited about two weeks before the dedication ceremony but was told they already had their keynote speaker in the person of Edward Everett. Everett was the former president of Harvard College and had held every political office there was in Massachusetts. He was also the most renowned orator of his day, as Daniel Webster had been a generation earlier. So Lincoln's only assignment was to add his presidential presence to the ceremony and to offer "a few appropriate remarks." Actually, some of the organizers were nervous about having him say anything at all, fearing that his home-spun, frontier style might detract from the solemn dignity of the occasion.

Contrary to the mythology, Lincoln didn't dash off his memorable 272 words on the back of an envelope while bumping along on the train to Gettysburg. That would not have been his style, for although little was expected of his remarks, he was anxious to make them convey how he felt about what had happened there, about the sacrifices the soldiers he commanded had made, and about what those sacrifices meant in the midst of the country's bitter struggle for its very survival.

The president began work on his speech at the White House a few days beforeleaving Washington, once he'd cleared his schedule enough to make the trip, and there he composed those famous first words that set the tone for all that followed. Even if most Americans know nothing more about what he said, they can probably start with "Four score and seven years ago" and come pretty close to finishing that sentence. Lincoln did travel to Gettysburg by train, but he spent that time talking war and politics—and kissing babies held up to him whenever the train stopped along the way. There's no evidence at all that he made any attempt to flesh out his speech during the trip.

When the president arrived in Gettysburg on the afternoon before the ceremony, he was put up at the home of local attorney David Wills, the young event organizer. It was during some time alone late that evening, amid all the boisterous celebrations going on outside, and then early the next morning, after an emotional tour of the still-ravaged battlefield, that the final address came together. Every word was chosen to convey the precise tone and meaning he was hoping for—we know that because the papers he read from contain a number of last-minute edits.

By the time Lincoln finally stood to speak, Everett had gone on for almost two hours, with a full account of the battle and with dozens of obscure classical and historical references. Many in the audience of 10,000 may have been settling in for more of the same. No one was prepared for what they heard—and then in about two minutes it was over.

Most accounts say Lincoln spoke slowly, but in a clear ringing voice to make himself heard as far back in the gathering as possible. Some said that he seemed to struggle to check his emotions as he spoke. Many of the wounded who had returned, and the families of those who had died in that very place, were unable to hold back tears. The line that seemed to resonate most forcefully was, "The world will little note nor long remember what we say here, but it can never forget what they did here." The president underlined that word himself, to make sure he gave it the proper emphasis.

Despite the reverence we now feel about what President Lincoln said, some early newspaper accounts called the speech an "insult to the memory of the dead". In fact, when he sat down, the president himself thought he had failed. "That speech won't scour," like a bad plow, was how he put it. Ironically, it was Everett who immediately realized what he had heard, saying in his letter to Lincoln the next day, "I should be glad if I could flatter myself that I came as near to the central idea of the occasion, in two hours, as you did in two minutes."

Eventually, nearly all those who were there realized they had witnessed something timeless. Many of those 10,000 passed down to their children and grandchildren the stories of their experiences that day. There's a 1938 radio interview with an elderly man who was still telling how 75 years before, as a young boy, he had slithered up to the front and stood just below Lincoln. When President Obama was inaugurated in 2009, a woman stood in that huge gathering wearing the same cloak her ancestor had worn that day in 1863.

President Lincoln had freed the southern slaves earlier that year, though Dr. King would remind us a hundred years later that "the proposition that all men are created equal" was not yet a reality. The Union was eventually saved, but not without another year and a half of desperate fighting and many more graves filled and dedicated. The long battle for civil rights has been a bloody one, as well. Lincoln himself became a casualty, assassinated just five days after the surrender at Appomattox by a racist fanatic not unlike the one who ended Dr. King's life in 1968. Their words were so powerful that their enemies resorted to murder to silence them.

Just three days now and it's the 50th anniversary of President Kennedy's assassination. I was a junior in high school that Friday and was walking out of Mr. Lenci's English class when the guys coming in said the president had been shot. We didn't pay much attention at that point— rumors fly around schools like bats in a barn.

When we heard very quickly that the president was dead, though, it still seemed impossible, but everyone ran for where they might find a radio. The teachers soldiered on through the end of the day, but no one heard a word they said. I had a long bus ride home and it was usually a mad house of stupid adolescent behavior. That day everyone sat looking blankly out the windows, as though they'd been drugged.

Thankfully, there was no school on Saturday, and most businesses were closed, too. Everyone sat together in front of their black and white sets and watched the pieces of the puzzle come together. Lee Harvey Oswald was quickly arrested, but no one had any confidence that he'd acted alone, a feeling that will likely persist forever. On Sunday we went to church, a rare occurrence for our family that underscored how people mourned for the Kennedys. When we arrived home, we watched as Jack Ruby killed Oswald on live television. The holidays seemed like an afterthought that year. Finally, the stupor was broken late in December by a song on the radio called *I Want to Hold Your Hand.*

Kennedy's death was the first real tragedy I lived through, and it felt like everything suddenly came unhinged. If he'd lived, the long nightmare of Vietnam might have been avoided. If he he'd lived, though, there might not have been the resolve for passage of the Civil Rights and Voting Rights Acts that President Johnson was able to arm-twist into law. So much else might be different, too.

An op-ed in *The New York Times* on the first anniversary of the school massacre in Newtown, Connecticut, lamented that even the loss of those 26 lives—20 of them 1st graders—hasn't led to any national action whatsoever to curb gun violence. Some states have even cut gun purchasers/owners more slack since then.

The article also pointed out that since 1970, 1, 450,000 people in this country have been killed by guns—that's 50,000 more than have been killed in all wars the country has fought in its 237-year history. That's 43 years of civilian gun victims compared to what happened at Bunker Hill, Saratoga, Shiloh, Antietam, Gettysburg, the Marne, the Bulge, Okinawa, Iwo Jima, Normandy, Tet, Kosovo, Iraq and Afghanistan, all rolled into one—and those are just the ones I thought of in about 30 seconds. And in another Times op-ed just last Sunday, following the recent Charleston church and Oregon college shootings, the author pointed out that "more preschoolers are shot dead each year (82 in 2013) than police officers in the line of duty (27 in 2013)."

Let all that sink in for a minute. . . . OK, so since the overall number of deaths—even of little kids—isn't making a ripple, how many people would it take to be killed in one incident to tip the scales? 50? Not likely, there were almost that many killed at Virginia Tech a few years ago and nothing happened once the memorial services and empty rhetoric ended. 100? 200? 500?

We haven't seen those numbers so far, but you can be sure there's a kid/man—a male, for sure—in his basement somewhere right this minute who's stockpiling his automatic weapons and ammo clips and planning how to make the biggest splash yet. He's probably a loner or a loser, someone no one would suspect ahead to time—not a wild-eyed, drooling escapee from a mental institution. But because he can buy all the fire power he needs, with few or no questions asked, he'll be loaded for bear when his moment comes. Let's just hope that none of us or our friends or families are at the mall or the theater or the school, or just walking down the street—you know, one of those really high-risk places we should have avoided—when the guy finally emerges from under his rock and starts shooting.

Still more guns. A number of the domestic violence skirmishes we see involve a woman's claim that the guy threatened to shoot her, pointed a gun at her, or, in some cases, actually shot it near her as a form of intimidation. And I've picked my pronouns carefully, to conform to the facts. In a quarter century of hearing these cases, I can't recall a gun ever being pointed in the other direction—even once. It's also made me wonder why that should be.

I mean, it's not that women aren't allowed to own guns—they got that right even before they could vote (think Annie Oakley)—or that they can't afford them because they don't make as much as men (which is true as far as the income part goes), or that guns are too heavy for fragile women to lift (probably true of those Rambo-style assault weapons), or too complicated for women to figure out where the bullets go or how to pull the trigger (not a chance).

So if it's none of those factors, what might it be? How about that men are bigger jerks—I think we're getting somewhere now—or that their evolution as social beings ceased somewhere between when they stopped dragging their women around by the hair and when the first episode of *Duck Dynasty* appeared—bingo! Still, even those evolution-stunted males of the species need guns to defend their caves against slobbering wooly mammoths—and non-human animals, too, right?

The fallacy there is that in 25 years I've never seen even one—I repeat, even one—instance where a gun was actually used for personal protection—you know, the way the NRA and my old prof Justice Scalia say the Second Amendment is supposed to work.

So if self-defense is really such a red herring for having all those guns waved around out there, why do we perpetuate that culture? Even if you agree with Scalia and think the Second Amendment grants Americans the right to stockpile and strut around with all the guns they can carry, it doesn't have to stay that way. After all, the Constitution used to count African-Americans as 3/5 of a person, but we managed to restore the other 2/5. Women couldn't vote since the Pilgrims landed, but that finally seemed like a reasonable thing to change. We could probably do that with guns, too, if it was such a good idea. We wouldn't even need an amendment to legislate universal background checks on all sales (even to your brother-in-law), trigger locks, "smart" guns (like "smart" phones), or assault weapons bans. We'd just need legislators with enough backbone to keep their heads from where it's too dark to see the writing on the wall.

As far as I know, no other society in the free world is as rabid about its guns—and uses them as irresponsibly. How about some more statistics? Since the Newtown massacre, there've been more than 30,000 Americans killed by guns—and I'm not counting military deaths in Iraq and Afghanistan, where there haven't been nearly as many casualties. Apparently, it's now safer in the midst of an ISIS fire fight than in some neighborhoods of American towns and cities.

Let's face it, this whole "pry it from my cold dead hands" thing is about as idiotic as the voter ID laws that are cropping up in states where Republicans want to hassle the poor, elderly and minorities so they can't vote for Democrats—oh, sorry, to prevent voter fraud—because there was a case of that somewhere that no one can really remember, but it certainly would be a bad thing, right! If you can't see through that smoke screen, then you really shouldn't be wielding a loaded firearm either.

PS—It happened again here 48 hours ago. The police responded to a domestic violence call in one of New Hampshire's rural towns, and when they walked in the door, the big tough man of the house shot the officer in the head and killed him. I don't think that's what the Founders had in mind about self-defense when they were pulling together the Second Amendment. I'd like to think the NRA and Justice Scalia would agree with me on that, but I wouldn't ask them for fear of being seriously disappointed.

PPS—It's now happened several more times in just the past 2 weeks. Always some delusional—but probably not institutionalizable—male, and always some kind of assault weapon with a huge clip, so the damage is as devastating as possible. Which is what those things are for, of course, in military situations. If you're not serving in the active military, you ought to be serving a jail sentence just for having one lying around the house.

It's been awhile since we had a case with facts worth raising an eyebrow about, but both of them were twitching today. A clean-cut middle aged guy who looked like he could double for George Clooney in a pinch was charged with stealing a woman's laundry from a dryer at the local wash-and-fold. He was identified on the security cameras hustling various female unmentionables out of the premises and was probably easy to spot because most of the usual customers, frankly, don't look like they could have spent time on the red carpet.

After his fine was imposed, I asked if there was any need for restitution for the lady items. The officer said the woman was satisfied with what came back to her, apparently still fresh as a daisy—to the guy's credit—and that she was only missing a green bra, to the best of her knowledge. I was curious about the mention of that item, but decided to spare the guy further snickers in front of a packed courtroom.

Still, as he turned and left, I couldn't help wondering whether we might locate the missing garment if we asked him to strip down right then and there. I mean, Hollywood was [is] full of leading men who played for the other team—think Errol Flynn, Rock Hudson and Montgomery Clift, just to name a couple of the guys who portrayed many a macho customer but had a distinctly softer side, shall we say.

Before it headed off for its summer recess this June, the US Supreme Court announced the long-awaited decision in the case about whether the Massachusetts law that established a buffer zone for protesters outside abortion clinics was unconstitutional. Not surprisingly, I guess, the court struck down the de-confrontational zone, because it violated the right of abortion opponents to exercise their First Amendment free-speechiness.

We could probably debate the merits of that decision for about as long as it takes the Israelis and Palestinians to tidy up their differences, but it's the hypocrisy of the ruling that scorches my robe. I mean, you can get right up in the face of scared young women, but it's a no-no to picket or demonstrate anywhere on the huge plaza in front of the marble palace where that decision was carefully crafted.

People's views are already jaundiced when they consider pretty much anything courts do these days, and this outcome isn't helping their attitude improve. For me it's right up there with not allowing cameras in the courtroom during oral arguments. If it's the justices being self-conscious about asking stupid questions with the whole nation watching, I can understand that concern based on some of the resulting decisions; however, we have to allow cameras in our piddling little outpost of justice, and the chances of our saying something really dumb are probably exponentially higher. The last time I looked, not looking dumb was not a constitutionally-protected right.

As the clock runs down on my rung time, I must be getting too crotchety for my own good. This time it's about marijuana. Many states have now decriminalized small- quantity possession, some have turned it into a hot (smoking?) retail enterprise, and quite a few more now have elaborate medical marijuana programs, including a budding one (I can't help myself) here in New Hampshire. There's even a cultivation facility planned for the local warehouse building where our old Brookstone store used to be.

OK, here's the crotchety part. Marijuana may be no more harmful than alcoholic beverages when used responsibly, but it's still a federal offense. Sure, the feds may not be making a federal case out of it anymore, like their decision not to bust the undocumented servers at popular Capitol Hill eateries they (the DOJ guys) frequent. But come on, its taboo status remains on the books. And as long as that's the case, should we—and I only have standing to sound off about the Granite State—really be scoffing that federal statute by giving our statewide endorsement to any marijuana use at all?

When you come right down to it, how do we maintain any credibility about law enforcement when we decide on State nullification of the federal statute. I mean, why not just adopt a law that all funds due the IRS shall be paid instead to the State treasury and instantly solve our revenue shortfall? Is there really any difference, and are you prepared to draw that line? Either get the federal law off the books, or turn off all those grow lights until then.

I was about to shed the robe and head for the office yesterday when I heard there was a woman filing a stalking petition that I needed to wait for. Alright, that happens all the time, so no big deal.

When I finally saw her, though, it turned out she was from my town and knew me well enough to call me Phil when we ran into each other at the paper store. The problem was, we weren't at the paper store, and yet she felt she could be that chummy when I sat down to review her petition. We weren't in the courtroom and no one else was present except the bailiff, but I was still wearing my robe so she knew it wasn't quite the same setting as Sunday morning picking up the Times.

Maybe she'd never been to court before and thought this was just a cozy chat. Anyhow no offense was taken. We don't stand on a lot of top-rung formalities here, even in the courtroom, and if I let a minor irritation like this get under my skin, I'd soon have a rash worthy of the emergency room.

For the record, though, I do ask people to stand when they speak—I think the institution itself deserves that level of respectfulness. After all, you stand when they play the National Anthem even at a minor league game, as do the participants in Judge Judy's faux court. I know this is way over the top, but I make them ditch their gum, too, if I see them chewing it like cud out there (one of the local chiefs is actually the worst [repeat] offender, and you'd think they could take a two minute swipe at proper courtroom decorum at the police academy).

Still, I can't help feeling that if someone is calling me here by my first name, they may be expecting me to cut them slack or render a privilege that's not available to just anybody. In the end, I didn't say anything; I never do. I haven't figured out a way to say it without sounding pompous. But I won't have to worry about it again this time, because I'll be asking one of my colleagues to take over when the woman and her defendant come in for their final hearing. She may not see how the chumminess has clouded the water, but I do.

Saturday night the phone rang about 3:15. I must have been dead to the world because it took several rings before I registered what was happening. Once I did, I quickly ticked off the likely scenarios: Mom's fallen and broken something on her way to the bathroom but managed to push her Medic Alert and she's in the emergency room; one of the kids has had an accident on the way home from a way-too-late party and is now also at a hospital somewhere—I hope not charged with DWI; or it's the cops.

So when I managed to mumble "hello" and heard someone say "Judge Runyon?", I was mostly relieved. Sort of like the time I drill-pressed my index finger to the bottom of a woman's pocket book during a summer job at a local factory and thought I might lose the fingertip on my pitching hand—then learned all I'd done was generate a lot of blood and ruin one of my favorite shirts.

This wasn't just a local cop, though, it was some poor guy within an easy jog of the Canadian border who'd been calling judges for an hour trying to find someone to give him a warrant to search a house where there was a lot of Pabst Blue Ribbon but no one old enough to drink it. He said he'd tried judges in his area first, then started working his way down the length of the State, and that I was the first one who'd picked up the phone. I wasn't quick enough to ask how many calls he'd actually made, but maybe I'll check back with him some morning at 3:15 when I can't sleep and have a good chance of catching him back on duty.

To put the strangeness of this call in geographic perspective, it would take me as long to get to his tiny station on our patchwork quilt of largely two-lane roads as it would to be careening down the Henry Hudson Parkway and catching my first glimpse of the Statue of Liberty. So this was truly like a cop at a tough precinct in Hell's Kitchen looking for a warrant to search a crack house and deciding he needed me to help him out in a pinch because all the intervening judges in the Bronx and in Hartford and Springfield were out of commission.

I granted the warrant—fortunately not worded in French—then toyed with whether to wake Cathie up to tell her the whole story. Some things, though, are crystal clear even at that ungodly hour.

I'm closing in now on two years left on my rusty little rung, and I'm thinking it's going to be a real slog to the finish line. For any of you who may have run a marathon—or in this case the one in Boston—I envision being on Beacon Street at about the 24-mile marker and seeing the huge Citgo sign way up ahead in Kenmore Square. You put your head down and run for another 15 minutes and when you look up again, it's still about the same distance away. Your legs aren't sore any longer—you're way past that—and you know you're going to make it, but you're numb from the waist down and dazed from the neck up. Then, suddenly, after what seems like an eternity, you're crossing the finish line on Boylston Street and it's all over.

There are a number of reasons it seems like this. You've been at the race so long that you can't really imagine it ending. When I was 43 and saw 27 years of judging ahead of me, I couldn't fathom that much time. I didn't even think I'd live this long, much less still be out on the course at the 24-year marker. Even more so, though, I had no idea the nature of the job would change so dramatically. When I started, we kept our records on 3"by5" hand-typed index cards, and we wrote out orders and decisions in long-hand. There were a few forms, but most of what each court did was unique to it, and each judge had created a few basic forms that worked for him or her.

Now, in the interest of standardizing every aspect of the process—probably a commendable goal in the abstract—all our forms come down from the main court office in Concord, and they multiply like rabbits on Viagra. It seems like years since I did anything official without "populating" a form and hitting "print". The biggest challenge is that I might not be using the latest version of the right form or might forget that there's another form I also need to use to make something happen.

I know it's old fartish to go on this way and that everything newer should be better, but I'm not buying it without a final gasp right before I collapse at the finish line. Way back there on the course, I lamented that the State was sacrificing a lot of valuable experience by forcing everyone out at 70, but I'm reconsidering my opinion based on new information not previously before the court.

OK, I'm now, in fact, down to less than 2 years of struggling to cling to this modest perch, which I think about each time I impose a suspended sentence of that duration or longer. In other words, when these defendants come back for review of their compliance with the requirements I've meted out for them, someone else will already be the new decider (note to self: make sure to have robe de-loused prior to retirement festivities).

You may have noticed I've had a gnat in my ear about Justice Scalia on several occasions. What's got me riled this time isn't even what he says; it's how he goes about saying it. I'm not begrudging that he thinks he's smarter than all his colleagues on the other side of a big decision. I mean, you probably don't get all the way to the top rung without a pretty lofty opinion of your legal firepower. The trouble is, he can't keep his mouth shut about it, and he does it in such a snarky, condescending way that you wouldn't want him at your table in the lunchroom even if you thought he might help with your homework.

Of course, you only get a glimpse of this petulant streak when he's not getting his way or when someone has the audacity to disagree with him. Then whatever the offending opinion says is "gobbledy gook" or "pure applesauce" or "jiggery-pokery", and these are just from his most recent rants on the majority's death penalty, gay marriage and Obamacare decisions. Sure, they make for colorful sound bites in a place where pretty much everything is black, but is this really the kind of juvenile dissing we want from the folks we're counting on to keep our Constitution meaning what it says?

It's like, if I don't get my way, you're stupid and your mother is a scofflaw. And if I'm Ruth Bader Ginsberg and he says that kind of thing about an opinion I've worked pretty hard on, I'm thinking there's not enough room on this rung for both of us and maybe we'd all be better off if he took his fancy robe and went home—or at least climbed back down to where he could get some anger management and behavior modification.

And, you know, it's not like this was the first time one of these big guns didn't get his way and had his robe in a wad about it. Justice Oliver Wendell Holmes, Jr. (remember him!) is certainly in the top tier of the Great Deciders, but was known as the Great Dissenter because he was on the short end of so many decisions. Yet he still managed to act like a grownup. Oh, I'm sure Holmes thought his colleagues were idiots more than once, but he managed to keep that opinion to himself, at least publicly, and to confine his official views to the actual issues. If he had a ball at all, he left it in the game.

Scalia is dead, to paraphrase Dickens, and I feel bad about that last entry. That is, I'm sincerely sorry for his wife, his 9 children, and his more than 30 grandchildren –there may even be some great grandchildren by now. I wish he had had the chance to spend many years of blissful retirement enjoying their company.

That's as far as I'm willing to go, however, because I'm not sorry in the least that the Supreme Court will no longer have his vote. In that respect, my sentiments are not unlike those of US Grant when someone asked him about Robert E. Lee just after their surrender meeting at Appomattox: He was indeed a valiant foe, but his cause was one of the worst for which people ever fought.

Maybe you think that's harsh—and the Constitution gives you the right to voice your own opinion. This is my book, though, and I'm voicing that his vote made the 5th one in many cases that have changed the course of our history, and not in a good way. We've covered this ground before, but let's recap the low points:

> In *Bush v. Gore* his vote to stop the Florida recount handed the election to George W. Bush, who in turn sent our troops to war in Iraq without justification and cost thousands of young American lives, indeed many more than the terrorist attacks here that he was trying to avenge.
>
> In *District of Columbia v. Heller* he cobbled together an opinion that dismissed a whole section of the Second Amendment in order to "find" an individual right to own firearms for personal protection. Even his own court had never been able to do that before.
>
> And in *Citizens United v. Federal Election Commission* he decided that non-human things like corporations are entitled to the same First Amendment free speech rights as individuals, without any supporting language in the Constitution itself—it didn't start out with "We the artificially-created entities."

He claimed to be such an "originalist", yet what he did was create new law when he wanted a particular result, thereby making his candidate the president, making the country a dangerous place to be, and opening the floodgates of money pouring into election campaigns so his candidates would likely stand a better chance of winning future elections.

Sure, there were others who joined in those cases to tote up the necessary 5 votes, but Scalia was the most senior of them and their judicial pied piper. If he'd opined that the First Amendment applied only to "We the people"; that the right to guns was only to protect against oppression by the federal government, which was the sole concern when the Constitution was written; and that it was reasonable for the Florida authorities to continue counting their own votes, I guaranty that his arguments—advanced with the force of his personality—would have rubbed off on at least one of his robemates.

Now, of course, it will be mesmerizing to watch what happens as President Obama makes a nomination to fill Scalia's seat, and the Senate conservatives do their best to shoot down whoever is put forward, probably on the ground that his/her daughter once drove a friend to a Planned Parenthood appointment.

Last Sunday *The Keene Sentinel* published an op-ed by our Senator Kelly Ayotte, in which she argued that President Obama should defer to the next president the nomination of a successor to Justice Scalia. She said the American people have a right to a role in that choice by virtue of who they elect in November and inaugurate almost a year from now.

I doubt you'll be surprised if I dissent from that view, and I wrote the following response to submit for the paper's consideration. Of course, I couldn't really do that, because the issue of Supreme Court appointments is no longer about the "administration of justice", but is now a political hot potato that would get me yanked before the Judicial Conduct Commission for taking a public position about it.

Anyhow, here's what I think and what I wanted so much to say:

"I dissent from Senator Ayotte's view that President Obama should defer to the next president the nomination of a successor to Justice Scalia. She said the American people have a right to a role in that choice by virtue of who they elect in November and inaugurate almost a year from now.

"My reasons are grounded in the Constitution. Not only is a president's term—and his [her] obligation to govern—four years, not three, but it is the Senate's role, not the American people's, to hold the hearings and make the decision whether the president's nomination is likely to be 'a staunch defender of our Constitution and a brilliant jurist.' In addition, the reasonable inference from Senator Ayotte's suggestion is that a Supreme Court justice is nothing more than a president's advocate, rather than an independent decision-maker in a wholly separate branch of our government.

"If the Senate conducts its due diligence and decides that the president's choice is unqualified to serve or has a record as a partisan proponent of a particular agenda, then its obligation is to vote against the nomination. But if the president proposes a candidate who has established an exemplary record of accomplishment and gives every indication of respect for the Constitution and the rule of law, then the Senate's obligation is to confirm the nomination. President George H.W. Bush did the latter when he nominated our own David Souter, who served us with equanimity and distinction—and without petulant rhetoric when he found himself in dissent.

"If what the Senator means, however, is that the new president should have the right to name an agent in a black robe to advance his or her own political agenda, then the Senate should reject that candidate, no matter what party's nominee wins the White House.

"While it's rare in this climate of polarized partisanship to envision any candidate who can truly function as the kind of objective umpire that Chief Justice Roberts aspired to, I believe those judges exist and should be fairly considered if put forward. Several recent appointments to high federal judgeships have received almost unanimous bi-partisan support and have performed admirably in the meantime. It is reasonable to think that one of those judges would again be a worthy candidate.

"This is an important opportunity to begin restoring the public's confidence in the Supreme Court, by disengaging its members from lockstep decision-making at either end of the political spectrum. No one should be able to predict the outcome of a case simply by counting up the number of justices nominated by the president from one party or the other; yet that has become the reality. Instead, every litigant should have the opportunity to prevail if the facts and law are marshaled most convincingly and fashioned into the most persuasive argument.

"That outcome is not fostered by tying nominations to the winners of partisan elections, as Senator Ayotte would have it. If President Obama is unable to put forth a qualified candidate who can be vetted and confirmed by the Senate, acting responsibly and in good faith during his remaining term, then that task should and will fall to his successor. But that process should not be delayed or deferred at the expense of the important cases requiring decisions by the Court—and at the even greater expense of re-enforcing the American people's disgust with the partisan divisiveness they have come to expect from their representatives."

September or October is the month each year when the news of the latest indignity comes down from Concord, in the form of the number of court sessions we've been assigned for the ensuing calendar year.

This year, as the last few grains of summer sand slip to the bottom of the hour glass and I wax pathetically poetic, the news has arrived of yet another 20% cut in the number of days we'll be authorized to gather together to approximate justice. That means in the past 5 years our session days are almost exactly 50% of what they were back then, while as far as I can see, the number of cases hasn't dwindled in even remote proportion.

Consequently, on many days our dockets run to 60 cases, and the vision I conjure is of the little Asian guy who's trying to see how many of Nathan's Famous he can eat in the allotted time without barfing. It means that in most of those cases, I'm just rubber-stamping the prosecutor's sentencing recommendations and spending little or no time determining whether it's really appropriate based on the circumstances of the offense and whether this is the first or twenty-first trip to a courthouse for the person standing out there.

Then, heaven forbid, someone wants an actual hearing on his case and the gears lock up for a minimum of 20-30 minutes if it's, say, just a minor motor vehicle case—thereby throwing us into a ditch and accelerating the remaining docket to warp speed once we get back on the road. Oh, we try not to have the process look like making sausages—you know, too gross to watch—but maintaining the appearance of carefully considered and thoughtfully dispensed justice becomes harder by 20% each year.

The final thing is just the indignity of the same rote cutbacks year after year. If we actually had 20% fewer cases each time, I wouldn't have anything to complain about; the results would only be fair. But that's not the case, and it makes Cathie so angry that I just don't volunteer the information any longer. When she finally asks, I grudgingly admit what's happening, and then I cringe like a kid about to be spanked for something his sister did. If this annual process doesn't cause her to go into apoplectic convulsions before I'm finally finished here, it will be a small miracle.

And when these cuts are consolidated over the years, the financial outcome is that I'm making less as a judge that I was when I first put on my predecessor's smelly hand-me-down more than 25 years ago. In fact, it's less than half of what it was just 5 years ago. But at least I have a job, so the only place I'm blowing off steam is right here. Sorry to put you through this, but you're almost finished.

It's presidential primary season in New Hampshire once again, and if you've ever had the opportunity to see the great African migration, you would easily recognize the similarities. That's because both the primary process and the migration never really end. The critters roam from place to place in a large oval based on the seasons, just like the herds of zebra and wildebeest. You can tell they're here if you watch any TV at all, because you get barraged every 5 minutes by one of the scavengers searching for new prey and "approving this message."

Because there are so many candidates of one party in the hunt, they're all trying to convince you how vicious—er, tough—they'll be on terrorism and immigration and Planned Parenthood, and how they'll change just about everything we're doing now I guess this shouldn't come as much of a surprise, given the Hatfields and McCoys nature of current American politics, but there's a part of the party's pitch that's relevant to what we see here on the bottom court rung.

Based on what I've reported so far, you'll appreciate that many of our customers are in dire need of a public safety net because they're either totally submerged or treading water for dear life. They don't need to voice it; you can see the panic and desperation in their faces.

Maybe they did something really stupid that they regret now, because the consequences are going to put them farther under. Maybe they won't be able to get to a job now or they'll be spending whatever they do make to pay us off.

Maybe they're working—many of them very hard—but only for a nearly minimum wage. Then they or someone in their family gets sick or hurt, and suddenly they have a $10,000 uninsured medical bill, because they couldn't afford the coverage that might have paid it. So bankruptcy may be the only option, but they don't even have enough money to file.

Or maybe they financed a car to get to work, but they couldn't keep up with the payments, and it gets repossessed and sold for a lot less than the loan balance. So now they have a $5,000 judgment against them for the deficiency. At $50 a month that's a day's pay every month for 8+ years.

Yet this one party's candidates wouldn't be caught dead supporting an increase in the minimum wage, because it might hurt the "job creators". You know, those business owners and CEOs with the 6 and 7 figure incomes who don't want to share any of those os with their employees. Oh, there'd surely be a small business here and there that would have to lay off someone to save on payroll, but there'd be millions who'd actually be able to pay those medical bills and car loans with a few more bucks every week.

In case you haven't noticed, that's the difference between the parties. They both want to help people. The trouble is, the people the one party want to help don't really need it, and the people the others want to help need it desperately. Yet the irony is, many of the people who need help the most, each and every day, have been bamboozled into supporting the one party because of social issues like immigration and gun control that likely won't adversely affect them at all, no matter who's elected. Did someone already observe that politics make strange teammates? I'd have said "bedfellows", but that's too gay for an awful lot of the folks in that particular party.

Just please, no matter what your point of view, give the ads a rest— announce that you're giving the money to food banks for the people who need it. You'll get a big bounce in the polls—and you'll be giving us some credit for grasping your marginally accurate message after the third or fourth time you interrupt the programming we actually turned on the set to see. All you're doing at this point is making us mad as hell and hoping to get you out of our State as quickly as possible.

If you've hung with me during this entire journey in search of the elusive grail of justice, you deserve both a medal and a dope slap. Among other indignities, you've endured several installments of my rant concerning capital punishment. Now there's a new chapter.

You'll recall that I mentioned the black guy who shot and killed a

Manchester police officer and was sentenced to death. The guy was a career criminal, with a rap sheet as long and hopeless as a Russian novel, and he shot the officer in the head to avoid yet another arrest. So we're not talking about a single mother who was desperate enough to hold up a Walmart for diapers and baby food.

The problem is, we haven't executed anyone in the Granite State since 1939, and I'm guessing that during those 75 years there've been some other pretty grisly murders of officers, not to mention loving parents by their good-for-nothing children, helpless infants by their abusive parents, and beloved teachers by their ungrateful students. But once a black guy gets into the crosshairs, we start acting like it's 1939— in Mississippi.

After the guy was sentenced, the long appeals process started and the first stop was at the New Hampshire Supreme Court. The issue was whether the death penalty was "excessive and disproportionate" for the kind of crime involved. Of course, if you start from the premise that capital punishment isn't cruel and unusual per se, then you don't have far to go to find that other states where this sort of crime has occurred— most of them in the South, frankly—have dispatched their defendants without significant public pangs of conscience.

But why would you look at what other states are doing, instead of making sure the punishment fits the crime right here at home? I mean, if we haven't executed anyone in New Hampshire in 75 years, despite all those other horrific murder cases, doesn't that suggest we must think it's pretty excessive and disproportionate?

And why look at places like Arizona, Florida and Texas anyhow, when we don't buy into the way they run their states for any other purpose? Say, isn't Arizona where that crazy, hard-ass sheriff has been re-elected every time since 1992, despite being convicted of racial profiling and spending a lot of his time investigating President Obama's birth certificate? And I think I heard that Texas executed someone for dissing the UT mascot—on second thought, maybe he only got 20 years.

Not surprisingly, despite the apples and oranges nature of the whole exercise, the Supremes bought right into it in their decision, and—what a surprise—decided that executing our guy wouldn't be excessive or disproportionate at all in the Grand Canyon, Sunshine or Longhorn States. Of course, if they'd considered geographic proximity, they'd have seen that all the other New England states stopped killing people a long time ago.

The good news is that this is just the first stop on the long and winding road of capital appeals. Still, the sooner we start looking at this the civilized way, the sooner we'll get off the death watch and just throw away the key of our guy's cell, so he'll have the rest of his life to mull over what he did. I'd concur in that result.

Eight months from today will be my 70th birthday and my first day as a former judge. That's going to mean quite an adjustment after 27 years of 3:00 AM. calls for search warrants and protective orders, and I'm wondering how I'll cope. Maybe I'll have to transition by setting the alarm for 3:00 for a few weeks. I'm not the only one who's struggled with this change, of course, as there are plenty of "how to" guides like *Leaving the Bench* and *Hypothetical Cases for Former Judges*. The former is a real one; the latter is one I haven't seen, but it may be an idea to work on at 3:00.

I'll still have my private practice to fall back on, which isn't something most full-time deciders can count on, but as I said somewhere back here, that's never been quite enough for me. Politics might be one way to go—Bernie showed us there's no age limit there—but I don't have the demeanor for the day-in and day-out self-promotion that that process requires, and Cathie would freak if she thought she'd have to behave a certain way just to be the right kind of official spouse. So what's it going to be?

Don't hold me to this—I haven't fully committed yet—but I'm testing out whether joining the full-court press to get the death penalty off the books in New Hampshire is the issue to laser in on. It's not only barbaric (see my letter to *The New York Times*), but it no longer serves any of the purposes used to justify it. How could a consequence of crime that hasn't been employed in more than 75 years be seen as a deterrent to any kind of behavior, and the "eye-for-an-eye" argument to kill someone for murder makes about as much modern sense as cutting off the hand of someone convicted of theft.

Sure, getting out in front on an issue like this might cost me a few clients, but since most of my contemporary colleagues are already on the 1st tee, I may decide to take that chance. Plus—and this is a biggie for me—this might be one small way finally to put myself in the line of fire as atonement for stiffing the military those many years ago.

CLOSING STATEMENT

I n case it hasn't occurred to you, there's no big finish here like you'd get in a Grisham novel. The jury's not going to come in with a huge verdict for the tragic widow, and the murderer isn't going to confess on the witness stand to save the wrongly accused. The customers are just going to keep arriving every day, like mail at the post office, and we're going to keep trying to do the right thing with/to/by/for them, collecting the right postage as best we can, and trying not to damage the goods any more than we can help, to maintain the same metaphor for a change.

I could keep going with the vignettes and the pontificating almost indefinitely, or at least until my decider's permit expires on April 20, 2017 —but why push my luck. (By the way, if you're moved to send a birthday card, I love the irreverent ones, but please don't send cash or gifts of great monetary value; otherwise, my remaining bench time will be reduced pretty abruptly and you'll be able to read all about it in the papers.)

Whatever—as people say today when they can't think of anything intelligent to say. I think this is as good a place as any to wrap up. You've gotten the flavor of what's going on here, I hope; and I've gotten the chance to blow off some potentially coronary-clogging steam. And besides, I warned you at the get-go that this isn't some lofty marble sanctuary we're talking about. It is a critical rung of the ladder of American justice, however. I mean, you can't get to the top rung without starting with this one. I could also tout its importance to average Americans vis-à-vis the pronouncements that come down from the distant rungs in Washington and Concord, but suffice it to say that none of those gilt-edged decisions would be worth the 24-pound bond paper they're engraved on unless we bottom-rungers made sure everybody played by their rules down here. Which we do.

One final, final PS—Way back there, I mentioned spotting the father of a teenage ne'er-do-well while taking photos of a cross-country race. That was several years ago now. Recently I was reprising my paparazzi role at the same event when the same dad showed up right in front of me—literally not more than 20 feet from where we were standing for our prior encounter. He asked if I was the same guy who sent his kid to jail after he hadn't learned his lesson as a juvenile offender and had become an offensive adult. I wasn't sure I wanted to fess up about all that, not knowing what might be coming next, but I mumbled a "yes" and then got ready to dodge a flying fist.

Instead, he said he wanted me to know that the kid had come around dramatically and was now reconciled with his family, gainfully employed, and seeing a great young woman. He wanted to tell me the tough love had worked and that as painful as it was to endure at the time, the cold water in the face seemed to snap his son out of the dead-end funk.

The whole thing didn't take more than a minute, but it gave me a lift that's likely to last for months. Maybe the Supremes have moments like that, too, but I'm thinking this is mostly a bottom rung phenomenon. No matter what, it wipes the slate clean of all the other grousing I've done. So I'm opting to finish on a high note here, sort of like a Grisham novel after all.

ACKNOWLEDGMENTS

I couldn't have stayed balanced on my lowly but precarious rung without the support of lots of people, none of whom are responsible for what I've done there—or likely share many of the views I've expressed here.

At the court I appreciate all the folks who kept the cases coming and going for the last 27 years, notably Pauline, Danielle, Julie, Cindy and Larry, but also Pat, Brenda, Jen, Amy, Elizabeth, and Trisha. The guys who've kept me safe all these years—including making sure the hats were off, the gum was discarded (and not stuck under the benches!), and the people were on their feet when speaking, were, among many others, Bill, John, Doug, Roger, Bruce, Steve, and Lance (who fortunately never had to shoot anyone due to anything I said or did). We were also served extremely well and competently over the years by a host of lay and lawyer prosecutors, police officers, public and private defenders, juvenile service officers, CASA volunteers, and bail commissioners (who went out at all hours of the night to set bail for people often behaving at their very worst, for compensation totally unworthy of the effort).

Back at the office, Margot and Marge kept the law practice humming smoothly along—and the clients feeling like they really didn't need me after all—while I was two-timing them with my court family.

I also want to add sincere thanks to Cassie Baron, who helped me wrestle this unwieldy collection of ramblings into printable form, though she's not to blame in any way for its content. Sarah Bauhan of

Bauhan Publishing LLC and Grove Street Books also helped me along at many points in the process, but she, too, is innocent of any culpability for the final result.

Finally, I couldn't have remained on my rung and made it safely and successfully back to earth without the support of my family. LP and Grier behaved like model citizens (at least as far as I knew) and never created an embarrassing moment for me, managing to stay out of the courtroom during their formative years except as sheepish visitors on class trips. And finally Cathie, my loyal, loving and long-suffering partner of 48 years and my greatest supporter and defender—she was ready to go to battle for me whenever she thought the system wasn't treating me fairly, and she was always there to answer the phone at 3:00 a.m., even though it took her the rest of the night to get back to sleep! She will undoubtedly enjoy my retirement more than I will.